INSIDE THE REINVENTION MACHINE

INSIDE THE REINVENTION MACHINE

Appraising Governmental Reform

Donald F. Kettl
John J. DiIulio, Jr.
Editors

THE BROOKINGS INSTITUTION
Washington, D.C.

Copyright © 1995 by
THE BROOKINGS INSTITUTION
1775 Massachusetts Avenue, N.W., Washington, D.C. 20036

Library of Congress Cataloging-in-Publication data:

Inside the reinvention machine : appraising governmental reform /
   Donald F. Kettl, John J. DiIulio, Jr., editors.
       p.   cm.
   Includes bibliographical references and index.
   ISBN 0-8157-4910-4 (alk. paper). — ISBN 0-8157-4909-0 (pbk. :
alk. paper)
   1. Administrative agencies—United States—Management.
2. Administrative agencies—United States—Reorganization.
3. Executive departments—United States—Management.   4. Government
productivity—United States.   5. Bureaucracy—United States.
I. Kettl, Donald F.   II. DiIulio, John J.
JK469   1995
353.07′5—dc20   94-44708
                                                                                      CIP

9 8 7 6 5 4 3 2 1

The paper used in this publication meets the minimum requirements of the American
National Standard for Information Sciences—Permanence of Paper for Printed Library
Materials, ANSI Z39.48-1984.

Set in Garamond #3

Composition by Harlowe Typography, Inc., Cottage City, Maryland

Printed by R.R. Donnelley and Sons, Co., Harrisonburg, Virginia

Foreword

THE AIM of the Clinton administration's National Performance Review (NPR) is to make government "work better and cost less." Streamlining bureaucracy, cutting unnecessary regulations, and improving civil service personnel practices and federal procurement processes are among the NPR's official objectives. But can these goals be met? What are the political and budgetary roadblocks to real reform? And what does the new Republican majority in Congress mean for the success of the NPR and for "reinventing government" more generally?

This volume addresses these and related questions by examining in detail the successes and failures of the first full year of the NPR. It looks inside the federal government's "reinvention labs" and ponders the politics of reforming the bureaucracy. In the end, the authors are generally optimistic: the NPR can make a positive difference, but only if certain tough strategic and political choices are made soon.

This is the fourth volume produced by the Brookings Center for Public Management, which was begun in 1993 within the Governmental Studies program. The other works include *Improving Government Performance: An Owner's Manual*, by John J. DiIulio, Jr., Gerald Garvey, and Donald F. Kettl; *Deregulating the Public Service*, edited by John J. DiIulio, Jr.; and *Making Health Reform Work*, edited by John J. DiIulio, Jr., and Richard P. Nathan.

John J. DiIulio, Jr., is professor of politics and public affairs at Princeton University and director of the Brookings Center for Public Management; and Donald F. Kettl is professor of political science and public affairs at the University of Wisconsin, Madison and a nonresident senior fellow at Brookings. The editors and contributors would like to thank Thomas Mann, director of the Brookings Governmental Studies program, for supervising the project. Nancy D. Davidson edited the manuscript; Carey R. Macdonald provided research assistance and verified its factual content; Cynthia Terrels provided word processing and other project assistance; Susan L. Woollen prepared it for typesetting; and Robert Elwood compiled the index.

The views expressed here are those of the authors and should not be ascribed to the trustees, officers, or staff members of the Brookings Institution.

BRUCE K. MACLAURY
President

February 1995
Washington, D.C.

Contents

1 ||| Works Better and Costs Less? Sweet and Sour Perspectives on the NPR

John J. DiIulio, Jr.

ON DECEMBER 19, 1994, a front-page story in the *New York Times* declared "Clinton Turns to Gore's Proposal for Faster, Cheaper Government."[1] As leaders of the Republican-controlled 104th Congress vowed to raze the federal government (for example, to abolish the Department of Housing and Urban Development), President Clinton redoubled his efforts to reinvent it (for example, to cut HUD's staff by thousands and consolidate its scores of programs into just four). The president sought "to prove that his Administration can shrink the bureaucracy and was doing so long before the Republican electoral triumph" of November 8, 1994.[2]

As Christopher H. Foreman suggests in chapter 6 of this volume, the smashing Republican victory in the midterm congressional elections of 1994 has changed the politics of reforming the federal bureaucracy in ways that increase the chances of congressional support for some form of the administration's civil service personnel, procurement, downsizing, and reorganization efforts.

Reinventing, Razing, or Reforming Government?

The question, however, is whether a legislative-executive bidding war to raze or reinvent government is necessarily conducive to meaningful efforts to reform the federal service in a manner that improves performance and spares the public purse. Based on a careful analysis of the first year of the administration's reform efforts, this volume provides some preliminary answers.

On September 7, 1993, the Clinton administration released the first

1

report of its National Performance Review (NPR), headed by Vice President Al Gore. Entitled *From Red Tape to Results: Creating a Government That Works Better and Costs Less*, the NPR report contained 384 major recommendations for improving performance in the federal bureaucracy. The recommendations covered twenty-seven federal agencies and fourteen "government systems," including budgeting practices, information technologies, personnel procedures, and procurement regulations.[3]

The Rush to Reinvention

The NPR got off to a fast start, attracted an enormous amount of favorable media attention, and won early praise and encouragement from academics, union leaders, and policymakers of both parties.

The report was issued on Labor Day, just six months after the NPR initiative was announced, and less than nine months into the new administration. Inside government, the vice president made impassioned "reinvention" speeches before workers in each agency. Outside it, he waged a public relations campaign for the NPR that included several high-profile television appearances. Most memorable was CBS's "Late Night with David Letterman," during which he dramatized wasteful tests of government-issue products by shattering an ostensibly overpriced ashtray.[4]

On the day the NPR report was released, the president joined the vice president on the White House lawn for a widely televised briefing and photo opportunity in which they were flanked by forklifts loaded with government personnel manuals and related "red tape" documents.[5] At least at the outset, the NPR was a pure public relations triumph, resulting in a quick twelve-percentage-point bounce in Clinton's approval ratings.[6]

Intellectually, the NPR was animated by journalist David Osborne and former city manager Ted Gaebler's *Reinventing Government*, a treatise that stood the field of public administration on its head by identifying ways that government could alter or eliminate civil service personnel and procurement systems and become less top-heavy, more decentralized, and more committed to serving "customer interests."[7] Every generation of public service reformers has included some who believe that government can and should be run like a business. But Osborne and Gaebler went farther, arguing not only that government should borrow successful business approaches such as total quality management but that government should "reinvent" itself so that the "entrepreneurial spirit" could grow from within and new, performance-oriented organizational cultures could take root.

Like *Reinventing Government*, and unlike any other government-sponsored public service reform document on record, the NPR report made its way on to the *New York Times* best sellers' list and was quickly reprinted by several for-profit publishers. Many previous efforts to reform the federal service did make headlines and also made a positive difference. For example, the President's Committee on Administrative Management (the Brownlow committee) of the 1930s and the two Commissions on Organization of the Executive Branch (the first and second Hoover commissions) of the 1940s and 1950s left indelible organizational marks on the federal government and were treasured moments in the golden age of American public administration. But no previous government or private commission on the federal service— including the NPR's two immediate predecessors from the 1980s, the Executive Committee of the Private Sector Survey on Cost Control in the Federal Government (the Grace commission) and the National Commission on the Public Service (the Volcker commission)—captured public attention in quite the way the NPR did.

Beyond the favorable public reception, many of the early political and academic responses to the NPR report were quite favorable. In Congress, the initial Republican response to this early effort by a Democratic administration showed a degree of bipartisan spirit that, with the exception of the final vote on the North American Free Trade Agreement, was nowhere else in evidence during the first year of the Clinton presidency.[8] Republican Senator William V. Roth, Jr., endorsed the thrust of the report, stating that it "offered some important recommendations" that "provided an excellent starting point for reorganizing, streamlining, and reforming federal program structure and operations."[9]

In December 1993 the General Accounting Office (GAO) issued an analysis of the NPR report's 384 major recommendations; it officially agreed with 262, offered no comment (for lack of sufficient information) on 121, and rejected only 1. (The GAO rejected the NPR's recommendation for a creation of a multiagency coordinating council within the Department of Labor.)[10] The Alliance for Redesigning Government of the National Academy of Public Administration (NAPA) bolstered efforts to get policymakers, the public, the academic community, and the press to "really take the NPR's message seriously."[11] A number of prominent journalists, including nationally syndicated columnist David Broder, wrote highly favorable articles about the NPR's promise and progress.[12] And the NPR was acknowledged as a model for reform efforts abroad.[13]

Much Motion, Little Reinvention?

But it was not long before these largely favorable early returns on the NPR were swamped by political problems and negative reviews. As the first year of the NPR drew to a close, there were basically two schools of thought about it, one on balance positive, the other on balance negative. On the one side were those who, like public management expert Laurence E. Lynn, Jr., found problems with the NPR but concluded that

> the Gore report already has been catalytic, and public administration is enlivened by a palpable new energy. Properly mobilized on behalf of good policies, the movement to reinvent government will enter the history of administrative reform as a useful step forward.[14]

On the other side were those who, like former NAPA trustees Herbert N. Jasper and Anita F. Alpern, looked "favorably on the intent and general direction" of the NPR but concluded that

> the report is flawed by a number of omissions, inconsistencies, and questionable judgments. Further, the implementating actions to date . . . contain significant defects. . . . We think it contains both good and bad ideas, and a lot of overblown rhetoric which is mostly irrelevant to solving federal management problems.[15]

By the end of the NPR's first year, however, the negative perspective had found many more adherents than the positive one. Many came to the conclusion that the NPR report was, in the words of budget analysts Louis Fisher and Albert J. Kliman, "rife with contradictions, misstatements, and inaccuracies that call into question the overall quality of the report."[16]

Politically, the rush to reinvention began to stall just two months after the NPR report was released with such great political fanfare.[17] The haste with which the report was prepared became a source of criticism and embarrassment for the NPR. For example, most of the footnotes in the NPR report were to "accompanying reports" that were not released until months later and varied greatly in quality.[18] Another embarrassment came when, in early congressional hearings on the NPR, administration spokespersons were unable to explain precisely how the NPR had arrived at a work force reduction target of 252,000 (since revised upward to 272,900).[19]

Although trivial in their own right, such journalistic quibbles and political nitpicks were magnified beneath the thick lens of cautions, criticisms, and quasi-moral condemnations that eventually surrounded the NPR. Among other things, the NPR was criticized for overstating potential cost savings and for ignoring what many believed to be the twin sources of government's burdensome personnel and procurement regulations, namely, the proliferation of political appointees within the executive branch and the rise of legislative micromanagement within Congress. And the NPR was charged with everything from an abject failure to understand the Constitution to a complete misreading of the lessons of private-sector and state and local government reforms.[20]

Assessing Governmental Reform

This volume represents a preliminary effort to assess the NPR's freshman year of governmental reform. The first section, an extended essay by Donald F. Kettl, examines the NPR's underlying theory of reform, its track record in overcoming political and other obstacles to reform, and its significance in bringing about new laws and actual administrative changes that are likely to have the effect of making the federal service "work better and cost less."

The second section offers a diversity of perspectives on the NPR in relation to Kettl's synoptic analysis. In chapter 3, Gerald J. Garvey offers a critical historical perspective on the NPR. In chapter 4, Beryl A. Radin profiles six federal organizations that the NPR's leaders have identified as "success stories." In chapter 5, Carolyn Ban assesses the NPR's efforts to forge new partnerships between federal unions and management. And in chapter 6, Christopher H. Foreman, Jr., assesses the political progress and prospects of the NPR within Congress.

In August 1994 the Brookings Center for Public Management released a report on the NPR's first year based on a draft of Kettl's essay in this volume.[21] The report drew an enormous amount of media attention, which in turn quickly transformed the report into a "report card." When the NPR's own first-year report was released in September 1994, the press pushed the vice president to give the effort a single grade. He gave it a "B +."[22] While mindful of grade inflation, neither Kettl nor any of the other contributors to this volume feels that a "B" or "B +" is a bad way to measure what the NPR achieved in its first year. Our ultimate purpose, however, is not to grade the effort but to begin to develop a set of reasonable expectations and standards by which this and future broad-scale efforts at governmental reform may properly be judged. Although the contributors differ with each other about just how much the NPR has achieved to date and what it is likely to achieve in the future, they agree wholeheartedly that much that is good has already gone on inside the reinvention machine, while public awareness of and political attention to the need for major public service reforms at all levels of government have seldom been greater. Our collective aim, therefore, is to identify strengths and weaknesses in the NPR that will enable those in and out of government who truly care about improving government performance to make the most of this and other reform initiatives.

Whatever the administration and the 104th Congress make of the NPR, let no one suppose that meaningful reform can occur in defiance of certain basic facts. For example, at 2.1 million employees, the federal civilian work force is smaller today than it was in 1960.[23] Then as now, nine out of ten federal civilian workers lived outside the Washington, D.C., metropolitan area. The only part of the federal bureaucracy that has consistently grown over the last three decades is the ranks of political appointees. That has happened under presidents of both parties and shows no sign of abating. Every major domestic federal program enacted since the end of World War II has been administered directly not by federal workers but by state and local government employees and networks of private contractors. The Reagan administration made several serious efforts to "devolve" responsibility for social programs to the states. But those efforts did not, in the end, limit the scope of these programs, shrink their overall budgets, change the behavior of program staff or clients, or decrease the number of government employees who were responsible for administering them. Finally, while many, perhaps most, federal agencies could function well with less staff, some federal agencies and subunits within given agencies clearly need more staff to monitor pensions, manage prisoners, or perform other nontrivial functions.

No strategy for reforming federal bureaucracy can succeed unless it confronts these realities. As Kettl argues in the next chapter, in its first year the NPR took some important first steps on the road to real reform. But the biggest political and administrative challenges are yet to come.

Part One

2 Building Lasting Reform: Enduring Questions, Missing Answers

Donald F. Kettl

WHEN VICE PRESIDENT Al Gore released his National Performance Review (NPR) report in September 1993, some cynics dismissed it as just another hollow piece of rhetoric. Academic critics attacked it as dangerous to the public interest. They were both wrong. In its first year, the NPR has proven one of the most lively management reforms in American history. It has helped reorient the federal bureaucracy toward a far more effective attack on problems that it must learn to solve. Public support has been overwhelming.

Indeed, a careful review of the NPR's first year shows impressive results that disprove the cynics:[1]

A quick start on culture change. The report's theme that government had to work better and cost less resonated profoundly. Measuring the precise impact of the report on the culture of government agencies is impossible, and sustaining such an ambitious change will take a generation. But one conclusion is already certain: After the report, neither the behavior of government workers nor the debate about their jobs can ever be the same. The NPR's four key principles—cutting red tape, putting customers first, empowering employees to get results, and cutting back to basics—provided new, if rough, guideposts by which to steer and judge the federal bureaucracy.

Simplification of rules and processes. The NPR has also helped disentangle some of the rules and procedures that hinder effective federal management. In particular, the Office of Management and Budget (OMB) has issued waivers to make it easier for agency officials to survey citizen satisfaction with public services.[2] The Office of Personnel Management (OPM) eliminated the huge Federal Personnel Manual and the government's monstrous all-in-one application form, SF-171, as it delegated personnel decisions to government agencies.

A reform of the procurement process. The Clinton administration's enthusiastic support and hard work dovetailed with ongoing congressional effort on procurement reform. The result is an important simplification of the procurement process—the Federal Acquisition Streamlining Act of 1994—the first major reform of the government's contracting rules and procedures in a decade.

Improved coordination of the government's management activities. The NPR recommended designating a "chief operating officer" within each cabinet department to oversee management and promote culture change. In addition, the NPR suggested that the chief operating officers comprise, together with a handful of other top officials, a President's Management Council (PMC) "to lead the quality revolution and ensure the implementation" of the NPR.[3] In just a few months, the PMC has become a valuable weapon in the Clinton administration's efforts to marshal support in the agencies for the NPR. It has also proven an important mechanism for focusing governmentwide attention on key management issues and for organizing political support for major legislative issues. The coordinated efforts of PMC members contributed greatly to the passage of the first piece of the NPR legislative program.[4] The PMC also provided a secluded forum in which top officials could compare approaches—a "counsel council," in the words of Alice Rivlin, who chaired the PMC as OMB deputy director before being named the office's director.

Widespread innovation by federal managers. The NPR encouraged agency heads to establish "reinvention labs," and more than one hundred sprang up throughout the government.[5] Although there is no systematic survey of what these reinvention labs have accomplished, mounting evidence suggests that they represent exciting innovations in the federal government. Not all of the labs are likely to produce successes; the whole point of experimentation is to find what works and what does not. But the labs are generating an impressive amount of fresh ideas and information about how government workers can do their jobs better.

Vice President Gore has recognized governmental "heroes of reinvention" who slashed government red tape. One hero, the Department of the Interior's Roger Patterson, cut the process of approving fish ladders over dams from two and one half years to six months and from thirteen steps to just eight. The old process, Patterson said, "wasted a lot of time. It wasted a lot of money, and it wasted a lot of fish." Rodney Martin, a Small Business Administration employee in Texas, introduced a simple loan application for small business operators that replaced a far larger form. Meanwhile, General Services Administration (GSA) officials replaced long approval forms, which cost $50 each to process, with a new credit card for routine purchases.[6]

The NPR has unquestionably generated an enormous amount of activity, enthusiasm, and positive effort. Not all of the initial results can be traced directly to the NPR. Indeed, some of the earliest successes came from experiments started during the Bush administration. The NPR, however, unquestionably accelerated the pace of change and provided political cover for managers trying to break out of hidebound routines. The NPR has also generated a fresh sense of the possible. Managers were amazed that ideas that had lain fallow for years suddenly sprang to life. Small but important reforms that top managers had previously dismissed suddenly received higher-level approval.[7] The frenzy of activity did not convince all of the cynics, especially longtime mid-level government workers who had watched waves of reform wash over the bureaucracy for years without effect. But the NPR unquestionably fueled new excitement and energy.

Finally, for an administration under siege after the 1994 midterm congressional elections, the NPR gave Clinton's political strategists ammunition in their new battle with resurgent congressional Republicans. As one of the most significant political successes of the Clinton administration's first two years, the NPR quickly became part of the foundation for the president's 1996 reelection campaign. The first year of the NPR generated more progress than almost anyone—indeed, perhaps more than the reinventers themselves—imagined possible. The flurry that followed the 1994 election, however, sharply focused the NPR's vulnerability. The concept of "reinventing" government was so attractive, yet so broad that virtually any reform could fit within it.

Indeed, to get the NPR moving, the reinventers understandably made short-term tactical decisions to produce quick wins. The quick wins, however, came at the cost of building the foundation for lasting success. As a result, *the NPR is not now sustainable*. Indeed, some of the tactical decisions made to get the movement under way have undercut the chances for building in the long run a government that meets the Clinton administration's goal of a government that works better and costs less.[8] When the 1994 election produced a frenzied bidding war over further cuts in public employees and programs, the gap between the NPR's "costs less" and "works better" elements threatened to widen even further. Symbols of size overwhelmed debate over results.

This does not mean that the NPR is destined to fail. But its ultimate fate will depend on the reinventers' success in solving four critical problems.

First, *tensions*: The NPR has played an outside game focused on downsizing the federal government and an inside game focused on transforming the government's culture. At the most basic level, both interconnect in the effort to improve government's performance. Some of the movement's biggest headlines, in fact, came from the pledge to produce $108 billion in savings, especially by reducing the number of government employees and transforming the procurement process. At the operational level, however, it was natural for government employees to see the downsizing as yet another explicit attack on their jobs and behavior. By alienating public employees, NPR's strategy for public support—shrinking the federal government—risks undercutting its efforts to transform the government's inner workings.

Second, *capacity*: The NPR was dominated by arguments about dysfunctional forces—processes and structures that interfered with performance. Indeed, there was considerable suspicion within the NPR about the government's existing supervision, authority, and oversight. The report argued the need to bulldoze away these forces. The report, however, was far weaker on what ought to spring up in their place. The overwhelming lesson of the last generation of policy experimentation in the United States is that government programs do not manage themselves. Rather, success depends on finding the institutions, processes, money, technology, and especially people—that is, the capacity—to do the job. Will a reinvented government transform itself into a leaner government, faster on its feet and better able to adapt to the dizzying pace of change? Or will the legacy of reinvention be an even more hollow government that has far less capacity to do its job and is managed by employees with even less incentive to do their jobs well? The former would produce a truly revolutionary change. The latter would worsen the cycle of raised expectations, disappointing results, increased inefficiency, and greater public cynicism.[9]

Third, *ideas*: The NPR built on ambitious ideas about cutting red tape, putting customers first, empowering employees, and cutting back to basics. Far less clear, however, was what the concepts actually meant. Where do procedural due process and proper administrative safeguards become red tape? Who are the government's customers and how can they be served? Does customer service contradict other public goals? What would it take to empower employees, and what risks would empowerment create? Who decides what the basics are? In *Reinventing Government*, a driving spirit of the NPR, David Osborne and Ted Gaebler make the case that government should "steer, not row."[10] In what direction should government steer, and how good are the ideas that serve as its compass? Fuzzy thinking could staff the oars with government employees rowing simultaneously in conflicting directions. The lessons from reinventions in other countries is that a clear sense of purpose and sharp guiding principles are critical to success. Is the NPR intellectually mature enough to define such a purpose and provide guiding principles?

Finally, *glue*: The NPR builds on a philosophy of "empowering" government workers to make better decisions. It argues for a more entrepreneurial philosophy, with competition replacing monopoly-based command-and-control management. In short, the NPR seeks to shift power from Congress to the bureaucracy and, within the bureaucracy, from top to bottom levels. If empowered bureaucrats behave entrepreneurially, what glue will prevent government from disintegrating into a vast network of quasi-independent operators? What processes will ensure democratic accountability to elected officials? What processes will ensure that the public interest dominates private behavior?

The NPR has the potential, together with the New Deal and the Hoover commissions, to be one of the three most important administrative initiatives of the twentieth century.[11] Moreover, the NPR has demonstrated several important things. The public constituency for bureaucratic reform proved far larger than anyone anticipated. Many public managers, as eager as anyone to make government work better, quickly embraced the opportunities the NPR presented. Positive results, in the form of both lower costs and improved performance, are palpable. Its themes resonate with great political appeal. Most important, however, the knots tangling the work of the federal government and the jobs of federal executives have proven far tougher to cut than the initial waves of enthusiasm suggested.

The stakes for the NPR are huge: the public's trust in its government and government's own ability to adapt to ever-growing demands in an era of tight resources. Launching the revolution was the easy part. Sustaining the revolution will require much harder, and far less glamorous, work.[12] It will require considerable creativity, far more than either the NPR's leaders or their critics have demonstrated, in recognizing and solving the critical underlying problems that lie beyond the beachhead.

Tensions: Which NPR?

Assessing the NPR is difficult: there is no such thing as *the* NPR. In practice, the NPR has been a messy and sometimes disorganized multifront war against the government's performance problems.

The Three-Front Revolution

There are, in fact, three different NPRs. First, the NPR's supreme commanders, especially senior staff members working out of the vice president's office, have focused on how the NPR can help the Clinton administration attract voters. The administration's political strategists have worried constantly about how to win the approximately 19 percent of American voters who supported Ross Perot in 1992. They have focused single-mindedly on the NPR's cost savings and personnel reductions as critical elements in the Clinton administration's reelection strategy.

Second, the NPR's skeletal staff has concentrated on preaching the gospel of reinvention to anyone who would listen and on coordinating the crosscutting reform issues, like procurement reform and customer service. The NPR has relied heavily on presidential management interns and staff from government agencies on short-term detail to the effort. There has been only a small continuous core to the NPR staff, which has limited its ability to ensure consistent follow-through.

Third, an army of reinventers throughout the executive branch has had primary responsibility for most NPR efforts. Nearly all of the 384 recommendations in the NPR report, in fact, relied on actions by individual agencies.[13] For example, the report charged NASA with improving its procurement practices, the Department of Labor with creating one-stop career management centers, and the Environmental Protection Agency with supporting market-based instead of regulatory approaches to pollution control. Agency-based commanders carried the reinvention flag into the bureaucratic trenches to apply the movement's broad principles to their agency's specific problems.

Because it has operated simultaneously at such different levels and pursued such varied objectives, it is difficult to assess fully the NPR's results. Indeed, the revolution has proceeded on many different fronts, and the fighting has mattered as much as the winning. In part, this was because the movement's leaders believed that front-line bureaucrats were the best judge of the right direction. In part, this was also because they believed that inertia posed the greatest problem. Forcing innovative action was the quickest way, in their minds, to ensure success, and activity became NPR's immediate measure of success. The NPR's six-month status report was little more than a study of motion (laws passed, executive orders issued, action started).[14]

Assessing the NPR's more fundamental results is difficult because it has pursued radically different, indeed conflicting, goals. The NPR seeks, in the words of its subtitle, a government that "works better and costs less." On one level, of course, more effective programs can save money. On a deeper level, however, the subtitle represents an uneasy truce between opposing camps in the reinvention effort. During the Clinton administration's six-month performance review in 1993, the "costs less" forces, led especially by political strategists within the White House, argued that nothing mattered as much as shrinking the size of the government. They also contended that without significant savings the NPR would not be taken seriously. The "works better" team argued for changing the culture of federal agencies to improve public programs. The August 1993 budget battle helped define the outcome. Senators holding the critical votes to approve the administration's first budget insisted on even bigger cuts. The administration's bargains with key members of Congress pushed some of the NPR's money-saving ideas (like elimination of the government's helium reserve) off the table, but it also underlined the critical political importance of making the NPR a money-saver. The promised $108 billion in deficit reduction soon became the bedrock of the movement.

As a result, the ghost of deficit reduction lurked behind every promise of empowering workers or improving performance. The short-term pay-off from the tactic was huge. Public support for the NPR report was overwhelming and delivered the Clinton administration the strongest bump in approval during its first eighteen months in office. Moving from the headlines to the front lines, however, surfaced the conflict implicit in the "works better–costs less" theme. Because the largest single piece of the promised savings was to come from reducing the number of federal employees, the threat to their jobs became the defining element of the NPR for most federal employees.

There was a major conflict between the "works better" and "costs less" objectives. The NPR staff trumpeted "doing more with less." Government workers, however, believed that they had already been stretched to the limit by a decade of budget cuts; struggling to do their jobs with even less help could only mean doing less with less, they worried. The focus on using the NPR to produce cost savings risked undercutting both the government's capacity to do its work and bureaucrats' incentives for taking the considerable risks that the NPR demanded. Indeed, some government employees began calling the reinvention movement "reinvent-sham."

The disparity between the two objectives of the NPR had an important tactical advantage for each camp. The downsizers could allow the performance improvers considerable latitude so long as the promised savings materialized. The preoccupation of the downsizers with the budget cuts gave the performance improvers considerable maneuvering room in charting fundamental change. Thus, in the first year the lack of connection gave the Clinton administration good headlines, yet insulated the front lines from political interference.

This tactical advantage, however, hurt the movement's long-term potential. Actually producing the savings proved far more difficult than the report promised. And the search for quick deficit reductions undercut the long-term effort to improve government performance.

Delivering the Savings

Most of the $108 billion savings the NPR promised was to come from three categories: a smaller bureaucracy ($40.4 billion); program and organizational changes in individual agencies ($36.4 billion); and a 5 percent reduction in procurement costs achieved by streamlining the contracting process ($22.5 billion). [15]

In its first year, the NPR in fact did produce substantial savings. Its first-year status report outlines $12.2 billion in likely savings (based on actions taken before August 1994 and actions pending in Congress), nearly the $12.6 billion the NPR projected for the first year in its original report. Looking into the future, the NPR could proudly argue that its first-year actions, projected over five years, would produce almost 60 percent of the $108 billion in savings promised in 1993. [16] Two important facts about the savings, however, stood out. First, most of the remaining savings the NPR hoped to obtain were based on tactics that were notoriously hard to implement (reducing intergovernmental

Figure 2-1. NPR Savings, Fiscal Years 1995–99

Billions of dollars

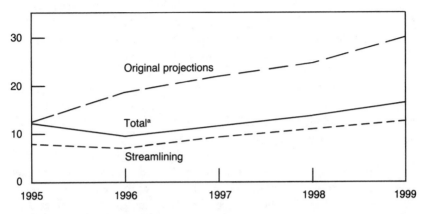

Source: National Performance Review, *Creating a Government That Works Better and Costs Less: Status Report* (Government Printing Office, 1994), p. 121.
a. Decisions as of September 1994.

administrative costs, for example) and even harder to measure (how can any analyst know what administrative costs might have been in the absence of a reform?). Second, nearly all the savings the Clinton administration quickly produced came from streamlining and downsizing the federal work force, as figure 2-1 shows.

Downsizing the bureaucracy was the keystone of the cost savings. Where did the magical figure of 252,000 (later 272,900) come from?[17] Although many observers believed that the figure was an arbitrary one, Robert Stone, NPR project director, had an explanation:

We made a head count government-wide of supervisors, budget specialists, financial specialists, procurement specialists, personnel specialists and headquarters people, plus regional offices. The total count was—I think the report says 690,000. We have a little later count that's about 670,000. We said, "This is twice as big as it ought to be."

But if you cut that group in half, you have to substitute for them—for example, groups that measure progress, that set goals. So you can't just cut 335,000. The judgment was that maybe a quarter of what you cut out you ought to put back to perform these other functions. So half of the control and micromanagement force is 335,000, a quarter of the 335,000 is 85,000 or 83,000. That leaves you at about 252,000. That's roughly the arithmetic.[18]

Stone and his NPR colleagues believed that government's problem lay with the layers of checkers and cross-checkers. By reducing those employees, they believed, the government would be leaner and more effective. About 55 percent of the cuts, moreover, were to come from the ranks of middle managers, although neither the report nor subsequent discussion made clear exactly who was in the "middle."[19]

Several problems plague that logic, however. First, the target came from an *assumption* about where and how large government's problem was, not the result of any careful analysis nor of an assessment of what kind of government was needed. There was no assurance, therefore, that the downsizing would shrink government in the right places.

Second, there was considerable risk that the downsizing plan would induce the wrong workers to leave first. Indeed, many of the officials who quickly took advantage of the buyout were some of the most seasoned managers, in whom the government had invested a great deal for decades. (They, of course, had the most opportunities in the private sector.) The downsizing threatened to be indiscriminate, and government managers worried that they would lose some of their best people.[20]

Indeed, the GAO found that, although most departments had not been hurt by the work force reductions, several agencies argued that the losses hurt their ability to do their jobs. Officials in one agency said, "The buyout has 'gutted' corporate memory. . . . The number of key managers who left has resulted in a deleterious domino effect. Depth and coverage in certain offices . . . has been negatively impacted."[21]

Third, the NPR argued that the government's problem was its layers, not its people. In particular, the report argued that the federal government had far too many middle managers. As Paul Light has found, however, government's most significant layering problem occurs at the very top, not in the middle. The 3,000 political appointees who populate the top of the bureaucracy can produce layers upon layers of officials between the president and the career service.[22] Attacking the middle would do nothing about the problems at the top. The debate soon became moot, though, as the incessant downsizing pressure made the NPR team preoccupied with the numbers instead of the layers.

Fourth and most important, the targets quickly became the political acid test of the NPR. Strategic planning initially was to drive the cuts, but the head-count game quickly replaced the planning. The downsizing goal became the administration's most politically visible target and hence its most vulnerable front. By committing itself to an arbitrary reduction, the NPR eliminated any chance that a serious look at the composition of the work force and the skill mix of government would drive the reductions.[23]

There was a widespread assumption that the downsizing would be imposed across the board. In fact, during the first full year of the personnel cuts (fiscal year 1995), two-thirds of the reduction was to come from the Defense Department as part of the broader reduction in the defense establishment. Some other agencies were to be held even while others were to achieve relatively small reductions. Nor was the downsizing uniform across the levels of the bureaucracy or between Washington and field offices. That made it all the more difficult for the administration to describe clearly what the downsizing would accomplish and where it would occur (which, of course, only increased the anxiety of government workers, even those who in the end would not be affected). Moreover, having harvested strong public support in the polls simply by *announcing* the reduction, administration officials were left with the tough job of achieving it with little additional political capital to be won.

The savings, however, proved far easier to promise than to deliver. In October 1993 the administration packaged some of the reforms in H.R. 3400, the Government Reform and Savings Act. Administration officials estimated that the bill would produce $6 billion in savings over five years.[24] However, the Congressional Budget Office reviewed the bill and estimated that savings would be only $2.5 billion, less than half the amount claimed by the administration. The CBO's scorekeeping embarrassed the administration and undercut the confidence of many observers in the NPR's other savings estimates. Administration officials and members of Congress alike had looked hungrily at the promised $108 billion in savings as a funding source for new programs, such as the administration's crime bill. If the savings proved hard to deliver, the enthusiasm of many policymakers would shrink. The dispute with the CBO also caused the administration immediate trouble in winning congressional support for the buyout legislation, on which the downsizing and hence the largest piece of the NPR's deficit reduction depended.[25] Members of Congress were unwilling to pass the bill if they could not be confident whether it would, in the calculus of the deficit reduction process, save or cost money. In the end, the OMB and CBO reconciled their disagreement over the savings estimates, and the administration won passage of a buyout bill in March 1994, but not before the dispute underlined three serious issues.

First, although the savings proposals were only a small part of the

NPR, they became its driving theme. Cost reductions take up only a few pages out of 172 in the NPR report. Nevertheless, because of the pressure on the administration to produce savings through the NPR and the administration's own efforts to sell the reform, the cost savings became the movement's touchstone. In the high politics of the NPR, nothing meant as much as the cost savings.

Second, amid all the rhetoric of "empowering employees" and "serving customers," the dollar savings seemed the most solid feature of the NPR. In practice, the savings proved perhaps the hardest element of the NPR to judge. Producing long-term savings sometimes required short-run costs, such as providing payments to government employees willing to leave the government. Sometimes short-term savings risked incurring long-term costs, if downsizing, for example, led the wrong employees to leave or weakened government management. In almost all cases, putting hard numbers on actual savings, beyond the downsizing of the federal work force, turned out to require extraordinary feats of budgetary analysis. That complexity not only increased the difficulty of assessing the NPR's savings but also sometimes surrounded the NPR with debates of such technical complexity as to undermine their political value.

Finally, Congress proved eager to support the savings proposals in general but often backed away from taking particular actions required to achieve them. In late April 1994, for example, the House voted to exempt the Veterans Health Administration (VHA) from any personnel reductions. The VHA accounted for 212,000 full-time employees, about 90 percent of all the staff at the Department of Veterans Affairs and more than any other civilian agency. The Senate later voted to exempt Treasury law enforcement staff from personnel cuts. A few months later, when the Transportation Department submitted an NPR proposal to turn the nation's air traffic control system over to a government corporation, congressional opposition forced a hasty retreat. All three actions proved frightening omens for the reinventers' efforts to shrink federal employment.

Despite the support for the NPR that many members of Congress showed, they also demonstrated that they could easily unravel, strand by strand, its critical threads. As the NPR staff were drafting their report, they had devoted virtually no attention to building congressional support for their recommendations. They therefore had no offensive plan to build congressional support for the plan and no defense against forays against individual elements. When they first announced their report,

NPR staffers argued that they could implement a majority of the recommendations without congressional action. The first year of their efforts demonstrated that they could launch and sustain *none* of the recommendations without at least congressional acquiescence.

Improving Performance

On the front lines in the federal agencies, a quite different movement developed. The watchwords were *employee empowerment* to produce *culture change*. Commerce Secretary Ron Brown, for example, distributed "permission slips" to his employees, and Education Secretary Richard Riley issued "reinvention licenses." Secretary Brown's permission slips asked bureaucrats a series of questions: Is what I want to do right for my customers? Is it legal? Is it something I am willing to be accountable for? Is it consistent with my agency's mission? Is it a wise use of my time? The permission slip then told employees that, if the answers are "yes," they already have permission and should press ahead. The presumption was that employees too often hold back for fear of retribution, but that empowered employees will take more initiative and solve problems more effectively.

Many federal employees, however, argued that such slogans were hollow and simple-minded. From previous reforms that had swept over government, they had learned two lessons. Bold rhetoric often had little substance behind it. And new revolutions soon replaced old ones, so they could easily wait out any new reform. Indeed, there had been total quality management, which replaced the Reagan administration's privatization initiatives, which followed on the heels of the Carter administration's reorganizations, which came after the Nixon administration's management by objectives, which succeeded the Johnson administration's planning-programming-budgeting system. "This, too, shall pass" was the watchword among countless managers (and "none too soon" others added under their breaths). Many managers had little confidence that reinventing government would produce any better results or prove any longer lasting than earlier initiatives.

Not all federal managers wanted to be empowered, moreover. Being empowered meant taking risks, and the reinventers could offer little more than broad assurances that employees would not be punished if "empowered" behavior produced criticism. The impenetrable maze of forms and regulations, furthermore, worked to the great advantage of those who knew how to maneuver through them. One senior government official found that some senior bureaucrats were resisting the reinvention movement. "They have figured out how to maneuver within the current system," the official explained. "'Don't change it,' they say, 'because I've already figured out how to work within it.'"[26] Their power and comfort came from learning how to survive an admittedly dysfunctional system.

Finally, empowerment requires a top-down commitment to bottom-up decisionmaking. Many of the Clinton administration's top officials embraced the principle but were so overwhelmed by the demands of their offices that they had little time to promote it. "How do you tell political appointees who are already working fourteen-hour days that they ought to be more committed?" one government employee asked.[27] As many lower-level officials worked on reinvention projects, they worried constantly about the degree to which they could commit their superiors to the process and, without their sustained commitment, how much real change they could effect.

Empowerment therefore remained a broad goal with shallow support. It was a heady concept only vaguely defined. It required new political leadership that was hard to produce under the press of regular business. It asked government employees to abandon an admittedly dysfunctional system, through which they nevertheless had learned to negotiate, for a far riskier way of doing business without any guarantee of compensating political support. Many government employees asked why they should take such risks when empowerment seemed only a rhetorical cover to threaten their jobs.

Reinvention throughout the federal government thus has proven a wildly uneven initiative.[28] In some departments, harried top managers paid almost no attention to reinventing government's goals. It seemed a distraction from what, to them, were far more important issues, and they followed only the letter of the presidential executive orders and directives. Other agency heads decided that reinventing their offices would have to wait until the endless appointments process produced a full complement of presidential appointees. Some cabinet secretaries and agency heads, however, saw in the NPR a license for broad managerial discretion. It allowed them to seize the reins of their agencies more quickly and to help sweep troublesome rules and processes, such as OMB clearances, out of the way.

However, for most federal managers, the defining reality of the NPR soon became the work force reduction. Despite the bold phrases in the

NPR report about empowerment, customer service, reduction of red tape, creating market dynamics, forming labor-management partnerships, and investing in greater productivity, the immediate threat of fewer employees was what grabbed their attention.

Capacity: What Will It Take to Do The Job?

Stripped of the rhetoric and stories, improving government performance is fundamentally about people and the tools they need to do their jobs. In 1986, Charles H. Levine warned of a "quiet crisis" steadily but surely eroding the capacity of the federal government. Levine cautioned that the quiet crisis, "if left unattended, could produce major breakdowns in government performance in the future."[29] The Volcker commission echoed Levine's concern and worried that "if these trends continue, America will soon be left with a government of the mediocre, locked into careers of last resort or waiting for a chance to move on to other jobs."[30]

The evidence of America's performance problems might appear in ridiculous rules or tangled processes. Bulldozing through those rules and processes undoubtedly can help clear the way for real reform. But what will replace them? And more important, who will be there to do the job? After committing itself to sweeping away the detritus of a century of public management, after pledging employee empowerment and customer service, the NPR has not yet forcefully articulated a vision for the public service of the future. There is still time. Indeed, the NPR is preparing a civil service reform package for late 1994 or 1995. Without solving the people problems of American government, however, the NPR will be worse than incomplete. It will sow the seeds of its own undoing. Having dismantled an admittedly dysfunctional system without designing its replacement, it could leave public management even more impoverished and government performance even worse.

Public Employee Unions

The keystone of the NPR's people strategy lay in building bridges to public employee unions. The NPR learned one lesson from its survey of private organizations: "No move to reorganize for quality can succeed without the full and equal participation of workers and their unions. Indeed, a unionized workplace can provide a leg up because forums already exist for labor and management exchange."[31] Building a partnership with the unions thus became the centerpiece of the NPR's relationship with government employees, and the core of union relations was to be a new National Partnership Council (NPC).[32]

The NPC has a dozen members, including the heads of the three major federal employee unions (the American Federation of Government Employees, the National Federation of Federal Employees, and the National Treasury Employees Union), a representative from the Public Employee Department of the AFL-CIO, representatives of seven federal agencies, and a special representative of the vice president. Its charge is broad:

advising the President on labor-management relations; supporting the creation of labor-management partnerships and promoting partnership efforts; and proposing legislative changes related to labor relations, staffing, classification and compensation, and performance management.[33]

The NPC's importance lay both in the administration's desire to frame a new partnership with federal employee unions and in short-term political imperatives. When the NPR became committed to a dollar target for cost savings, and when a reduction in the number of public employees became a prime vehicle for producing those savings, the NPR acquired an immediate political problem. For a Democratic administration already embroiled in controversy with the unions over the North American Free Trade Agreement, another battle with unions was distinctly unappealing. The administration tackled the problem with a two-front effort: it aimed the personnel cuts at middle managers, who tended to be less unionized than lower-level workers; and it promised union leaders the NPC as a forum for dealing directly with the administration.

The political strategy worked. The NPR avoided a quick counterattack by the unions and in fact won their endorsement for the report. Moreover, the NPC got to work and helped lead the charge for abolishing the 10,000-page Federal Personnel Manual. In January 1994 Clinton administration officials and career civil servants joined together to throw the stacks of volumes into a dump truck parked outside the Office of Personnel Management. OPM Director James B. King, in celebrating the event, said, "It is written in such gobbledygook that it takes a team of Washington's finest attorneys to understand what is required to hire, fire, classify and reward employees. . . . and that's nonsense."[34]

OPM continued to eliminate core elements of the existing system. Three months after abolishing the Federal Personnel Manual, OPM officials dumped the much-hated SF-171, the standard federal personnel application form. "I just think the ordinary citizen has no idea of how bad this form is," King said at the time. He demonstrated the fact by unfurling his own SF-171, which stretched to more than his own height of six feet, four inches.[35]

These actions reflected serious ongoing talks within the NPR about four different issues:[36]

—Bargaining on workplace issues, including empowerment, the rights of managers in hiring and disciplining employees, and compulsory union membership for government employees in units already composed of at least 60 percent union members;

—Constructing a agency-based hiring process;

—Collapsing the fifteen-level General Schedule classification system into a smaller number of so-called broad bands; and

—Promoting performance management systems, including assessment of employees' work. Although such systems had been around for years, the NPR galvanized support for them. The discussion included streamlining the process for firing underperforming workers but was less clear on how underperformers would be identified.[37]

The NPC arrangement defused what could have been serious union opposition to the NPR. However, it also created difficult ongoing problems for the NPR. Representatives of government managers' associations, notably the Federal Executive Institute Alumni Association, the Federal Managers Association, and the Senior Executives Association, were furious that they had been excluded from the process.[38] These managers "were flabbergasted to hear of the creation of the NPC," said Allan Kam, a senior attorney in the National Highway Traffic Safety Administration and president of the Federal Executive Institute Alumni Association. "It was as though we were being disenfranchised."[39]

Representatives of nearly twenty different managers' groups organized their own committee, the Coalition for Effective Change, to counter the NPC. The coalition began meeting regularly with NPR officials, but the administration's early deal with the unions, coupled with the downsizing targeted at middle managers, unquestionably worsened the NPR's relations with many federal employees. Managers came to believe that the NPR was a two-track system, with different treatment for the unions and managers. In fact, they "were stunned that career managers, executives, and nonunion professionals had been excluded from the National Partnership Council."[40] The coalition made the point in its report to the NPR:

> The [NPC] Report . . . is silent on the role and treatment of managers and supervisors as *employees* in a changed system. Supervisors, managers, and management officials who are excluded from the bargaining unit also are employees who have certain inherent rights to fairness and equity both individually and collectively that are not addressed in the Report. Who will speak for these employees . . . ? Who will represent their interests . . .?[41]

Despite the central role that the public employee unions played in the NPR's first months, no one really knew how broadly the unions actually represented government workers. OPM statistics show that 59 percent of federal government employees (or about 1.3 million) work in units covered by bargaining agreements.[42] Only a relatively small fraction of employees in these units, however, are dues-paying union members; the actual number is a secret closely guarded by the unions.

Union organization, moreover, varies tremendously across categories of federal employment. Nearly all (91 percent) of blue-collar employees work in union shops, while only 53 percent of white-collar employees are in units with exclusive bargaining agreements. On the other hand, the number of white-collar employees who work in units with exclusive agreements is three times greater than the number of blue-collar employees. Thus, although blue-collar workers are more unionized, they represent a much smaller share of federal employment. The white-collar unions are far more important. Union activity, however, varies widely across federal departments.[43]

That means a union-based strategy plays out very differently: by an employee's level (since lower-level employees tend to be far more unionized and top-level employees were excluded in the NPC); by kind of work (since white-collar employees tend to be far less unionized); and by agency (since unions have been far more successful in organizing some agencies than others). The political advantages of the tactic are obvious, but the potential for building a long-term strategy for solving the quiet crisis of the civil service is far less.

When the Clinton administration turned to civil service reform in late 1994, the fragile foundation of its partnership with the unions became starkly clear. When early drafts of the legislation omitted any mention of labor-management relations, union officials called it "really sad." As Robert M. Tobias, president of the National Treasury Employees Union, explained, sweeping reforms of the hiring and performance management process unaccompanied by responsiveness to union concerns "would constitute the worst of all possible worlds."[44]

Managers and Management

The NPR's tactics worried managers throughout government. Headlines of personnel newsletters ranged from "GORED!!! 'Reinventing Government' Plan Creates Spoils System" to "From Rowing to Steering to Abandoning Ship."[45] The Federal Executive Institute Alumni Association surveyed a group of senior federal managers and found that 61 percent said that morale was low in their agencies, compared with 34 percent a year before.[46] "There are lots of angry SESers [members of the Senior Executive Service]," one federal manager explained. He was an administrator of a federal "reinvention laboratory," a strong reinvention advocate working the front lines of the reform. Nevertheless, he was discouraged by the downsizing campaign. Middle managers, he believed, were the targets of the campaign. "The middle chunk is a very disenfranchised group right now. They see little incentive to play because they weren't involved in framing the goals."[47]

Just who *are* middle managers? In the debate, the "middle" sometimes seemed to cover everyone just above front-line workers and just below political appointees. The NPR continually insisted that the cuts were addressed at the system, not the people. A memo from NPR staffer John Ayers to project director Robert Stone underlined that "the attack on the central control structures is not an attack on the employees."[48] Despite such assurances, however, virtually everyone who could potentially be considered a "middle manager" felt threatened by the NPR.

As the NPR evolved, the disconnect between the downsizing pressures and union partnerships and the strategy for improving government work and supervision grew wider. Managers—middle managers in particular—felt vulnerable and under attack just as they were being challenged to take more risks. Many middle managers laughed cynically at the NPR's charge to "do more with less," convinced that in the long run the only enduring legacy of the movement would be the cuts in government employment. A favorite slogan among the reinventers is "get on the train or get under it"; charting a course through high demands and inescapable conflicts is the only option, they quite rightly argue. If the problems are inescapable, so too are the anxieties of government workers. There is, quite simply, no easy way out and no way to avoid the turmoil.

Middle managers play a critical role in the reinvention effort. They occupy the key positions throughout government that determine how well programs work. They are the project managers, branch chiefs, and section heads who shape programs and the behavior of their agencies. They model the behavior of their subordinates.

Vice President Gore has spoken enthusiastically about how a "shift of our understanding of human capacity" has led us to realize that "individuals within organizations are capable of producing more than had been previously thought possible." Revolutionary information technology has created the potential for flatter organizations with quicker response. Speaking to federal managers, Gore said, "We can't achieve [major changes] simply by making a report. It can only be done by individuals. We are relying on you to lead this charge."[49] Federal managers have heard the message, but the voice of large cuts in the government service has spoken even louder. Fulfilling the promise of the NPR depends on their action, but the NPR has singularly undermotivated them.

If the NPR is to have any real staying power, the movement will have to motivate the managers who most determine government's results. They have sensed the large conflict between downsizing the bureaucracy and reshaping the bureaucracies they are trying to manage. Some members of the career bureaucracy have quietly noted the irony that, although Ronald Reagan waged war on the bureaucracy, it remained largely unscathed by his presidency. Bill Clinton, on whom they had counted for support, produced the cuts that Reagan could never manage. Many federal managers worried out loud that enthusiasm for the "culture change" would evaporate, leaving behind only the residue of the cuts: a bureaucracy with even less capacity to tackle the challenges of a new century.[50]

Dealing with labor-management relations is not the same as dealing with supervisor-subordinate relations. The issues have always been different. In the context of the NPR, the distinction is even more critical. The report calls on managers to motivate their employees, to build broad partnerships, to cut across agency boundaries, to take chances.

By building on a partnership with unions, the NPC approach reinforces much that helped to create and maintain the very forces the NPR is seeking to change.

This is not to criticize the active role and significant accomplishments that the NPC has to its credit. Using such a partnership as the primary mechanism for dealing with the government's work force, however, carries grave risks for the NPR. It has alienated many government employees who are not union members, especially managers on whom partnership with the unions will ultimately depend. Most important, it has missed a chance to redefine the nature of government work and determine how the relationship among government workers ought to be transformed. It is a less-than-half-a-loaf solution that all too easily can lead reformers to convince themselves that they have in fact solved the problem.

Solving the Quiet Crisis

There is little question about what needs to be done to create a high-performing civil service. Levine outlined the elements nearly a decade ago: strong political leadership; pay for performance; greater freedom for workers in entering and leaving the federal service; and a carefully designed pay scale to recruit and keep the best workers (an issue growing more important and more complex as increasing numbers of women and minorities join the federal work force).[51] To that can be added greater freedom for managers in hiring, promoting, and firing workers (to which the NPR is committed); and a system for measuring government performance (to which I will return below).

More than anything else, however, what is needed is an aggressively defined vision, bolstered by top-level support, of the new job of the federal executive.[52] In a March 1994 speech on "The New Job of the Federal Executive," Vice President Gore laid out seven principles to guide action: developing a clear vision, creating a team environment, empowering employees, putting customers first, communicating with employees, cutting red tape, and creating clear accountability.[53] The speech was useful indeed. It was, however, more an outline for future thinking than a clearly developed set of principles. Any set of principles has to take account of four important issues.[54]

REDEFINING THE CAREERS OF CIVIL SERVANTS. The existing civil service builds on a system of clearly defining administrative tasks and finding the best people to fill them. Both the rapid pace of change and the complexity of administrative demands have rendered that system obsolete. The modern civil service—indeed, all of American government—needs to be far quicker to adapt and change and better equipped to deal with the challenges it faces. A reinvented civil service will have to invest more in people than in process. People will have to be more mobile and faster to learn; agencies will have to acquire more flexibility to attract the people they need, if only on a temporary basis. Government employees will be working across organizational boundaries instead of being surrounded by them. In short, the American civil service must learn the lessons being taught around the world: the key reality is "the shift from a career service based on ongoing structural certainties to one based on agreed, ongoing values and principles" to compensate for rapid structural, procedural, and programmatic changes, as Denis Ives, the director of the Australian civil service, put it.[55] The NPR must resist the temptation to replace the existing civil service procedures with new ones, when the problem is far deeper than just procedures. Macro-level values must drive the micro-level repairs.

SUPPORTING PUBLIC SERVANTS WITH TECHNOLOGY. It is not unusual for college students who have left behind their campus computer labs for federal internships to complain when they return about the prehistoric technology they found. Over the last few years, the government has made great strides in better equipping federal managers with the technology they need to do their jobs. Nevertheless, managers lag behind their private-sector colleagues in workplace tools. For example, managers are under heavy pressure to develop more customer-friendly processes, like single application forms for related programs. Federal workers often say that they would love to do just that, but they lack a computer system to link different offices and data bases together. The reinventing government initiative has largely been sold as a cost-cutting measure, and undoubtedly huge cost savings are possible. However, many long-term cost savings and increases in effectiveness will require up-front investment. The government cannot leapfrog into the twenty-first century with decades-old technology.

TRAINING. One of the most important investments is in training. The NPR has recognized the importance of training government employees, especially to reinforce the messages of employee empowerment and culture change. The principal approach has been a cascading method: training trainers, who in turn train others to spread the word.[56] Although this is a valuable first step, it is not the basis on which to institutionalize the NPR's goals. Making it stick over the long run will require a far larger investment in much more sophisticated training. Australia, by contrast, has been at government reform work far longer. Its public service invests 5 percent of the personnel budget in training and recognizes that failure to provide adequate training "may cause confusion about overall organisational aims and structure, with loss of motivation and decline in performance."[57] In the United States, by comparison, the federal government spends only 1.3 percent of its personnel budget on training.[58] Moreover, senior Australian officials have argued after reflection that it was the training they organized, especially for their middle managers, that proved most useful in their reforms.[59] Without far greater attention in the United States to training, and significantly more investment in the government employees who will do the job, the result may be confusion, loss of motivation, and performance decline.

PROVIDING CENTRAL STEERING. The NPR pledges to reform the personnel system by untying the central personnel rules and vesting more power in agency managers. Indeed, it has already moved to a surprising degree in that direction. What, then, is the role of OPM if it gives away most of its work and authority?[60] The NPR suggests that OPM needs to transform itself into a consulting organization, providing "leadership for the cultural change."[61] That, to put it mildly, is not an easy process. It is not simple to change the internal culture of OPM from a regulatory agency into a consulting firm. Former regulators are not always good consultants, and in any case a new consulting agency ought to be far smaller than the old organization. But OPM's role needs to be more than advice giving. It needs to be the collector and analyzer of information on the 2 million workers in the federal service, tracking trends and forecasting future problems. It needs to oversee the newly empowered agency-based personnel systems, for a set of core values surely will remain. Most of all, OPM needs to set the tone, to transmit the values and principles that a reinvented work force will follow.

Ideas: What Are the Guiding Principles?

Vice President Gore and his staff launched the NPR with an overriding preference for action over ideas. They cared far less about theory than about quick results. Nevertheless, important ideas were implicit within the movement they launched. These ideas, moreover, proved crucial in steering the movement. They defined the broad themes, communicated to government employees the kind of behavior the NPR desired, and helped shape the way the news media covered the NPR. The lesson of every major government reform around the world has been that ideas drive action and frame the standards by which others judge that action. So taking stock of these ideas is critical in appraising the NPR.

For the NPR, two ideas were central. First, the reinventers argued, if implicitly, the need to transfer power from Congress to the executive branch. In the NPR report, Congress makes few appearances except as the source of overregulation and micromanagement, and those problems are critical to the NPR's diagnosis of government's performance problems. Reinventing government requires ending overregulation and micromanagement. That implicitly demands that Congress give up its penchant for tinkering with the bureaucracy and leave more of management to the managers.

Second, the Clinton reformers argued, much more explicitly, that government employees needed to be empowered. Real empowerment meant, in the jargon of private-sector reformers, putting more decisions on the shop floor. In a production process, the ultimate symbol and reality of empowerment is the ability of any employee to stop the production line. That, in turn, demands that top managers decentralize power to front-line workers. The NPR builds on just that philosophy and envisions, both literally and figuratively, giving front-line government workers the power to stop the line. This approach implies a transfer of power from Congress to the bureaucracy and, within the bureaucracy, from top-level to lower-level officials.

The reinventers built heavily on Osborne and Gaebler's *Reinventing Government,* earlier reform classics like *In Search of Excellence,* and management gurus like Peter Drucker.[62] Newer ideas, from "continuous improvement" to "reengineering," crept into the reinvention lexicon as well, and private-sector experience with these movements heavily flavored the early days of the NPR.[63] They also borrowed heavily on the lore of government reform abroad, especially in Great Britain, Australia, and New Zealand.[64] The reinventers rarely stopped to make clear the intellectual provenance of their actions. They quickly looked for ideas, any ideas, that promised some purchase on American governmental problems. As a result, they often seized on concepts that were complex, occasionally contradictory, often far beyond existing public management theory, and sometimes in advance of anything written down. That makes deducing the guiding principles of the NPR difficult, but it also makes it all the more important to outline and analyze them.

What mattered to the staff of the NPR was finding principles that could spark the movement or notions that could fan the flames of reform. What they promoted has sparked many critics, especially among public administration scholars who contended that the movement was wrong-headed or even dangerous to American democracy.[65] In fact, the NPR builds on some time-tested administrative reforms. It also adds some ideas unique to American administrative reform. Together they constitute a surprisingly robust body of thinking with significant implications that sweep far beyond the NPR.

Continuities

Two important tensions from administrative history helped shape the NPR: the ageless battle between Hamiltonians and Madisonians over the proper role of executive power in American democracy, and the eternal debate within administrative theory over how to balance central control over policy with decentralized power to fit policy to particular problems.

On one level, the NPR is a recurring skirmish in a battle over executive power that has raged since the founding of the Republic. Followers of Alexander Hamilton have long pressed for a stronger executive; long opposing them have been followers of James Madison, who argued for powerful democratic checks on executive power. Had Alexander Hamilton been alive during the NPR's 1993 campaign, it would have been easy to see him as reinventer-in-chief. In the *Federalist Papers*, he argued for "energy in the Executive" and contended that "a feeble Executive implies a feeble execution of the government. A feeble execution is but another phrase for bad execution; and a government ill executed, whatever it may be in theory, must be in practice a bad government."[66] Hamilton believed that only a strong central government, led by a powerful executive, could help the country realize its potential.

Hamilton, of course, had a difficult time convincing most of his contemporaries, and in the end his strong views cost him his life in a duel with Aaron Burr. If the Framers of the Constitution agreed on anything, it was that the mischiefs of the king's rule over the colonies would not be repeated. James Madison's genius lay in constructing a system that simultaneously recognized the inescapable need for an executive and constructed a system for holding executive power in check. The checks-and-balances system, in fact, is most fundamentally a strategy for checking and balancing *presidential* power. Congress was the first branch; its role was to assert the people's primacy, especially over the potential abuse of executive power.[67] If the judiciary was the least dangerous branch, the executive was the most dangerous one. True Madisonians, therefore, saw any attempt to increase executive power as dangerous.

The reinventers are Hamiltonians. Their views produced what Hamiltonian arguments always produce: strong, fierce reaction from Madisonians who quite predictably warned about the dangers of concentrated executive power. The attacks were strongest among many traditional public administration scholars who were, in their hearts, Madisonians, and who saw the NPR as a dangerous aberration from increasing and rightful congressional control of the executive branch. The reinventers, meanwhile, reacted as Hamiltonians always do. They argued that a feeble executive threatened government performance and that only more energetic, empowered bureaucrats could shrink government's performance deficit.

On another level, the NPR is about where power ought to rest over those decisions that policymakers put in the executive domain. This debate is even older than the Madison-Hamilton dispute and is, indeed, one of the ageless questions of administration, public or private. Centralization strengthens the hands of policymakers and their control over the actions of their subordinates. Such control, however, weakens the ability of front-line workers to match broad policy with the problems they find. Lower-level workers inevitably have at least some discretion. (Just how many drivers traveling over the speed limit should the highway patrol arrest—and how much speed over the limit warrants an arrest?) The centralization-decentralization issue frames an eternal dilemma: too much higher-level control limits the flexibility of lower-level workers; too much flexibility by lower-level workers risks transforming the policy they are charged with administering into little more than the accumulation of ad hoc decisions.[68]

To argue for employee empowerment is also to argue for greater decentralization of decisionmaking. That, in turn, brings the NPR all the well-known risks of subversion of broad policy. The reinventers quite explicitly sought to take those risks, for they believed that excessive top-level control was choking innovation and undercutting performance. But in choosing sides, the reinventers quite predictably led critics to warn of the dangers that decentralization could produce: risks to equal protection and democratic accountability, which are limited by centralized power.[69] Neither the Hamiltonian-Madisonian nor the centralization-decentralization dispute presents a sharp either-or choice. Indeed, the question is always how much executive power to trade for democratic control, how much decentralized discretion to trade for less central policy control. A reading of this intellectual history produces two important insights. First, critics from opposing camps have always struggled over how much power the executive branch ought to have. The opponents of reinvention saw it for the Hamiltonian thrust that it was and argued forcefully, as Madisonians always have, about the risks it posed for accountability. Many of the intellectual battles over reinventing government thus reflected ageless contests over power in American government. Second, the very fact that American society has been fighting these battles for more than two centuries suggests that the reinventing government solution—indeed, any solution—is unlikely to endure. The reinventing government movement is, in fact, only the latest and certainly not the last solution. History suggests that reinventing government carries within it the seeds of the next reform; Hamiltonian reforms like reinventing government tend to give way to Madisonian reforms to restrain executive power. It is reinventing government's part of the eternal search for balance rather than its inherent virtues that, in the end, matters most.

Discontinuities

Beyond the continuities with previous reforms, however, the NPR built on a genuinely fresh notion that private-market incentives ought to drive public-sector performance. The following ideas based in the "new economics" of organizations laid the foundation for this approach.

CONTRACTS. The key relationships in government can be viewed as a series of contract-like connections. Although never explicitly acknowledged by the reinventers, this idea drives the innovative portion of the NPR.[70] It builds on interrelated theories that flow from formal economics. First, principal-agent theory holds that organizations can be understood as a series of relationships between principals (who have work to be done) and agents (who agree to do that work). This theory explains not only the basic relationships but also the typical problems: agents tend to have more information than their principals, and principals therefore have a hard time supervising their agents, which is known as the "information asymmetry" problem.[71] Second, transaction-cost analysis argues that such information and control problems impose important costs on managers, who naturally seek to minimize their costs while maximizing their gain.[72] Such information problems, if not carefully managed, can cripple managers. Although these theories are abstract, they have powerfully and quite explicitly driven reform movements abroad.[73] They have also subtly but clearly flavored both Osborne and Gaebler's *Reinventing Government* and the NPR.

GOALS. If basic relationships are contract-like, then the contracts need to be explicit. And if supervision is tenuous, supervisors ought to focus instead on the results that their subordinates produce. Performance agreements, based on clear definition of goals, can set the standards by which managers will be judged. In fact, several cabinet secretaries have signed performance agreements with President Clinton. On one level they are a rhetorical exercise, but on a deeper level they represent not only a clear statement of each secretary's goals but also "a leadership commitment to achieving results," as one NPR official explained.[74]

COMPETITION. Even with clear goals, however, employees left to their own devices will tend to underperform, by substituting leisure or personal goals for the organization's goals (what theorists call the "moral hazard" problem). The information asymmetry problem prevents supervisors from knowing what their subordinates are really doing. Competition (among both employees and organizations, for pay and other resources) can create strong incentives that can substitute for authority-based supervision.

CUSTOMERS. No one knows better than customers whether an organization's goals are being met. Driving organizations to serve the customers, from the bottom up, can help solve the supervision problems that plague organizations from the top down.

For government to follow such a prescription, it would have to give more power to front-line workers, focus more clearly on the needs of its customers (leaving aside for a moment the tough problem of defining just who the "customers" are), use the customers to define goals, induce competition to serve these customers, measure results carefully, and stimulate entrepreneurial behavior on the part of government workers everywhere. In fact, that is precisely what the NPR recommended in chapters 2 and 3 of *From Red Tape to Results*.[75] Although the theoretical foundations of the NPR are never made explicit, its provenance in the "new economics" approach is clear.

Conflicting Theories

Terms like *downsizing, reengineering*, and *continuous improvement* have dominated the NPR as, in fact, they have driven private-sector reforms. The concepts often float in and out of discussions as if they were interchangeable pieces in an administrative puzzle. In fact, the ideas behind them are deceptively complex and, in many cases, even contradictory. Making sense of the NPR's reform movement requires sorting out the driving concepts behind it.[76]

DOWNSIZING. Downsizing is quite simple. Its strategy is simple—shrink the public sector—and its tactics straightforward—do whatever is politically feasible to reduce the number of agencies, the level of government spending, and the number of government employees. The approach is nothing more than this: do what can be politically done, set arbitrary ceilings on taxes or personnel, promise across-the-board cuts, or pledge to trim the middle of the bureaucracy. Angry taxpayers have increasingly voted to wield blunt axes in making cuts, even if good programs or key managers are eliminated, if that is what it takes to get their message across.

In the United States, such blunt-edge downsizing originated at the state level, although the target of angry state voters has most often been the reduction of property taxes imposed by local government. The movement began in the mid-1970s, as inflation fueled real estate prices, which in turn drove up property taxes. New Jersey, California, and Massachusetts led the campaign by passing limits on taxes and spending.[77] State legislators passed scores of other tax limitations or special tax breaks in the following decade. From just 1976 to 1982, legislators and voters in nineteen states agreed to limit revenues or expenditures.[78] In 1994, Michigan voters agreed to shift a substantial amount of local property tax revenue for education to state taxes, while Wisconsin legislators voted to replace local property taxes with state aid, to be financed by undetermined state government spending cuts and new state tax revenue.

The problem, several surveys in the 1980s revealed, was not that citizens were unhappy with the services they were receiving. Rather, they believed that the public sector was fundamentally inefficient.[79] Elected officials discovered that the mantra of cutting the unholy trinity of "waste, fraud, and abuse" resonated well with voters. For better or worse, both elected officials and voters came to believe that public inefficiency was so great that expenditures and revenues could be slashed without hurting the quality of public services. Tax and spending limits would force government bureaucrats to wring waste out of the system. E. S. Savas wrote approvingly of the measures, saying that the public, "despairing of the ability or will of its elected government to reduce expenditures, has taken the matter directly into its hands and reduced revenue, like a parent rebuking his spendthrift child by cutting its allowance."[80]

The downsizing movement spilled over onto the federal government in the mid-1980s, but with far more uneven results. In 1984, the President's Private Sector Survey on Cost Control, better known as the Grace commission after its chairman, J. Peter Grace, produced 2,478 recommendations that its report said would save $424.4 billion over three years. The commission concluded that the federal government was "suffering from a critical case of inefficient and ineffective management." Only more businesslike practices and, in particular, huge cuts in government programs could reduce the deficit hemorrhage.[81] Critics argued that the report built largely on an ideological, probusiness, antigovernment base. They contended that the report contained misrepresentations and that following the report's recommendations could actually hurt the work of the federal government.[82] Partisan battles doomed the report; Ronald Reagan championed it while battling a Democratic Congress.

The Grace commission report did, however, help fuel a downsizing movement at the federal level. In 1985 Congress passed the Balanced Budget and Emergency Deficit Control Act, better known as Gramm-Rudman after two of its key sponsors. Gramm-Rudman set deficit reduction targets backed by automatic budget cuts if Congress and the president could not agree on a deficit reduction plan. The strategy never worked quite as its sponsors had hoped, for the targets proved economically difficult and politically impossible to meet. Gramm-Rudman evolved through several incarnations as supporters tried, with only modest success, to fix it. But Gramm-Rudman did have a signal effect: It forced both Congress and the president, Democrats and Republicans alike, to begin bringing the burgeoning federal deficit under control. It also made downsizing an inescapable part of politics at all levels of American government.

By the early 1990s, the tax and spending limitation movement helped fuel the presidential campaign of independent H. Ross Perot. Perot's surprising popularity forced President Clinton to attack the issue head-on, and Vice President Gore's NPR was integral to the effort. Streamlining the government would permit government officials to cut public functions, eliminate layers of the bureaucracy, and save billions of dollars. Haunted by the ghost of Perot, the NPR offered the Clinton administration leverage on one of the issues that resonated best in the 1992 campaign and that promised to return in 1996.[83]

The state and local tax limitation movement, coupled with the Clinton administration's effort to reinvent the federal government, underlined a series of important points about the downsizing movement. First, the movement itself has been largely atheoretical. One principle has guided it: the only way to force greater efficiency is to put a cocked gun, in the form of tax and spending limits, to the heads of public managers.

Second, although there often has been bold talk about using strategic planning to drive downsizing, the downsizing generally has driven whatever planning took place, not the other way around. Government decisionmakers and managers alike have struggled to find short-term adaptations to the spending and taxing targets far more often than they have developed long-term plans. Indeed, the tougher the targets, the shorter the time horizon of government strategists.

Third, while downsizing has in fact limited the growth of government spending and tax revenue in the United States, its effect on the quality of services and the efficiency of administration is anything but clear. Government at all levels in the United States has increasingly underinvested in the capacity to understand the quality of what it buys.[84] In appealing to the deep-seated anger of the voters, elected officials have become bolder in proclaiming the pathologies of the governments they head while promoting the very policies that have helped to create the pathologies.

Downsizing has thus largely become a symbolic tactic, a way for elected officials to resonate with the concerns of the voters without directly attacking the problem of making government work better. Public officials, both elected and appointed, have turned instead to reengineering and culture change for that purpose.

REENGINEERING. Michael Hammer and James Champy's *Reengineering the Corporation* sat near the top of the best-seller list for months.[85] They tell a tale of corporations faced not only with new challenges but with threats to their very existence. To succeed, even to survive, they argue, business leaders must jump past incremental improvements to a fundamental reexamination of their operations. They contend that completely new work processes and organizational structures can produce quantum leaps in performance. That argument has proven powerful in the private sector, and its influence has spilled over into government.[86]

Reengineering begins by putting everything on the table. It "means starting all over, starting from scratch" through "discontinuous thinking."[87] Too often, Hammer and Champy believe, managers tinker at the edges when they need to start over. Reengineering begins by having managers consider the "three Cs": customers, competition, and change. Meeting customer expectations is the foundation. Today's reality builds on customers who know what they want, what they want to pay for it, and how to get it on the terms that they demand. The successful companies will be those that build their operations to serve customers' needs. More intense competition means that companies that do not incorporate cutting-edge technology into their operations will not survive. And as change becomes constant, only organizations that are quick to adapt will prosper.

Reengineering requires fundamental and radical redesign of work processes. Indeed, *process* is the fundamental building block of reengineering. Effective managers redesign the processes within their organizations to ensure that customers' needs are met. They incorporate the latest technology, especially information technology, to wring extra efficiency out of their operations. Hammer and Champy emphatically argue that reengineering is not the same as downsizing, which is not driven by the need to improve performance. It is not the same as administrative reorganization, because reengineers view process as far more important than structure. It is not the same as total quality management, which seeks to improve quality within existing processes through continuous improvement. Reengineers, by contrast, search for breakthrough strategies instead of incremental improvements. Rather than trying to do a job 10 percent better, reengineers look for strategies that can make work ten, or one hundred, times better.[88]

As private managers popularized reengineering, public managers found the movement irresistible. The state of Massachusetts, for example, reengineered its child support collection system. Previously, collection rested on complaints by the care-giving spouse against the nonsupporting spouse. Case workers, through a labor-intensive system, tried to track down scofflaws and intervene to try to win support. The state instead began relying on computers to find cases with similar characteristics, to search the data base for parents who owed support, and to launch letters insisting on payment. After two years, according to one report, 85 percent of collections occurred without a caseworker's intervention. The number of cases in which payments were collected increased 30 percent, and the compliance rate jumped from 59 to 76 percent. In Merced County, California, new software designed for individual workstations replaced mainframe-based programs for processing welfare eligibility claims. The time from initial application to interview decreased from four weeks to three days or less.[89] The state of Texas, meanwhile, launched several major initiatives to improve the state's tax administration system that supporters believed could produce an additional $51 million in annual revenue.[90]

Reengineers aggressively present their arguments as fresh and novel, all the better, of course, to promote book sales and consultancy contracts. In fact, their focus on customers, radical change, nimble organizations, and information technology represents a creative combination. However, since the early days of scientific management, organization theory has concentrated on an organization's purpose and how to maximize its efficiency.[91] Process was central to much organizational thinking in the 1930s, especially to the work of Henri Fayol. Luther Gulick's famous paper, "Notes on the Theory of Organization," written for the Brownlow commission, which advised President Franklin Roosevelt on reorganization of his office, explicitly tackles the issue of "organization by major process."[92]

In the decades that followed World War II, process became of less interest to organizational theorists—especially *public* organizational theorists. James Q. Wilson's brilliant book, *Bureaucracy*, however, talks about "procedural organizations" as those where "managers can observe what their subordinates are doing but not the outcome (if any) that results from those efforts."[93] Nothing could be further from the focus on process that the reengineers have in mind: they insist that designing the process to control the results is central.

Indeed, the very single-mindedness of the reengineers is also their biggest weakness. Hammer and Champy unself-consciously point to a single book as the predecessor to theirs: Adam Smith's 1776 classic, *The Wealth of Nations.* "We believe that the application of the principles of business reengineering will have effects as significant and dramatic as those created by Smith's principles of industrial organization," they write.[94] Like most modern organizational reformers, Hammer and Champy are unabashed in their enthusiasm for their idea and unreserved in arguing its promise. They strongly argue, moreover, that halfway measures will always prove inadequate. (That, of course, provides the perfect excuse, since any failure can be traced to a failure to reengineer strongly and thoroughly enough.) Reengineering provides scant guidance for more measured tactics, what to do when problems emerge except try even harder, or how to sustain change over the long haul after the revolution has ended and routine has set in.

In general philosophy and specific proposals, reengineering helped drive the NPR. Indeed, the NPR report promises that "we will reengineer government activities, making full use of computer systems and telecommunications to revolutionize how we deliver services."[95] The vice president's reinventers argued the need to eliminate or consolidate obsolete and duplicate organizational structures, replacing governmental units with improved technology to link them together better.

Even its most ardent fans admit that process reengineering is a high-risk venture. Some reports suggest that up to 70 percent of private-sector reengineering projects fail. "In the public sector," writes one expert, "there's less motivation to change, and many more structured impediments," so the odds might not even be that good.[96] Nevertheless, the pressures on government to reduce costs and improve services is so severe that managers, public and private, are often willing to try to risk the odds. Although reengineering has barely entered the public management landscape as more than a slogan, its promise has proved alluring. More important, it has provided a battle flag under which armies of reformers have marched.

CONTINUOUS IMPROVEMENT. Other management reformers have pursued a very different direction. In the place of the discontinuous, top-down, revolutionary change that the reengineers recommend, they have advocated a more gradual, continuous, bottom-up movement. In the last decade, the movement has been most strongly associated with total quality management (TQM), which was launched by W. Edwards Deming, but has far deeper roots.[97] Other theorists have adapted TQM to drive a broader movement toward continuous organizational improvement.

TQM builds on the notion that the quality of the product matters most. "Better quality leads to lower costs and higher productivity," one Deming admirer explains. "The consequences for an individual company are that increasing quality leads to higher productivity, lower costs, higher profits, higher share price, and greater security for everyone in the company—the managers, the workers, and the owners."[98] Instead of looking backward into an organization to determine how to squeeze out more profit, industry should look forward to improve quality, and profit will take care of itself. Workers dominated by the profit motive tend to be unhappy, while employees pursuing quality take more satisfaction in what they do, feel more secure, and work more productively. Thus, according to the TQM movement, a total commitment to continuous effort to achieve quality, in everything the organization does, should be managers' central focus.

To be sure, the reengineers care a great deal about quality. They believe, as do the continuous improvement advocates, that quality matters and that customers are the ultimate arbiter of quality. The reengineers, however, believe that fundamental organizational processes too often get in the way of achieving quality, and that only radical change in those processes can improve results. TQMers, by contrast, argue the need to "think small," to build from the bottom to the top of an organization. In TQM, workers themselves are the experts who know best how to solve problems, serve customers, and improve the work.[99] TQM, moreover, views reengineering as only one part of management improvement. Changing the process alone is not enough. One of TQM's foremost advocates, in fact, argued that process is but one of the "five pillars" supporting management improvement (along with product, organization, leadership, and commitment).[100]

Total quality management, in part because of its precepts and in part because it has been around longer, has been far more broadly deployed in American government than reengineering. The Environmental Protection Agency used the technique to improve its management of a program dealing with leaking underground storage tanks, while the Air Force Logistics Command improved the readiness rate of its fighter planes from 40 to 76 percent. In the New York City sanitation department, TQM helped resolve labor union problems. The Philadelphia regional office of the Department of Veterans Affairs used TQM to improve service to veterans applying for loans. Two students of the process concluded, "Quality improvement projects have resulted in significant cost savings, improved services to agency customers and clients, and measurable improvements in employee morale and productivity."[101]

The quality movement has bred a broader range of progeny than reengineering. Some advocates delete "total" from the label to distance themselves from the zealotry that alienated some managers from TQM. Other writers have advocated a broader approach based on shaping continuous improvement to help organizations learn and on having individuals assume personal responsibility for organizational results.[102] TQM and its progeny focus far more on people than on organizations. They tend to be more holistic than reengineering and its cousins, less inclined toward radical transformation of organizational structures, more driven by a concern for operating-level workers rather than top leadership, and more convinced in the ability of workers to improve organizational results as they improve their own work.

This approach also builds on a long tradition of organization theory, beginning with Mary Parker Follett and continuing through Abraham H. Maslow to more modern motivation-based theorists.[103] This tradition has argued that individual factors, from motivation to personal satisfaction, matter as much as structure and process in determining organizational results. The tradition has always been influential, but it has never been central to organization theory. It does not promise quite the same magic in such a short time as reengineering. Indeed, its basic precept is that the movement toward quality, once launched, is never finished. No level of quality is ever sufficient, and only the constant search for quality can keep an organization and its workers sharp.

These ideas, not surprisingly, found deep resonance within Gore's reinventing government task force. The report promised to "give customers a voice—and a choice" and to "put citizens first." Employees were to be "empowered to get results." Indeed, the footnotes at the back of the report are littered with references to TQM. More than any other set of ideas, the continuous improvement movement drove the Gore report. The discussion of continuous improvement, however, sits side by side with the argument for downsizing and reengineering. The advocates of continuous improvement would argue quite vigorously that managers cannot be expected to take risks when their jobs are on the

Figure 2-2. Major Management Reform Movements in the United States

	Downsizing	Reengineering	Continuous improvement
Goal	Lower expenditures	Efficiency	Responsiveness
Direction	Outside-in	Top-down	Bottom-up
Method	Blunt targets	Competition	Cooperation
Central focus	Size	Process	Interpersonal relations
Action	Discontinuous	Discontinuous	Continuous

line. Nor, in their view, can reengineering comprehend the full range of reform needed to make any organization work better.

Weighing the Reforms

The result, in the National Performance Review as in many government reform movements, is an uneasy alliance among these three ideas. A side-by-side comparison reveals stark differences. Figure 2-2 arrays the reforms according to the goal they seek, the direction in which they are implemented, the method that drives them, the central focus of managers following them, and the action that drives them.

Downsizing, enforced from the outside in by angry citizens, seeks lower government expenditures. Its methods are blunt targets, driven by the assumption that there is ample waste in government to accommodate the cuts. Downsizers seek to shrink the size of government by firing a weapon of sufficient size to signal their fundamental disdain for existing policymakers and managers.

Reengineering seeks greater organizational efficiency by seeking a radical change in organizational process. Top leaders, with the broad strategic sense of where the organization needs to go, attempt to harness competition and the urge to serve customers and thereby transform their organizations.

Continuous improvement, by contrast, seeks greater responsiveness to the needs of customers by launching an ongoing process to improve the quality of an organization's products. Advocates of continuous improvement believe that workers know best how to solve an organization's problems, so unlike reengineering, continuous improvement builds from the bottom up. Cooperation among workers replaces competition, and stronger relations among employees are more important than organizational structure and process.

The fundamental precepts of each movement directly conflict with the other two. Assessing the conflicts is itself an important problem. No one knows which one works best. Finding out is impossible, not only because governments tend grossly to underinvest in program evaluation but also because no organization adopts any reform in its pure form. Elected officials and managers shop around among the reform elements that most attract them. As a result, managers often find themselves attempting to cope with externally imposed downsizing targets by reengineering their processes from the top down while encouraging their employees to improve quality from the bottom up. The advocates of each approach often are aghast at such hybrids, which send out contradictory signals to workers and create conflicting expectations about results.

These contradictions, however, have scarcely prevented both public managers and policymakers from embracing the basic ideas. The labels themselves have strong symbolic appeal. The overall goals of each technique, moreover, are unassailable. Citizens and elected officials alike find alluring the promise of a smaller government, engineered with better processes and devoted to greater responsiveness to citizens and quality. Vice President Gore's report promised radically restructured programs that would be more quality-oriented and would result in $108 billion in savings. The savings, however, were calculated by using downsizing principles. The strategic planning that reengineers would argue ought to come first came much later, if at all, and continuous improvers were aghast at the prospect of attempting to motivate employees to take more risks and improve quality as their jobs were being threatened. The contradictions of management reform ideas were both fundamentally unresolvable and politically unavoidable.

Most important, the conflicts buried in the theories led to fuzzy prescriptions in the Clinton administration's reinvention movement. Two tensions in particular plagued the campaign. First was the basic strategy of the movement. Should it be a revolutionary reengineering and downsizing, or should it be a sustained campaign for continuous improvement? The three strategies send contradictory signals, raise different expectations, and often create radically different motivations for the workers who have to do the hard work of reinventing. Reengineering and downsizing are inevitably more threatening; continuous improvement by its very nature is more cooperative. By its embrace of all three strategies, the Clinton administration sent conflicting signals to government employees and made it far more difficult to get those employees' cooperation.

Second was balancing top-down centralization with bottom-up decentralization. The administration eliminated the Federal Personnel Manual and delegated responsibility to federal agencies, but did not define the Office of Personnel Management's new role. It aggressively pursued the drafting of customer service plans, which put far more power in the hands of front-line managers, without defining how to balance the need for central control to ensure accountability. Indeed, in far-flung corners of the NPR, finding the uneasy balance between centralization and decentralization continually resurfaced as a critical problem. Few problems in public administration have deeper or more lasting roots. But the driving themes of the reinvention movement rendered the conflicts even sharper and made resolving them even tougher. By promising substantial decentralization without clearly defining those functions and processes that needed to be centralized, the Clinton administration launched a ship without the right ballast—and as a result it rolled sluggishly through turbulent seas.

Assessing the Critics

Public management scholars have long resisted private-sector sloganeering that asserted government would be much better if run more like the private sector. Indeed, Wallace Sayre's axiom, that business and government are alike in all unimportant respects, drives much of the literature.[104] This rich tradition provoked the NPR's critics to several counterarguments.

Real entrepreneurialism cannot be created in government. The critics object both to the notion of citizens-as-customers and to the case for entrepreneurialism. H. George Frederickson contends that "governments are not markets" and that "citizens are not the customers. They are the owners."[105] The critics add that, even if entrepreneurialism were a good idea, the concept could never be applied to government. There frequently is little private competition in most public functions.[106] Government exists to take on those jobs that citizens view as important and that the private market cannot or will not assume. Because the public and private sectors are so fundamentally different, entrepreneurial, competitive, private-sector models create more confusion than clarity in public management, the critics conclude.

Market incentives cannot substitute for the law. More fundamentally, critics argue that democratic government requires that law, not competition, drive public bureaucracy.[107] The reinventing government argument undermines the constitutional system of top-down democratic accountability. It gives front-line managers too much power to decide for themselves what the law is and how it ought to be executed. That, the critics argue, is a dangerous departure from traditional democratic government, in which power flows from the people to elected officials and from elected officials downward to administrators, under close supervision by superiors. Congress ultimately is the source of administrators' power, yet in the NPR, "Congress is viewed largely as a nuisance," Ronald Moe wrote.[108] No matter how inconvenient it might be, the critics strenuously object to any attempt to substitute marketlike behavior for the rule of law.

The reinventers undercut critical public management capacity. In the effort to empower front-line bureaucrats and to meet the administration's downsizing goals, the NPR advocated reducing the number of middle-level managers throughout government to allow managers to manage.[109] OMB followed with a major reorganization that eliminates management analysis as a separate function within the agency (which I will examine later). Such reductions, Frederickson worried, could diminish the government's capacity to function. Moe added that the NPR was a major attack on the "President as Chief Manager."[110] The reduction of central management reinforced the fear of the critics that government would prove unable to manage itself effectively and to hold bureaucrats democratically accountable for their behavior.

The real problems are primarily political, not administrative. Nothing separated the reinventers from their critics more than their analysis of where the core problems lay. For the reinventers, the vision of good people trapped in a bad system—a bad administrative system, that is—drove their recommendations. Their critics, on the other hand, defended the administrative system and argued that the problem lay in failures of political judgment and will by elected officials. "The problems are power and politics, not bureaucracy," Frederickson contends. Moe argues that bureaucrats have done their best within a balance-of-power battle between the president and Congress that inevitably undercut their effectiveness. [111] Laurence Lynn adds that the reinventers have also engaged in the folly that technocratic strategies "can somehow short-circuit the political process and be made precise and unambiguous." [112] Efforts to replace politics with management reform, the critics conclude, risk paralyzing the government by weakening political support for administrative leadership.

One thread of the critics' attack was telling. The NPR largely ignored fundamental differences between public and private management as well as centuries-old thinking about how to hold bureaucratic power democratically accountable. In particular, the NPR dealt poorly with both the political and the constitutional roles of Congress in American bureaucracy. Finally, the critics struck a telling blow in pointing to the fundamental political causes at the root of many administrative problems.

However, the academic critics missed two important points. First, existing administrative theory has not served the performance of American government well. The roots of the government's performance problems extend past the political problems into fundamental dysfunctions of the executive branch. Administrative theory does not have a very good diagnosis or prescription to attack these problems. Just what is the connection between political institutions and administrative practice? And how can they mutually support each other to improve government performance?

Second, many of the critics' points represent problems in theory more than in practice. In fact, administrative practices are already far in advance of much theory in the field. Treating citizens as customers *and* as owners, for example, need not be inconsistent (as I will later explain). Entrepreneurial incentives can produce better results within the framework of public law. In Phoenix, for example, Public Works Department workers competed with private contractors for the garbage collection business. In the end, city workers won a sizable share of the work and, under the pressure of competition, greatly increased their productivity. [113]

Much of the criticism grew out of two traditional theories of accountability: legislative supremacy over executive discretion and administrative action through hierarchical bureaucracy. The problem is that neither well describes administrative behavior today. Although Congress retains the ultimate power to write the laws that govern bureaucratic behavior, the sources of political influence (over both Congress and the bureaucracy) are vastly more complex. Moreover, especially at the federal level, little administrative action takes place through traditional hierarchies. Most program implementation depends instead on complex partnerships among federal, state, and local governments, together with private and nonprofit organizations. The critics build at least in part on assumptions about the workings of government that no longer hold. Furthermore—and this is the reinventers' strongest point—they would have little need for a fundamental reinvention if the old theories continued to work well.

There is, in short, a large gap between the theories and the tough realities that government managers must daily face. The managers have not much concerned themselves with the intellectual battles and have struggled to cope pragmatically with their problems. But the evidence from the front lines is that such practice is far in front of theory, and that buzzwords like *customer* are too poorly thought through to support sustained action. The theorists, on both sides, badly need to catch up.

Glue: How to Hold the Movement Together?

Two central problems lie at the core of the NPR. First, the NPR is moving far in advance of the ideas driving it. The central themes (cutting red tape, putting customers first, empowering employees, and cutting back to basics) are more a call to arms than a battle plan. Second, especially because the NPR builds on putting far more power in the hands of bureaucrats, the weakness of its underpinnings carries grave risks. If empowerment drives the NPR, and empowerment means delegating far greater discretion to bureaucrats, what will direct the exercise of that discretion? What will ensure that bureaucrats use their discretion to promote the public interest instead of their own, perhaps idiosyncratic, views of what ought to be done? Indeed, an important implication of the economic theory of bureaucracy, on which much of the reinvention movement is based, is that unsupervised bureaucrats will simply pursue their self-interest, which in turn will create an ever growing and ever less efficient government.[114] What glue will unify governmental policy and prevent it from spinning off centrifugally into thousands of directions?

The ultimate success of the NPR depends on solving three important problems: defining a new approach to the public interest to replace the old version that no longer fits administrative practice or America's political life; sharpening the notion of customer service to serve as a proximate compass for bureaucratic action; and developing a mature approach to performance measurement to provide long-term guidance to American public management.

The New Puzzle of the Public Interest

The experiments with government reform in the United States over the last decade teach three important lessons. First, there is no government service that could not be delivered by nongovernmental organizations. From libraries to police, prisons to social services, fire protection to sophisticated planning, private and nonprofit agents have eagerly stepped in as governments have tried to shrink. Although the results of the American version of privatization have varied widely, the overriding lesson is that there is no function left that only the public sector can deliver.[115] However one chooses to define what government alone ought to do, one cannot do it by function.[116] Because the private sector *can* do anything, there is less certainty about what government *ought* to do.

Second, the thrust of government reform has been to impose market-style incentives on public managers. It is the "entrepreneurial spirit" that drives *Reinventing Government*, and for the NPR the keystone of creating a government that works better and costs less is "using market mechanisms to solve problems."[117] Reformers have argued that competition, rewards, and sanctions will prove far superior to authority-based, monopolistic governmental agencies. In brief, they suggest that many private sector–based mechanisms could usefully replace public sector–oriented ones. The debate over incentives has made it less clear *how* government employees ought to do their jobs.

Finally, the increasing contracting out of government services over the last two decades has increased the mutual dependence of both parties: government depends on private and nonprofit organizations to deliver services, and private and nonprofit organizations depend on government revenues to sustain their business. In addition, the rules and procedures accompanying the sharing of government's power have created a complex fabric of organizational linkages. The harder reformers have tried to separate the public and private sectors, the more blurred the boundaries between them have become.

What these three lessons have created is a fundamental challenge to defining and achieving the public interest. A generation ago, the precepts of traditional public administration made clear what public managers ought to do and how. It was the job of public managers to administer the law by the best of their technical ability. Indeed, in 1948, Leonard D. White could write in the leading textbook of the day:

> The need, incessant and urgent, is for the administrative mind that can hold fast to the public interest and bind conflicting special interests to it by skillful contrivance, based on knowledge but exceeding mere *expertise*. In the highest reaches, the administrative art touches the political, but it grows out of different soil. [118]

In the years that followed, however, the notion that the public interest ought to guide administrative action slowly evaporated as the difficulty of defining it grew. Students of the process worried about the growing complexity of political influences on managers, which created multiple back channels of influence on administrative behavior, and the increasing interconnections among government programs, which made it hard to determine who was responsible for anything. [119] They worried about growing professionalization of the public service, which risked making managers more accountable to narrow professional norms than to the broader goals of the law. [120]

The "public interest" consequently disappeared from most debate about public management, in part because it became so hard to define and in part because some critics wondered if the new entrepreneurial spirit might not be superior to the old notions that drove it. Resurrecting the concept along with the old definitions clearly will not help the debate over the NPR. The classical approach does not fit an administrative world of high technology and instantaneous communication, interdependent organizations (public as well as private and nonprofit), and institutionalized political tension between the executive and the legislature. [121]

On the other hand, allowing a careful consideration of the public interest to slip from the discourse risks substituting one set of problems—control of empowered bureaucrats—for another—bureaucrats with little incentive for high performance. As Don Hunn, head of New Zealand's Public Service Commission, explains, "We spent so much time trying to 'let the managers manage' that we forgot that government owned these institutions and that there is a set of common, core values."

New Zealand, leading the movement for public-sector management reform, therefore found itself seeking a new definition of the "collective interest" as a counterpoint to administrative autonomy.[122] Indeed, the New Zealand experience helps chart the mines lying ahead in the NPR's eager push for reinventing government. Sweeping away the old notions of accountability will not work unless something new and equally powerful rises up to replace it.

The success of the NPR depends on establishing and promoting a new definition of the public interest that would include the following.

—A full understanding of how enhanced employee discretion helps government tackle its new challenges better than the old procedure and rule-based approaches;

—A sophisticated approach to interorganizational networks of public, private, and nonprofit organizations, instead of the old approach that assumed a single agency was in charge of each program;

—Outputs instead of inputs, results instead of activity;

—A fully developed comprehension of what customer service and performance measurement really mean; and

—In particular, a fresh but sound approach to ensuring accountability of government workers for the jobs they do—promoting high performance and low cost while remaining responsible to elected officials.

Customer Service

If empowering employees is the "how" of the NPR, customer service is the "why." The reinventers worked from a set of beliefs that drove them away from traditional top-down management: they believed that traditional approaches made bureaucrats unresponsive, self-absorbed, and inefficient. British Prime Minister John Major's 1991 "Citizens Charter" white paper, as well as other movements abroad, heavily flavored the NPR. The reinventers also borrowed from the American private-sector reform movement.

Introducing the idea of customer service to government enraged traditionalists, as discussed above. In part, the customer-based approach smacked of importing business management into government. In part, they argued that accountability in a democratic republic works from the voters through elected officials to bureaucrats, not directly between citizens-as-customers and government managers. They also quarreled with the drumbeat of customer service rhetoric.

In fact, there are three important conclusions about the customer service idea. First, the critics are right. Government is indeed different from the private sector, and any public-sector reform has to begin from that point. Second, there is nevertheless genuine value in the customer service approach. Bureaucrats at every level, throughout every bureaucracy (public or private), have great discretion in how they do their jobs. The customer service notion says they should use that discretion to satisfy citizens rather than to serve the purposes of government agencies and employees. Third, the notion nevertheless has proven a weak compass for the NPR. The concept is poorly developed, and overenthusiastic rhetoric has often substituted for clear thinking. If there is something to customer service, that something needs far more careful development.

The NPR's enthusiasm for customer service builds on the self-evident observation that citizens are truly unhappy with the performance of their government and view government as too often pursuing its own internal goals instead of solving the problems of citizens. "Quite simply," the NPR report concludes, "the quality of government service is below what its customers deserve." To solve that problem, the NPR pledged to provide "customer services *equal to the best in business*."[123] The Social Security Administration, for example, promised that callers to its toll-free service would reach a person on the first call. The Postal Service pledged to deliver first-class mail anywhere in the United States within three days and counter service within five minutes.[124] On September 11, 1993, President Clinton backed that pledge by issuing Executive Order 12862, which mandated agencies to define customer service standards. All executive departments and agencies providing "significant services directly to the public" were required to identify the customers who are, or should be served by the agency; survey customers to determine the kind and quality of services they want and their level of satisfaction with existing service; post service standards and measure results against them; benchmark customer service performance against the best in business; survey front-line employees on the barriers to, and ideas for, matching the best in business; provide customers with choices in both the sources of service and the means of delivery; make information, services, and complaint systems easily accessible; and provide means to address customer complaints.

It would be hard for even the most cynical critic to object to serving citizens in this way. As employed by the NPR, "customer service" essentially requires that government be responsive to citizens' needs and wants. The presumption is that too often government becomes inward-directed, toward the myriad rules, procedures, and forms that preoccupy public managers. Forcing these managers to focus outward on citizens, for whom public programs were originally created, is intended as an antidote. Such an approach is consistent with traditional theories of accountability.

The executive order does not call for the exercise of discretion beyond the boundaries of existing law. Rather, it calls for government employees to use the inevitable discretion embodied in congressional delegation of authority to ensure that government services are responsive to citizens. As *Improving Customer Service*, a report accompanying the NPR, concluded, customer service "is probably the simplest way to tell the federal work force what kind of service to deliver."[125]

Some of the most spectacular early successes of the NPR came from reinvention labs that dramatically improved customer service. In the Department of Veterans Affairs claims processing center in New York, for example, the manager set out to improve service to veterans. Workers previously had focused narrowly on specialized parts of the claim process. The lack of coordination among the pieces of the process produced long delays in processing checks. The manager reorganized part of his staff into a team composed of each of the specialists required to process a claim. Team members focused on individual veterans and worked together to solve the veterans' problems. Processing time dropped from years to weeks or months. The job satisfaction of the workers improved, and the veterans were much happier with the friendly and prompt action on their claims. Focusing on the customer instead of process dramatically improved the office's performance.[126]

The NPR has helped launch several such customer service initiatives, including one-stop career centers in the Department of Labor's Employment and Training Administration and improvements to the Treasury Bureau of Engraving and Printing's public tours. These experiments demonstrate that customer service need not be incompatible with bureaucratic accountability. In fact, customer service can improve accountability while it increases satisfaction. Frederickson has noted that citizens are owners, not customers.[127] However, even owners appreciate being treated responsively as customers. A stockholder (that is, owner) of an automobile company, for example, certainly expects responsiveness when entering a car dealership. Indeed, the owner's concern for the bottom line can even drive attempts to improve the quality of customer service.

The real problem with the NPR's customer service initiative is not that it is incompatible with democratic accountability. Rather, the notion of customer service in government itself is so new the concept is underdeveloped. Using the idea to drive bureaucratic performance therefore requires substantial intellectual innovation, which, to date, has not accompanied the NPR. Moreover, as currently employed, it is a crude fit at best for what government does and how it does it, for three reasons.

MULTIPLE GOALS. Responsiveness to citizens is not the only, or even the principal, goal of public programs.[128] As service recipients, citizens naturally expect responsiveness in the form of prompt, friendly, and generous service. In a big snowstorm, the road that needs to be plowed first is always in front of one's own home. As taxpayers, however, they demand economy and efficiency from government. "Pork barrel programs" are those given to someone else. Responsiveness to citizens as service recipients inevitably and eternally conflicts with the demands of citizens as taxpayers. Government managers therefore tend to face greater demands than they can ever possibly meet and clashing views about how to meet them. Should the Department of Health and Human Services seek to make it as easy and painless as possible for medicaid recipients to qualify for health care? Or should the department attempt to manage the program as strictly as possible to reduce costs?

Moreover, as service recipients, different citizens often want very different things. Should the Interior Department reintroduce gray wolves into Yellowstone National Park, as environmentalists have advocated, or should it try to clean out the wolves, to satisfy ranchers?[129] Should the Federal Aviation Administration supervise new but small airlines relatively more, on the grounds that with less experience they might have greater problems? Or should they focus relatively more attention on the older but larger carriers that transport far more travelers?

Such conflicts create a dilemma for bureaucrats attempting to follow the customer service mantra. Asking government bureaucrats, within the realm of their discretion, to pursue both efficiency and responsiveness creates an impossible problem. And leaving bureaucrats with impossible problems only further increases their discretion and the difficulty of holding them accountable to either the law or customer service standards.

CONNECTING WITH THE CUSTOMER. Second, many federal programs—and most federal bureaucrats—do not provide "significant services directly to the public," in the words of the executive order. There are, to be sure, federal programs and bureaucrats that do have substantial contact with citizens: air traffic control, patrol of waterways, operation of dams, operation of social security, customs collection, the national parks. But the nature of many federal functions and the complexity of program implementation both create large challenges for customer service.

Some government functions, like regulation, tax collection, and criminal justice, present tough customer service problems. Government officials must find the difficult balance between making their programs user-friendly and preventing abuse. Nevertheless, the IRS has devoted itself to making its tax forms easier to use and to improving the quality of telephone tax advice. The Customs Service in Miami has received one of Vice President Gore's "Hammer Awards" for improving service for the airlines and their passengers. There has even been tentative discussion about applying the customer service approach to prisons to reduce violence and costs. The ingenuity of both the reformers and government managers has been remarkable, but the nature of many government functions makes pursuing customer service far more difficult than the rhetoric suggests.

Working through the long and complex implementation chain of most federal programs presents additional challenges. Most federal government employees never encounter a citizen while performing their official duties. Their job, rather, is to help others do their job so that citizens eventually are served. It is not unusual, for example, for a federal manager to distribute a grant to a state agency, which adds state money and state requirements and then passes it on to a local agency, which then contracts out to a nonprofit organization to actually deliver the service to a citizen—who then must negotiate a system providing related services through similar complex relationships. It is, quite often, a government by proxy.[130] It is the job of the federal employee to work with the next person in the chain (whether another federal employee, a state government worker, or a private contractor). Under such circumstances, it is easy for the concerns of the citizen as customer to get lost.[131] It is also easy for everyone along the chain to claim lack of responsibility for how the citizen is handled. If everyone is in charge, no one is responsible for results. Making customer service work means focusing everyone along the chain on how well the system works (or does not) for the ultimate recipient of services.

In July 1994 Oregon officials proposed a novel, head-on attack against these system problems. State officials proposed shifting the intergovernmental programs in Oregon from an agency- and program-based effort to one focused on results. The plan would begin by having the federal government join with Oregon state and local governments to "identify results to be achieved." From there, the Oregon officials suggested,

> we will be contracted to achieve them. To help us achieve these results, the federal government will merge funding categories and streams, create funding incentives which reward desirable results, and reduce micromanagement and wasteful paperwork. This collaboration will empower our communities to identify local needs to be met by federal and state programs, to make their own decisions about how to address those needs, and to be accountable for results.[132]

The state had already developed a twenty-year strategic plan, with specific benchmarks (quantified policy objectives) defined.[133] Its officials argued that its basic approach (defining goals, building programs around people instead of levels of government, and constructing the system to serve those goals and people) fit into the NPR's philosophy. Furthermore, they contended, their approach would cut through the barriers that hindered "efficient, integrated, client-centered service."[134]

Although the proposal was embryonic, it attracted widespread interest in Washington. The meeting in Washington to discuss it attracted top officials from OMB, the Departments of Health and Human Services, Education, and Labor, and 170 other senior agency staff. To many observers and participants, it suggested an alternative solution to the intergovernmental dilemma: to focus on outcomes instead of inputs and on people instead of programs, and to use that approach to transform the organizational arrangements. The administration approved the plan in late 1994 as part of its effort to transform intergovernmental service delivery.[135]

HYPERSENSITIVITY TO CUSTOMER WISHES. Finally, a large part of government's performance problem is a hypersensitivity, not an insensitivity, to the demands of citizens. Elected officials, in particular, are preoccupied with the demands of their constituents. They have few incentives to worry about broad public management issues like performance, quality, or cost; they have every incentive to deliver the goods, from new dams to protection for social security, to the voters. That problem led George Frederickson to argue, tongue only partially in cheek, that real reform lies in employing "total quality politics" as well as "total quality management."[136] The danger—and it is the most subtle, yet most important, element of the customer service initiative— is that government managers' focus on customer service could reinforce the constituent-based pressure of elected officials and produce a government hypertuned to micro-level needs yet without capacity or incentive to deliver broad or sustained performance.[137]

This is not a case against customer service but a brief for thinking it through thoroughly and implementing it carefully. That, however, has not yet happened in the NPR. The customer service initiative has proven little more than an executive order demanding action and a rhetorical base for virtually any enterprise. The British have considerably more experience with the customer service notion. Their experiences teach several important lessons.[138]

—Defining customers is much harder than it looks. Different people tend to want very different things, and these preferences are not easily aggregated.

—A focus on customers—users of services—tends to avoid the question of who ought to pay for services. It can even accentuate the conflict between taxpayers and service recipients.

—A service-based approach works poorly for public goods, like defense and pollution control, for which it is impossible to define individual beneficiaries.[139] A large share of the federal government's activities, of course, centers on such public goods.

—The customer service approach encourages individuals to develop, express, and advocate preferences just as government's ability to satisfy them shrinks under the weight of fiscal stress.

—Excessive zeal in measuring citizen preferences can produce an information overload.

—Customer service can easily be put to partisan use. Critics of the party in power have used information about citizen complaints as ammunition. This, naturally, leads the ruling party to collect information most likely to put programs in a favorable light. Many elected officials complain about spending any money for citizen surveys.

Customer service is an undeniably attractive notion. But the notion raises as many problems as it solves. Customer service does, however, have two overriding values. It gears "the organization to serve its public rather than the other way around," as one participant in the British effort explained.[140] It also provides a fresh approach to the eternal search for the Holy Grail of program coordination.

The customer service initiative therefore has enormous potential. It is most useful as a proximate goal in directing the exercise of bureaucratic discretion. It can never fully steer government action, however, in part because of the inherent contradictions rooted deeply in the concept and in part because at best it is only a weak guide. Achieving its potential, however, will require a far more sophisticated exploration of what customer service means, how to do it, and how to fit it within the demands and constraints of democratic government. It also requires a frank admission of the value conflicts and dilemmas that the customer service initiative creates. The NPR has done neither, and without taking both steps the drive toward customer service will suffer.

Performance Management

In the long run, building a government that works better and costs less depends on strengthening OMB's ability to guide it. If government is to steer effectively, OMB will have to stand at the helm. But to do so it will have to have a compass more precise and more far reaching than an annual review of the budgetary process. It needs a mature performance management system to assess what government actually accomplishes with taxpayers' money.

The most promising source of glue to hold the movement together and promote the right incentives lies in the reorganization of the Office of Management and Budget launched in March 1994 under the banner of "OMB 2000" and the Government Performance and Results Act (GPRA), passed in 1993, which seeks to link budget inputs with performance outcomes. The OMB 2000 reorganization was the most fundamental change in the agency since its creation. OMB Director Leon Panetta and Deputy Director Alice Rivlin forcefully argued the need to escape from routine budget reviews and to "better integrate our budget analysis, management review and policy development roles."[141] The reorganization eliminated virtually all of the existing "management side" of OMB and integrated management functions with the budget review in new "resource management offices."[142] These new offices would be responsible for formulating and reviewing the budget, assessing program effectiveness and efficiency, conducting mid- and long-range policy and program analysis, implementing governmentwide management policy in areas such as procurement and financial management, and conducting program evaluation. OMB created five resource management offices: National Security and International Affairs; Natural Resources, Energy and Science; Health and Personnel; Human Resources; and General Government.[143]

OMB 2000 sought to help the budget agency move from the deadlines and short time horizons of the annual budget process to a longer-term, results-oriented perspective. OMB officials said they wanted "to be more strategic in the way we prepare the budget."[144] Some analysts have harshly criticized the reorganization because it eliminated the management arm.[145] However, the management division within OMB had long been a weak player, especially in overseeing general management issues. OMB officials had only two real options: pursuing the reorganization to provide integrated analysis, but risk having short-term budget issues drive out long-term management concerns; or creating a separate office of federal management to assess administrative issues, but risk having the office become a eunuch in a setting where budgetary decisions inevitably drive policy.[146] Faced with these choices, Panetta and Rivlin followed the first option.

The reorganization promised several important innovations. First, it strengthened a weak linkage between budgetary and management issues. Second, it committed OMB to adopt a broader and longer perspective on budget and management issues. Third, it provided the potential for integrating performance questions into the annual budgetary process. Finally, it sought to change the incentives for the way departmental budget officers communicated their requests.

Transforming the deep-seated budget-review culture was a huge job. OMB also faced a big problem of training its budget examiners to take the broader view and integrating its management experts into the resource management offices without undercutting their morale. OMB had never been successful in combining management and budget analysis in the same agency. Nor was it ever truly successful in combining long-term strategic planning with short-term attention to details. OMB 2000 attempts to do both, but by making the transformation within people, especially budget examiners, instead of within their organizational structure.

In the best of cases, OMB will acquire the capacity to link outputs and inputs, budget and management. In the worse of cases, central attention to federal management will disappear from the top circle in government—something that cannot be allowed to happen. Although the challenges are great, the direction is sound. The annual budget process remains the single most important way of focusing the attention of federal managers at every level. Transforming that process offers the means of transforming the behavior of those managers.

OMB's reorganization was designed to support the GPRA. The GPRA is part of a far wider movement, in both the United States and abroad, to focus managers' attention on accountability for results. It aimed at improving the effectiveness of federal programs and citizen satisfaction by improving "the confidence of the American people in the capability of the Federal Government, by systematically holding Federal agencies accountable for achieving program results."[147] In the long run, moreover, the GPRA may well prove to be the keystone of the federal government's reinvention movement. It defines performance as the critical touchstone of the government's programs; it defines the linkages among the government's activities; and it provides important incentives for government managers to focus on results.

Under the act, each federal agency, by the end of the ten-year phase-in period, will prepare a five-year strategic plan that is updated every three years; a comprehensive mission statement that links the agency's current operations with its long-term goals; an identification of the goals and objectives, along with the resources, systems, and processes required to achieve the goals; a description of the most important external factors that could affect the agency's success in achieving the goals; and annual program evaluations to help agency officials assess their success, explain why goals might not have been met, and revise the goals if necessary. OMB and the president would then use the process to set future budgets and to revise programs, if necessary. The law called for at least ten pilot projects. By the summer of 1994, federal agencies had put forward seventy-one pilots in twenty-seven departments and agencies.[148]

OMB did not expect the transition to performance-based management to come easily. In their briefing documents, OMB officials asserted that change will require a long-term process, even though they quickly encouraged performance measures as part of agency budget submissions.[149] This process, in turn, required fundamental changes in the culture of government management and the assumption of more responsibility by managers throughout the government. OMB officials repeatedly stressed that agency officials would be the leaders in the GPRA. They did not intend for this to be a top-down management reform.

Most important, the GPRA depends on technology that does not now exist. There is no budgetary system, no performance measurement system, and no career track within government for the people to do the work. There are few incentives for such a long-range perspective, and only a passing audience among elected officials, citizens, and the media for the results.[150] That is not a prescription for failure, but it is a measure of the work to be done if the promise of the GPRA is to be met.

The federal government's ragged experience with management and reform, from planning-programming-budgeting and management by objectives through zero-base budgeting and total quality management, suggests caution in pressing ahead without building the technology for the GPRA. But several things are clearly different this time. First, this is the first reform launched by law instead of by executive order or administrative action. The GPRA's base in law ensures both congressional and executive branch involvement and discourages retreat by its sponsors. Second, unlike previous reforms that began with an across-the-board effort, the GPRA builds slowly from pilot programs to governmentwide implementation. This provides an opportunity for learning along the way.

Third, the early evidence suggests that this reform enjoys far broader and more enthusiastic support throughout the bureaucracy than earlier efforts. The surprising eagerness of federal agencies to volunteer for the pilot phase of the act underlined the desire of federal managers and top political appointees to grab the leverage that the GPRA offered.

Finally, the GPRA speaks with unusual clarity to problems that citizens want to have solved. It would be hard to find anyone who finds government performance satisfactory or thinks that linking budgets with results is not a good idea. The 1992 Perot presidential campaign underlined that point.

Like the OMB 2000 reorganization, the GPRA offers considerable promise for linking the big politics of reducing the size of government and the little politics of improving its performance. OMB 2000 potentially provides the incentive for agencies to pay more attention to performance; the GPRA provides the language to discuss it. Past experience with aggressive budget and management reforms argues for caution in predicting results. If the NPR is to have lasting meaning, however, linking the two revolutions is critical.

The problem is that it is far easier to talk about performance management than to do it. Goals are notoriously difficult to define. Greater specificity attracts greater political conflict. Moreover, even if goals can somehow be defined, measuring progress is even harder. Public programs are often public because the private sector cannot or will not produce them. Their very nature makes outcomes even harder to judge. Managers often have little choice but to substitute input or activity measures (money spent or people served) for outcome measures (what the money accomplishes).

If the technical problems of measuring progress can be surmounted, building the capacity throughout the government to do the job will be difficult indeed, especially with the NPR's pledge to shrink the federal bureaucracy. And if measures emerge, comparing data across widely different programs is a daunting job. How can decisionmakers compare the results of health programs against highway construction, social security against defense?

Finally, even if results can be measured and compared with goals, it is hard to gain an audience for the findings. Elected officials frequently gain far more value by supporting new programs than by overseeing performance.[151] Administrators have few incentives for allowing anyone to measure what they actually do.

Nearly everyone agrees that "the budget process is not likely to be changed substantially until and unless decisionmakers use information on program performance when making allocation decisions," as the Congressional Budget Office argued.[152] Only by changing the incentives for managers, by focusing members of Congress on performance issues when they make budgetary decisions, will performance management become a reality. The difficulty is that elected officials understandably concentrate far more on the front end of the process. Even if measuring performance were easy, changing the political culture to focus on outcomes runs against the driving incentives of the American system. And measuring performance is decidedly not easy. If it were, it would not have taken the federal government decades to commit itself to the effort—and then to give itself another decade to put the idea into place.

Management and Measurement

The biggest difficulty in thinking through the problems of performance management is that reformers and managers alike far too often consider it simply as a problem of measurement. Committing the government to performance-based management, of course, requires that officials identify and measure results. The more fundamental question, however, is what to do with these measures. Too often, reformers pursue measurement for its own sake. If that becomes the case with the GPRA, then it will simply become a new procedural shibboleth to replace an old one.

Performance-based management is most fundamentally about communication, not measurement. Moreover, this communication occurs within a broader political process, in which the players have a wide array of different incentives. Performance-based management will have meaning only to the degree to which it shapes and improves those incentives. If managers think about performance-based management only as a measurement problem—how to gauge the results that public programs produce—they will miss the big questions: How does what they know about results shape how they manage public programs? How does their knowledge about results shape decisions about what programs they ought to adopt? And how does the process of measuring results affect the behavior of political institutions?

This leads to several important lessons for GPRA:

—Performance measurement is different at different levels of the bureaucracy. Front-line supervisors might be interested in assessing the quality of work done by their subordinates, but higher-level officials are likely to want to judge the quality of the programs under their control. Top administration officials and members of Congress will be looking not only at program performance but at where they can squeeze out extra performance for the same amount of money, cut spending without losing performance, or get additional results with extra money. In short, debate at the political level revolves around broad strategic measures and outcomes. On the front lines, supervisors focus on outputs. Managers in between need to build the linkage between these very different questions.[153] Measures that work at one level will not necessarily work well at another.

—Aggregating performance measures from lower levels is likely to produce meaningless noise. A temptation in performance measurement is to layer measures from lower levels on top of each other and pass the information along to higher-level officials. Such an approach produces information that is not easily digestible by top officials and creates the potential for hiding embarrassing details in a mountain of data. Officials at each level will have to define the kind of information they find most useful.

—Performance measurement will have to speak in a language that those listening can understand. Too often analysts who conduct sophisticated analysis complain that top managers and elected officials pay no attention to their work. If performance measurement is to be a successful language for political communication, those crafting the measures will have to use a language that those listening, especially busy elected officials and top political appointees, will understand and find useful.

—Moreover, performance measurement must speak in a language that those listening will want to hear. There is a special problem in giving performance information to Congress. Congress naturally tends to think of solving problems by passing laws; indeed, that is its constitutional charge. That makes Congress peculiarly input-oriented. Its oversight, moreover, tends to be haphazard and episodic. It has few incentives for regular and systematic review.[154] Performance measurement, by contrast, seeks a careful and systematic survey of results. Performance measurers must find a way to interest members of Congress in the GPRA and the results it produces, or it will have little staying power.

Missing Pieces

Despite the encyclopedic coverage of the NPR's report and the sweeping actions that followed, several important issues are either missing or have received scant attention. Without attacking and solving these missing pieces of the picture, the NPR risks undercutting its promise.

Civil Service

Reforming the civil service flows as a theme throughout the NPR report, and changing the rules of the civil service has been a major focus for much of the NPR's work since. However, as discussed above, creating a government that works better and costs less will depend ultimately on the movement's ability to build the capacity to do the job. Government's problem is a people problem as well as a process problem. Real reform hinges on government's ability to find, attract, promote, train, guide, and motivate the workers needed to do its work. Major pieces are missing from the NPR's personnel reform effort, and without them the movement will not have the capacity to accomplish its goals.

Investment

The NPR has great promise for cutting the costs of government. To produce some of these cost savings, however, the federal government will have to make short-term investments, as the NPR's report recognized.[155] In its first year, however, the incessant drive for deficit reduction has pushed the investment initiative off the stage. The different pieces of the NPR are, in many ways, an inseparable package. The reengineering of the federal government anticipates that advanced technology will make it possible to reduce the number of workers. The number of workers, though, is being reduced far before even the promise of new investment. The risk is that the NPR will deliver a government that, in the long run, costs more and works worse.

Steering

If the government's job is to steer, as Osborne and Gaebler suggest, whose hand will be on the tiller? Reforms abroad, in state and local governments, and even the reinvention experience at the federal level to date all reinforce the same point: Not only is strong political leadership necessary, there also has to be central administrative capacity to connect the person at the helm with the rowing mechanisms. To prevent the creation of a new government agency, NPR officials deliberately decided not to make the NPR an agency. Instead, the NPR has been staffed by detailees from other agencies rotating in and (often) out. Consequently few hands have been on board since the beginning. Meanwhile, OPM and OMB are undergoing major changes in mission and organization, and the General Services Administration is transforming its procurement functions and processes. All of the federal government's central management agencies are thus simultaneously undergoing major changes. The signals to managers throughout government therefore are unavoidably fuzzy and, sometimes, inconsistent.

The question for the NPR is not instability. Considerable confusion is inevitable in any reform of this size, and the experience of other nations suggests that it will take at least two or three more years for stable patterns to begin to emerge. Rather, the question is who will ultimately be responsible for maintaining the reform movement. The NPR has implicitly answered the question. There will be no central steering mechanism. The NPR report talked about the need for central management agencies to divest themselves of many of their powers, to decentralize those powers to the agencies, and thereby to empower workers. Although this tactic is a sensible beginning, it is no basis on which to build long-term success. Practical politics suggests that, when problems or embarrassments arise from the behavior of empowered managers, as inevitably they will, demands will surface that they be prevented from ever occurring again. In the absence of stronger forces to the contrary, someone at some central office will be charged, by the president or Congress, with doing just that. Practical management also suggests that it is unlikely that the accumulated decisions of millions of empowered workers will be consistent with each other, the law, or the public interest.

If government is to steer, someone will have to keep the compass. This does not mean the creation or reinforcement of large, overbearing central bureaucracies. But it does require careful thought about which functions (particularly information collection, long-range assessment, problem solving, coordination, and the articulation of driving themes) need to be central ones. One can safely predict that these, and perhaps others, *will* be needed. The question is where and by whom. The NPR can ignore the question and risk having others answer it in ways that might contradict the movement's principles. Or the NPR can aggressively seek to answer it and fix central responsibility clearly.

The logic of my argument for the OMB 2000 reorganization plan and the GPRA is that the OMB is the natural, perhaps inevitable, place for these questions to be answered. Indeed, the NPR's recommendations, OMB's reorganization, and the GPRA's long-term strategic planning and performance measurement requirements all are mutually supporting. The reinvented OMB is the logical place for the central steering role to occur, and it is time now to begin planning the transition from the NPR's short-term, jump-starting role to OMB's long-term nurturing and maintenance role.

Congress

When Clinton administration officials released the NPR report in September 1993, they received at least grudging support from Capitol

Hill. Most members of Congress recognized the appeal of a government that works better and costs less. In the details, however, Congress reverted to form.[156] Its members supported the rhetoric in general but micromanaged the details. Congress enthusiastically endorsed the downsizing initiative and even upped the ante from a cut of 252,000 government workers to 272,900. Members eagerly calculated how to spend the savings on the crime bill. When it came to individual decisions to produce the savings, however, Congress quickly retreated. They not only voted to exempt favored departments from downsizing, they also torpedoed the Department of Labor's plan to combine 154 federal job training programs, housed in 14 different federal agencies, into a coordinated effort.[157]

These actions teach an important lesson. Although NPR officials long contended that they could launch most of their reforms without Congress, the reality is that the NPR cannot sustain *any* of its reforms without congressional support, or at least the absence of opposition.[158] NPR officials began their reforms without a strategy for winning that support (or defusing that opposition) beyond the brave hope that the overwhelming logic of the reform would bring members of Congress to their camp. They have been struggling ever since, from the buyout bill through procurement reform, to recover.

Congress, by practice and the Constitution, attacks problems by passing laws. The NPR seeks to solve problems by improving performance. Congress as an institution works on the input side. The NPR focuses on the output side. Congress has little incentive to worry about results and uses the separation of powers to absolve itself from complicity in the executive branch's performance problems. Members of Congress, furthermore, have everything to gain from publicly embracing the broad principles of reinvention and then protecting their constituents and favorite programs behind the scenes in committee rooms and little-noticed riders to complex bills. If problems later develop, they will have been the result of a misdirected executive branch.

The NPR, however, has several advantages in tackling these problems. Many of the recommendations in its report, and much of its broad themes of performance and customer service, are of only remote interest to most members of Congress. Congressional disinterest gives the reinventers a great deal of initial maneuvering room to prove the success of their effort. Moreover, many of the recommendations depend on how individual bureaucrats deal daily with issues on their desks and with the discretion they have to solve problems. That is particularly true of customer service and program coordination issues. They can make substantial progress by changing the way they do business without changing the business they are in.

The NPR's long-term success nevertheless depends on creating at least some incentives for members of Congress to support the reinvention process. The biggest incentive would be clear evidence that government does indeed work better and cost less, although that would scarcely prevent members of Congress from tinkering with details to benefit their constituents. Even that, however, has lost some of its appeal, for local television reporters and newspaper columnists across the country have begun to point out the hypocrisy of embracing broad reforms while undermining them with pork barrel votes, even if the pork is flowing back home. Many members of Congress are struggling with some way to make government, and therefore their own jobs, more palatable to voters. They are seeking ways to wring extra performance out of government to obtain at least a small amount of money to spend on new programs. Indeed, savings from improved performance promised to help fund the Clinton administration's 1995 middle-class tax cut and the Republicans' more ambitious alternatives.[159]

Furthermore, some members of Congress who serve on committees that have long been relatively dormant, like the House Government Operations Committee and the Senate Governmental Affairs Committee, have discovered that the NPR has given them new, high-profile issues, such as procurement reform and performance measurement. In an era when fiscal constraints prevent most committees from taking major initiatives, these high-profile issues have given some members new standing. Because they cut across so many government programs and agencies—and thus across the jurisdictions of so many other congressional committees—these issues have also created the potential for new power centers in Congress.

The Media

The news media, particularly television's news magazine shows, have proven especially important to the reinvention revolution. They have focused on the Clinton administration's expectations and pursued the effort to make government more efficient. In the process, the media have become a critical element in an ongoing cycle that threatens the reform movement's success.

Much of the reinvention movement's ambitious agenda requires government employees to take greater risks in the hunt for improved performance. With risk taking comes the potential for failures, small or catastrophic. The key is not to avoid all risk—playing it too safe can paralyze performance—but to develop bureaucrats' judgments about which risks are prudent and to improve the system's ability to reduce the level of risk in general.

The "gotcha" syndrome that plagues much media coverage about government, however, has produced strong disincentives for taking bureaucratic risks. Aggressive management sometimes produces problems. The news media all too often seize on these problems as news, and television shows often present the problems as part of an ongoing pattern of poor performance. The media attention raises the salience of the problems to a level that neither members of Congress nor senior administrators can ignore. They respond with steps to try to ensure that the problems do not recur. This usually means tightening rules, limiting discretion, and increasing oversight, all of which run counter to the reinvention movement's focus on empowering bureaucrats. Recurring cycles of perceived abuse, media attention, and crackdown have encrusted the ship of state with barnacle-like regulations that tend to pile up over time. These barnacles are hard to remove and make the ship much more sluggish, more difficult to maneuver, and especially harder to adapt quickly to rapidly changing problems.

This is not an apologia for poor government performance. Such problems need to be aggressively identified and rooted out, and the news media have a critical role to play in that campaign. All too often, however, the media's voice is shrill and their portrayal of problems is inaccurate or uncharacteristic. For reinvention to succeed, the news media must become a partner in the effort to reform government. This certainly does not mean abandoning its independent judgment or its tough eye. But it does mean exercising its voice with a sense of civic responsibility, in ways that promote rather than undercut citizens' ability to govern themselves.

High-Risk Programs

The NPR paid scant attention to the government's "high-risk programs," identified by both OMB and the General Accounting Office (GAO), which have the potential for costing the federal government billions of dollars.[160] The Department of Energy (DOE), for example, has more than $19 billion in contracts under management by major firms and academic organizations. The NPR recommended that DOE improve its contract management, but the steps required do not fit neatly into the NPR approach. GAO found that

> historically, Energy's contractors have operated largely without oversight or financial risk, and this has placed the government's multibillion-dollar annual investment in contractors' services at risk. Energy lacks the necessary staff expertise and information systems to monitor contractors, and its contracts provide few incentives for cost-effective contractor operations.[161]

The core of the problem, GAO found, lay in DOE's own administrative capacity and in the nature of the contracts it negotiated. Neither issue received major attention in the NPR. Most of the NPR's procurement focus lay in untying the red tape binding the procurement process. DOE's fundamental problems stemmed from precisely the opposite problem: the government's overreliance on private markets.[162] The same is true of many other high-risk programs identified by OMB and GAO, from medicare to superfund. The lesson is that because of underinvestment in management in order to squeeze money out of the federal budget, poorly managed federal programs have cost taxpayers dearly.

Savings from solving these and other management problems would probably surpass the savings promised through the NPR. Money saved by avoiding future management problems, however, will not show up on the budget as savings. It cannot be scored by the CBO. Nor can members of Congress take credit for saving it or turn around and spend the savings elsewhere. The money saved is real, but expenses forgone do not mean as much politically as bureaucrats shown the door.

The high-risk problems stem from causes rooted deeply in the government's personnel, financial management, and contract management systems, and they cannot readily be fixed through culture change, empowerment, customer service, or the NPR's other themes. Moreover, the short-term tactical decisions the NPR made to press the movement ahead, particularly to downsize the federal work force, may make the high-risk problems even worse. By cutting to meet a target instead of to carry out a plan, the downsizing could easily eliminate both the people and the skills needed to attack the problem. And the long-run costs could dwarf the short-term budget savings. The NPR needs to examine its strategy carefully to ensure that it includes a focused attack on the high-risk programs.

Learning

One of the most remarkable features of the NPR is just how much positive activity it generated the first year. And no part of that activity has been more remarkable than the creativity thousands of government employees across the country have shown in the reinvention labs. The NPR has worked hard to gather success stories from these labs. A series of new electronic networks has encouraged managers to share results, but the NPR's learning strategy is embryonic. There has been little systematic effort to learn what the labs, or the broader reinvention movement, have to teach.[163]

For example, a Department of Veterans Affairs reinvention lab in Milwaukee teaches several important lessons. Its staff has been working since 1992 to improve procurement for eight VA hospitals in three states. One of the department's respiratory therapists noted that the VA was paying for full refills of home oxygen tanks even if the tanks were still half full. In a new contract the lab negotiated, the VA specified that it would pay only for the oxygen actually used, saving the department $100,000 a year.[164] Since the lab's start, Milwaukee officials estimate that through this and similar reforms they have saved $2.8 million on contracts valued at $33 million, plus significant but unknown administrative savings.[165]

The NPR argued that procurement decisions would work best by decentralizing decisions as much as possible, and indeed the Milwaukee lab works in part by decentralizing legal review and approval authority of contracts from Washington to the field. However, the Milwaukee lab also *centralized* contract authority from the hospitals to a regional facility. It was, as the center's manager described, "a one-stop shopping approach."[166] That allowed larger purchases and therefore better economies of scale. It made the contracts larger and thus more attractive for potential bidders. It also allowed VA officials to market contract opportunities far more effectively to potential bidders and thereby increase the number of contractors interested in submitting bids. It allowed better specification of goods and services so that each side had a better sense of what was being bought and sold. It allowed more responsive service to both vendors and users. It allowed improved recordkeeping so that the office could better monitor the performance of contractors, and it allowed the office to assemble skilled employees to manage the technical side of the purchases. The lab followed only part of the reinvention prescription, learned some new lessons, and has important lessons to teach. The NPR, however, has devised no way to reach out, collect the information, digest it, and figure out how to sharpen the principles of reinvention.

Conclusion

In just its first year, the NPR has confounded its critics. It has accomplished far more than cynics suggested might be possible. It has also launched, for the most part, a broad reform movement in the right direction. If the NPR has not always had clear answers, it has at least asked the right questions. Nevertheless, and this is the NPR's critical problem, the short-term accommodations it inevitably needed to make to get the movement going have weakened the NPR's chances for long-term success. Considerable work needs to be done to move the invasion from a beachhead to a breakout, and then from a breakout to conquest.

Reinventing government centers on the intersection of the "high politics" of presidential-congressional struggles and the "low politics" of routine administration.[167] The connections between policymaking and execution, often called "governance," are indisputably fraying. The question is where the problem lies: with good people trapped in a bad system, as the reinventers claim, or with a good system hamstrung by a failure of political leadership, as the movement's critics assert? The critics contend that, in the mad rush of the Clinton administration's "high politics" ambitions, the reinventers have misunderstood the foundations on which democratic administration rests. They argue that the reinventers have no theory but a set of unspoken assumptions which, if exposed, would reveal the movement as a threat to democratic governance. The reinventers counter that it is the "low politics" of administrative routine that has handicapped governance in the United States, and that this routine must be transformed if government is to work better.

The most valuable contribution of the reinventers is their frank recognition that the top-down bureaucratic authority approach guiding American bureaucracy since the Progressive Era no longer effectively steers public management. The traditional approach is not obsolete; it never can be so long as the United States is a government of laws. But it must be adapted to a new reality of shared responsibility for common purposes. Customer service, for example, offers fresh insights to attacking new and inescapable administrative realities. Traditional bureaucratic theorists face the challenge of fitting old notions of neat hierarchical control to an increasingly messy administrative state where bureaucratic boundaries are the beginning, not the end, of the management process.

The reinventing government movement, however, too quickly brushes away the internal inconsistencies within its own theory. Three threads of the reinventing fabric—downsizing, reengineering, and continuous improvement—compete to define it. There is, moreover, little consensus on what "customers" really are or how to serve them. The movement also dances too easily across critical but unsolved issues. Reinventing government depends on resolving difficult political and technical problems in performance management. And, even if these are resolved, the combination of customer service, competition, and performance measurement can never really substitute for top-down accountability. That leaves the reinventers with the difficult puzzle of adapting the valuable pieces of their own movement to the driving forces of constitutional bureaucracy.

The problem of reinventing government really revolves around these issues: Just what *do* citizens expect government to do? How can the bureaucratic power required to do the job well be held accountable to elected officials and, in the end, to the people? In sorting through these problems, historian Garry Wills writes, "We have been eating into our intellectual as well as our financial capital."[168] We need to stop eating our seed corn and begin anew to build the capacity to solve these problems.

Neither the traditional administration theorists nor the reinventers have full answers to the problems. New administrative realities have overtaken traditional theory, while tough and often undiagnosed problems plague the reinventing movement. Furthermore, their debate surfaces, in a new way, the ageless question of how to balance energy in the executive with checks on potential abuses of executive power. If Hamilton, Madison, and their followers could not resolve this question, there is little chance that either side will find a permanent answer.

Nevertheless, even if reinventing government raises more questions than it answers, they are the right questions. Furthermore, these questions are not likely to go away, for the administrative issues are fundamental and the political stakes are high. The genie is out of the bottle.

The struggle now is for who will control it: which values will shape the administrative process? The 1994 congressional elections even more sharply underlined this question's importance.

History teaches two important lessons about that struggle. It is unlikely to be resolved to everyone's satisfaction at any moment or to anyone's satisfaction over time. However, periodic shifts—from the Progressive movement through the New Deal, from the Great Society through the Reagan administration's downsizing—have produced huge changes in both policymaking and implementation. The reinventing government movement marks one of those important historical shifts. It is neither the fad that its critics condemn nor the fountainhead of reform that its proponents claim. It is, however, a fresh opportunity to rethink the governmental system: to update old ideas to fit new problems, to experiment with fresh policy solutions for enduring dilemmas, to rethink the government capacity required to solve problems, to inject new energy into the effort, and to reshape the social contract between civic responsibility and governmental power.

The NPR's strategy of launching a revolution without prescribing its form was brilliant. It allowed a breakout from the dominant ideas that the size of the federal government could not be reduced and that federal bureaucrats could not change. The NPR, especially because of its fuzziness, produced enormous enthusiasm for change. By promising bureaucrats more power and citizens a smaller and more effective government, the NPR was able to gather many good ideas under the same broad tent. Under the tent, however, the ideas of the revolution crowded uneasily with each other.

In the short term, that was of little moment. In six very hectic months in the middle of 1993, the NPR produced an enormous contribution in jump-starting the bureaucracy. In the long term, however, these problems threaten to be the NPR's undoing.

The single biggest problem was that, although the NPR had a strategy leading to the release of its report on September 7, 1993, it had no strategy for September 8 and afterward. The NPR staff played a cheerleader role, coordinating a handful of crosscutting issues like procurement reform and customer service and leaving the other management reforms to executives across the government. What they did not do was to create an explicit strategy for linking the two revolutions or for inducing cynical or busy executives to join the battles.

As a result, downsizing became the dominant theme and driving reality. The tactics of reinvention had the strongest effect where they fit the preexisting strategies of managers, especially cabinet secretaries. They had little effect where managers did not see their utility in reaching larger ends. In those cases, the NPR had little leverage and scant success in creating incentives to lure busy, reluctant, or frightened executives into the revolution.

Any management reform, of course, has meaning only to the extent that managers throughout an agency adopt it. The problem was that the NPR developed no mechanism for converting the unwashed or the reluctant. Many managers throughout government understandably replied that they had seen it all before. Downsizing the federal bureaucracy only increased their cynicism.[169] Many managers said that they saw little empowerment or reinvention, but they certainly felt the reality of a shrinking work force and the pressures of doing more work with less help.

Without a much stronger foundation, the NPR now risks leaving behind a worse reality than the one from which it started. Government could be smaller, but the number of layers and regulations could be little changed. The quality of management could diminish even further. Worse yet, because expectations have been raised to great levels, continued performance problems could diminish even further public trust and confidence in government. And, should that occur, even the victory of producing a smaller government will be Pyrrhic, for voters and government managers alike.

This dismal outcome need not occur. In Dickens's *Christmas Carol*, Scrooge was given the gift of seeing the ghost of an unpleasant yule yet to come and the opportunity to prevent it from happening. The NPR has the same opportunity.

Taking advantage of that opportunity has to begin with a revolution in thinking about federal management. Every important federal management reform of the last generation has been derived from innovations from the state and local level, the private sector, or sometimes foreign governments. Elected officials, seeking new leverage over the bureaucracy or fresh ideas to please voters, have culled the "greatest hits" of other organizations. In particular, they have tended to extract the most attractive little-politics ideas to promote big-politics aims. In many cases these ideas were not well suited for the federal government.

Nowhere is this problem more obvious than in the enthusiasm to downsize. The federal government's downsizing movement derives heavily from private-sector initiatives of the late 1980s and early 1990s. The private sector, however, is already beginning to learn painful lessons from its own downsizing experiences; the federal government is on the verge of stumbling into the movement's worse problems. In analyzing private-sector downsizing programs, management expert Peter Drucker argued forcefully, "We are seeing way too many amputations before the diagnosis."[170]

Research is now beginning to demonstrate that the initial advantages of corporate downsizing have often produced higher long-run costs.[171] Stressed workers burn out, leave, or remain with lower morale. Large cuts in staff tend to "penalize departments that are slim and reward those that are oversized," management analyst Eileen Appelbaum concludes. The biggest performance differences, in fact, appeared due more to the quality of management than strategic downsizing (or upsizing).[172] Indeed, a study of 531 American corporations revealed that private-sector downsizing rarely helped companies achieve the goals of higher profits and lower costs. Moreover, employee morale and motivation among surviving employees suffered. More successful efforts, on the other hand, began from a clear vision for the future coupled with a fundamental restructuring of the organization, from top managers to front-line employees. The biggest private-sector successes came when people came to see change as an ongoing process instead of a short-term event.[173] These findings lead to five important lessons for the reinventing government movement.

—Successful reinvention requires coupling the driving ideas of the movement to the federal government's mission. Private management reforms teach an important but little understood lesson: reforms derived from some organizations and applied blindly to others typically create more mischief than success. Any successful reform has to be tailored closely to the fundamental mission and management problems of the organization.

The NPR gathered together ideas about reform from any source it could find and used them to start the revolution. Many of these ideas are disconnected from what the federal government does and how it does it, however, and they provide weak guidance to harried government managers. For example, no one can quarrel with the customer service goal of making government services more responsive. But as now framed, it is a weak guide for action. Simply charging managers to develop customer service programs without thinking carefully about what that means in the federal system will surely mean painfully relearning the most important lesson of private management reform: powerful ideas plucked out of context and grafted onto the wrong kind of stock will never take.[174] "Too often we end up reengineering trains that don't connect," one observant state government official said.[175]

Making reinvention work requires creative thinking about how to do the federal government's work better. The federal government cannot simply consume knowledge about management practice. It must move far more strongly into the business of developing new knowledge. Careful thinking about management must be encouraged throughout the bureaucracy. More important, such thinking, powered by an in-depth understanding of what the federal bureaucracy is and what it does, must be the driving mission of high officials close to the president—in OMB, OPM, and the White House staff itself.

—Successful reinvention requires linking the big politics of downsizing with the small politics of performance improvement. The biggest temptation in reinventing government is to reach for quick success by embracing downsizing without doing the hard work of improving performance, or to seek performance improvement while resisting the powerful political pressures to reduce the size of government. The single most important reality of American public management for the coming decade is the need to solve the paradox these two movements present. Big-politics downsizers will have to reckon with the fact that, without careful planning, they could "dumbsize" the federal government, worsen performance, and even further enrage voters. Little-politics performance improvers will have to reckon with the fact that expectations will increase as resources shrink.

Making reinvention work requires a frank recognition that neither piece of reinvention can proceed without the other—and that, to date, the movement has been singularly unsuccessful in charting a course to do that. The pieces sit uneasily next to each other within the NPR report, and in the agencies they have juxtaposed even more uneasily.

The missing link in the NPR's effort to bridge the gap is attention to the number, position, and role of political appointees. It is inconceivable that government could be invented, that managers could be empowered, and that programs could achieve results, if the political appointees who direct government agencies are not part of the plan. It is also inconceivable that the number of layers, especially at the top, could be reduced without dealing with what Paul C. Light has perceptively described as the "thickening" problem.[176]

—Successful reinvention requires developing a language for talking about it. Just as the reinventers have not yet reconciled the conflicting elements driving their reforms, they have not yet discovered an effective way of talking about their work. Part of the problem came from short-term tactics to appeal to the public through the mass media. The vice president broke ash trays and laughed about rules preventing the purchase of floor wax off the shelf. These symbols did represent deep-seated problems that had to be solved, and they did attract media attention to the typically dull problems of public management. However, these symbols celebrated the revolution without encouraging government workers to join in. Here, yet again, were public officials making fun of workers' best efforts to negotiate through an unforgiving system; in most cases, they did not make up such nonsensical rules for their own amusement but wrote them to fit the dictates of Congress and political appointees. The effort to build public support often undercut the NPR's ability to recruit government workers to the movement.

Making reinvention work requires reinventing the media and citizenship. As leaders, government officials have a responsibility to educate and shape public discourse instead of simply feeding its worst preconceptions. Many of the most publicized symbols of the NPR, like the ash trays and piles of regulations, have outlived their usefulness. NPR officials now need to develop symbols to communicate to the public what the work of reinvention requires and what it produces. Counting the number of executive orders issued or the number of NPR recommendations on which work has started will simply not be enough. Reinventing government depends on building a new partnership between elected officials and the government's managers and between government and its citizens. The Clinton administration has made an important start, in initiatives like food stamp "smart cards" and effective disaster relief for California earthquake victims, but the broader message has not yet begun to sink through. If the administration allows its new initiatives to be judged on the terms of past failures, the reinventing government movement will surely wither.

—Successful reinvention requires reinventing the job of federal managers, especially in government's middle. The most important failure of the early months of the implementation of the NPR's report was the widespread alienation of middle managers from the movement. The downsizing galloped far ahead of the strategy that was to drive it, and the spread of the NPR's empowerment initiatives was wildly uneven. The middle managers' reaction was scarcely surprising; they heard the talk about new partnerships but saw the overriding reality of personnel cuts amidst rising expectations.

To a degree that many cabinet secretaries—let alone top White

House and congressional officials—fail to realize, middle managers shape the work of government. Top officials can make policy and set priorities, but those priorities take hold only if the managers responsible for meeting them produce results. It is easy to talk about building partnerships with union officials and pass out permission slips to lower-level workers, but the partnerships and permission slips will work only if supervisors create an environment that promotes them. Managers on the front lines have come away from meetings with some NPR officials convinced that they simply did not understand what managers in the field had to do to make programs work.[177] NPR officials could reshape their rhetorical flourishes and better connect with the managers they are trying to motivate if they moved their headquarters out of Washington, or at least established an important field office beyond the Beltway, where the real work of reinvention is happening. "The NPR is as isolated as any other government agency," one government official said.[178]

More important, if the reinventers are serious, they must move from the bold rhetoric to the hard work of changing the systems. Unless they do, federal managers will be left with new demands, a smaller work force, obsolete management systems, higher expectations, and lower morale. Foremost is the need to reshape the personnel system in order to produce new job categories that reflect what future managers will have to do and create the incentives for attracting the best people to do them; allow managers more flexibility in deploying and rewarding their staffs; allow managers greater versatility in matching the personnel system to the needs of their agencies; and allow supervisors greater authority to hire the best, fire the worst, and reward the hardest-working employees. Civil service reform was a constant subtext of the NPR report, but the Clinton administration has struggled to devise a genuine civil service reform. Without fundamental reform of the civil service, the federal government will never be able to match its employees with the new jobs they must do or to attract the best employees to do those jobs.

—Successful reinvention requires creating the glue to bind the movement together. The NPR has operated under the assumption that, once launched, the movement would become self-directed. Federal managers, newly empowered, would exert their energy to manage more effectively. The history of management reform, however, demonstrates that managers are rightly skeptical of big changes introduced in their interest. Faced with a choice of taking large risks toward uncertain ends or riding out the storm in an admittedly leaky boat, many managers choose to take the conservative course. Conversely, some managers who take bold steps will surely walk in a direction different from the one supported by either their supervisors or members of Congress. Reining in the overeager or misdirected without eliminating incentives for bold action is a huge challenge for the movement.

The reorganization of the Office of Management and Budget (OMB 2000) to support its more fundamental look at larger performance issues is an important source of glue to hold the movement together and focus its attention more sharply. If OMB can combine budgetary and management perspectives, input measures and outcome results, and short-term budget marks and long-term performance, it will fundamentally alter the discourse about what matters in the federal government. The task is a large one, but to a degree that even NPR officials might not appreciate, the OMB effort is central to gluing together the two revolutions of reinvention.

Holding the revolution together ultimately will depend on how Congress reacts to it. The single biggest omission in the NPR was a strategy for dealing with Congress. The report seemed to suggest that its logic would be irresistible to members of Congress, that public support for its recommendations would make it impossible for members of Congress to disagree, or that the big picture supplied by the reinventing government movement would help Congress escape more parochial perspectives. The first months of the NPR proved the folly of an implementation strategy that did not include Congress. The struggles over the buyout bill, followed by House rejection of downsizing within VA hospitals and opposition to privatization of the air traffic control system, demonstrated that congressional support (or at least the absence of strong opposition) is critical to everything the NPR wants to accomplish. For a movement founded on building partnerships, the absence of a strategy for building a partnership with Congress was surprising. Success will surely require quick attention to constructing that partnership.

Even more fundamentally, achieving the NPR's promise will require linking more clearly the questions of *what* government ought to do and *how* government ought to do it. The NPR, in the report's own words, "focused primarily on *how* government should work, not on *what* it should do."[179] The lesson of a century of public management research, however, is that the distinction is artificial: the how powerfully shapes the what because means embody ends; and, from the beginning, the how has to be driven by the what.[180]

To a greater degree than even political noncombatants stop to recognize, and certainly far more than government officials ever acknowledge, many public performance problems are often the product of what government sets out to do. Government in fact does many things very well, from delivering social security checks to providing weather satellite maps. Often, when things work badly, it is because it tries to do things that are very hard or impossible, like preventing drug abuse, training unemployed workers, cleaning up toxic waste, or providing welfare without creating dependence.

Improving performance on one level requires focusing government most clearly on the things it does well and figuring out how to do them better. However, we (the NPR, policymakers, and Americans in general) have not thought clearly about what those things are. On another level, if we want government to do things that are hard to do well, we must be frank about the degree of difficulty and focus sharply on how to do the impossible better. Many of the most basic questions to which the NPR is addressed revolve around such issues. In the NPR's second round, launched in January 1995, Vice President Gore directed government officials to focus on just these questions. Prompted by both the Republicans' aggressive takeover of Congress and the Clinton administration's need to generate revenue to pay for its middle-class tax cut, he asked what the government no longer needed to do. However, whether this new tack would help the administration better couple the "what" of government with the "how" remained very much an open question.

The National Performance Review accomplished, in just its first year, far more than anyone thought possible. It energized employees, it attracted citizens, it drew media attention to government management, and it made the point that management matters. However, the NPR failed to build the foundation for success in the long run. It borrowed bits and pieces of management reform from both the public and private sectors and pasted them together in a patchwork that, while initially attractive, could not hold together. In the process, the NPR missed the most important lesson that other successful reforms teach: in the long run, management must match mission. The movement launched in September 1993, however promising, was not self-sustaining. Sustaining it requires hard work on tough questions, and this work, for the most part, has not begun.

Part Two

3 ||| False Promises: The NPR in Historical Perspective

Gerald Garvey

IS THE National Performance Review little more than a declaration of the Clinton administration's intent to achieve modest structural reform: a laudable goal, certainly, but if the truth be told, not a very dramatic or imaginative one? Should observers regard all that talk about "reinventing" as puffery, well within the rules of American political discourse—and therefore not to be taken too seriously? Or might the NPR in fact be the blueprint for radical transformation, as the hype implies? The measure of the actual reformist potential of the NPR may be assessed first by considering it in light of earlier attempts at fundamental change.

Early Administrative Reform Efforts

Administrative action in any political system, but especially in a democracy, must somehow realize two objectives simultaneously. It is necessary to construct and maintain administrative capacity, and it is equally necessary to control it in order to ensure the responsiveness of the public bureaucracy to higher authority, most particularly to elected representatives in the legislative branch. The first of these requirements implies a quest for administrative competence and energy ("state capacity" in the recent jargon of political science.)[1] The imperative of control equates, in a general way, to the familiar concept of democratic accountability, the idea that the behavior of career officials is reviewable through a line of supervision that runs up through the bureaucratic hierarchy to politically appointed superiors, on to elected officeholders, and eventually to the people themselves, who put the elected politicians in office and can recall them if they dislike current policies or the way their appointive agents are implementing those policies. This kind of control system is sometimes referred to as top-down control—a point of some importance, since one of the innovations proposed in the NPR involves the substitution of bottom-up control, that is, control of officials in their day-to-day work by those officials' "customers," the citizens whom they serve.

The historic challenges to administrative reformers have been to change the nature of the existing structures of capacity and control while at the same time serving both these values and, indeed, maintaining a proper balance between them. The reformist impulses of the Jacksonian and Progressive Eras arose out of contemporaries' dissatisfaction with the existing pattern of institutions and practices: with Federalist elitism (itself a basis for a theory of capacity) in the Jacksonians' case, and with the spoils system in the Progressives'.

Jackson, Popular Representation, and Democratic Accountability

The Jacksonians denied that effective public service required any special abilities, let alone special education or other kinds of unusual intellectual or experiential preparation. They believed the demands of governance were modest. Any reasonably right-thinking, well-meaning adult could perform them. This belief supported the Jacksonians' willingness to rely on the common abilities of the American people for good governance, to be secured through patronage appointments to public positions. As President Andrew Jackson himself put it, "The duties of all public officers are, or at least admit of being made, so plain and simple that men of intelligence may readily qualify themselves for their performance; and I cannot but believe that more is lost by the long continuance of men in office than is generally to be gained by their experience."[2]

The Jacksonians thus regarded capacity—in the sense of competence combined with requisite energy—as a feature of the democratic governance process that Americans could pretty much take for granted. More significantly (and subtly), control would automatically be achieved through spoils system appointments. The patronage system would guarantee a measure of popular representation, one of the three key administrative values in Herbert Kaufman's well-known trilogy of popular representation, neutral competence, and executive leadership.[3] In other words, the Jacksonians relied on popular representation as a technique of control; the theories of later reformers, especially the Progressives, would not necessarily permit such reliance.[4] Rotations in office with changes in administration would automatically produce staffs of civil servants bearing opinions reflective of recently elected leaders, and hence by extension, of the electorate itself.

The Progressives and Neutral Competence

The ensuing story is familiar. Abuses and inefficiencies in the patronage system gave rise, in due course, to the next round of reformist demands. For many Progressives, the scandal of filling public jobs on the basis of political connections became a defining moral issue, much as slavery had been before the Civil War. The civil service reformers, and their Progressive colleagues generally, also held a view of the intellectual demands of governance that contrasted dramatically with the older Jacksonian notion. Deficiencies of capacity, already serious enough in the public service, boded to become an ever more grievous shortcoming as the demands of governance grew apace with the problems of industrialization. The Progressives sensed a need for expertise and even science in the practice of government. This change in viewpoint underwrote the shift, perhaps best symbolized by the Civil Service Reform Act of 1883, from popular representation (or at least popular representation, Jackson-style) to neutral competence as the key value in American public administration.

The 1883 act enshrined the principle of appointment to the federal service by merit. The appointee would then enjoy tenure in the job. Federal statutes from as far back as the 1850s had anticipated in rudimentary form the third foundational principle of the civil service, classification. Under the Classification Act of 1923, personnel experts began to prepare detailed job descriptions, systematically linking civil servants' pay scales with their skills. Through merit-based appointment, tenure protections, and "scientific" position-classification procedures, the Progressives sought to ensure capacity by elevating and protecting expertise in the public work force.

But whereas the Jacksonians' method of capacity building automatically carried at least a plausible claim of control, the Progressives' strategy arguably opened the public service to serious problems. The Progressives' cadre of experts would be, by virtue of their competence, set apart from the run of ordinary citizens. The Progressive formula for building state capacity implied a need for a more complex theory of governance if capacity were to be reconciled with control.

The Challenge of Control

The scientific managers (disciples of Frederick Winslow Taylor) and the administrative lawyers (disciples of Lord Alfred Dicey) both contributed to the solution of the problem of control that emerged from the Progressive Era reforms. Members of both schools developed distinctive views of bureaucracy. Briefly, the scientific managers welcomed bureaucracy and contributed significantly to the development of the Weberian theory of a machine-like organization.[5] The disciples of Dicey suspected and feared bureaucracy. Members of neither group, however, questioned the effectiveness of hierarchy as a mechanism of control.

THE SCIENTIFIC MANAGERS AND THE ONE BEST WAY. Taylor and his followers popularized the idea that careful, scientific study of any production process would reveal the one best way to do any job.[6] Transferred from the field of industrial relations to that of bureaucracy, the theory of the one best way suggested a test for the expertise that the Progressives expected of public servants—and a possible solution to the problem of control. The proof that an administrator really was an expert in his field would lie in his mastery of the one best way of the subject (such as "generally accepted accounting principles," or "best engineering practice"). Legislators could—and Progressive legislators customarily did—pass vague laws that required administrators to exercise discretion, trusting that the experts would use their specialized competencies within the latitude allowed by the statutes to find the optimal means toward ends taken as givens. One-best-way thinking, complemented by the idea of the policy-administration gap, seemingly solved the problem of administrative discretion.[7] Legislators would define ends, leaving it to administrators to select the best way of achieving specified goals.

As most commentators on administrative theory emphasize, there is a direct line of descent from Taylor to the bureaucratic structure of modern industry and government. The Taylorite world was bureaucratic in its very essence. For bureaucracy is, essentially, a means of combining capacity (in circumstances requiring coordination of many different skills and functions) with control. Control is achieved through hierarchical supervision and administrative direction (in economist Ronald Coase's sense).[8] This all leads back to a basic problem of the Clinton administration: the desire to activate and galvanize government while curbing and even deconstructing bureaucracy. How do you retain control when you eliminate bureaucracy, whose essence is control achieved through the codification of knowledge, the inculculation of habits, and the structuring of hierarchical authority? The answer may be you do not retain control. Or, if the existing system of controls is too deeply entrenched, you just talk about eliminating bureaucracy—citing anecdotal instead of systemic evidences of radical change—instead of really doing it.

THE RISE OF ADMINISTRATIVE LAW. Although in theory the Progressives enshrined expertise and efficiency, in many fields of governmental practice they delivered decisionmaking to lawyers and judges, whose controlling professional values are often inconsistent with efficiency. The use of a highly legalistic method of control (one that is adversarial rather than organizational in its working ingredient) is after all very much within the American political tradition and was so long before the Progressives appeared on the scene.[9]

Over the course of the last few generations a large and complex body of administrative law has emerged that encompasses the statutory provisions legislators have passed, often to prevent abusive or arbitrary behavior by administrative officials. Rules have been issued over the years by administrative officials themselves, often because the statutes require regulations that will spell out the procedures they intend to use when interpreting and executing the statutes they are responsible for administering. And of course, judicial interpretations of all of the above constitute a significant portion of the body of American administrative law.

Today's rule-encrusted administrative process is the result of a century's worth of evolution, during which controls on the public bureaucracy seem to have gotten out of control. It is this rule-bound apparatus of formal structures and fussy procedures that many Americans associate with the word *bureaucracy*. The same dissatisfaction, but voiced now by the top officials in the land as well as by some of the bureaucrats who staffed the NPR, underlies the expressed purpose of the Clinton administration's reinvention initiative. President Clinton's fear and loathing of bureaucracy was perhaps most clearly revealed amidst the early press agentry of the National Performance Review. The president expressed it when he announced the NPR: "This performance review is not about politics. Programs passed by . . . both parties, and supported by the American people at the time, are being undermined by an inefficient and outdated bureaucracy."[10]

Alas, this discomfiture with the federal bureaucracy seems a somewhat dissonant element in the Clinton theory of administration, given the president's commitment to activist governance. Does Clinton need to dismantle bureaucracy in order to advance his political and programmatic agenda, or does he need instead to strengthen it?

Twentieth-Century Administrative Theory

President Bill Clinton took office intent to be what Erwin C. Hargrove and Michael Nelson have called "a president of achievement."[11] The president's plans included budget deficit control, health care reform, passage of the North American Free Trade Agreement and general moves toward freer trade, the "ending of welfare as we know it," and perhaps even some initiatives toward a resurrection of the kind of national industrial policy that his close advisers Robert Reich and Ira Magaziner touted in the early 1980s.[12] These ambitious objectives all suggested the scope of the changes in national policy that Clinton hoped to achieve while in the White House.

Clinton's position is in contrast with the viewpoints of some of his predecessors who also committed their administrations to critical reviews of the machinery and procedures of governance. Ex-President Herbert Hoover (who took a direct and even dominating interest in the work of the two commissions that bear his name), as well as Richard Nixon and Ronald Reagan, and to an extent even Jimmy Carter, all had positions of some consistency regarding the proper role of government and the value of bureaucracy as an organizational form. By and large, each of these four political leaders (in contrast with Bill Clinton) favored some retrenchment, or at least disciplining, of federal programs and commitments. They complemented their programmatic predilections with moves calculated to reduce the bureaucracy or to rationalize, streamline, and discipline it.

Clinton's outlook also contrasts with the outlook of earlier presidents who brought activist agendas into office. Theodore Roosevelt, Woodrow Wilson, Franklin Roosevelt, Harry Truman, John Kennedy, and Lyndon Johnson all believed both in energetic government and in the potentialities of properly structured bureaucracies as instruments of public action.

Presumably neither a TR nor an FDR would have thought it sensible to ask for programmatic expansion without expecting bureaucratic enlargement along with it. Implicitly, the activist presidents until now subscribed to what Ronald C. Moe has called the classical tradition in public administration: the Weberian organizational model, centered on such values as hierarchy, rationalization, specialization, and control.[13]

Thus for Bill Clinton the question, early in his term, became how to get more government (the "presidency of achievement") without building more bureaucracy? A key question for Clinton and his closest advisers, this presented an intellectual challenge of formidable proportions that called for a rethinking of the governance process and, perhaps, a new view of executive leadership. In this sense, the NPR responds to an intellectual problem that is both central and peculiar to the Clinton-Gore agenda.

The term *executive leadership* in twentieth-century American public administration (significantly, the third core value in the Kaufman trilogy) has referred above all to presidential leadership. A series of high-level study commissions symbolized the seriousness of the effort to devise mechanisms by which full presidential control could be exerted over the capacities of the administrative state. Not surprisingly, the Gore study has been regarded as the successor to a series of "landmark commissions," in Moe's term, that have been conducted to advance the agenda of executive leadership.[14]

The "First Series": Classical Public Administration

The landmark commissions can be divided into two series. The first series began with Theodore Roosevelt's Keep commission (1909), named for the assistant secretary of the treasury who headed it.[15] Next was William Howard Taft's Commission on Economy and Efficiency (1912).[16] It was followed by President Franklin Roosevelt's Committee on Administrative Management (1937) (known as the Bownlow committee).[17] In a real sense the series culminated in the first Hoover commission (1949).[18] A more or less coherent set of ideas underlay the first four landmark studies. Each study in the first series built on the Progressive legacy, and the later ones in the sequence built on the studies that had gone before. Taken together, the studies in the first series emphasized the following principles.

—Public law and formal organizational or jurisdictional arrangements: how work is divided, what formal charters empower the incumbents of particular positions in an administrative structure;

—The structuring of organization in accordance with certain universally valid "canons of efficiency," such as the famous scalar principle and the line-staff distinction, as explained in a famed compendium of classical organizational theories;[19]

—The desirability of a rationalized, national budget process as a primary instrument of presidential control. This emphasis, first hinted at in the Taft commission report, oriented administrative thought toward what today are called performance and program budgeting;[20]

—Unified executive power—particularly stressed by the 1937 Brownlow Committee on Administrative Management and the first Hoover commission—in the context of the institutionalized presidency.

According to public administration scholar Wallace S. Sayre, the Brownlow committee report marked the "high noon" of administrative orthodoxy in the United States.[21] Sayre's judgment is almost certainly accurate, particularly if the Brownlow report itself is regarded as integral to a somewhat larger body of administrative scholarship.[22]

"The President needs help," went a famous line from the Brownlow report.[23] The committee members felt that no chief executive—not even one with the leadership skills of FDR—could make efficient use of the disjointed administrative apparatus that had grown Topsylike, over the years, into the huge executive branch of the U.S. federal government. Fortunately, the committee members also believed, certain universal organizational principles had been worked out over the years and were available for use by the New Deal generation of governmental reinventers. In an oft-quoted line, Lyndahl Urwick asserted that certain general principles "govern arrangements for human association of any kind. These principles can be studied as a technical question, irrespective of the purpose of the enterprise, the personnel composing it, or any constitution, political or social theory underlying its creation."[24] How many layers of intermediate management should intervene between the top official and workers at the bottom? What span of control will maximize a superior's ability to manage subordinates? To such questions the classical thinkers thought they could give definitive answers, expressed in the form of the aforementioned "canons of efficiency." President Roosevelt could best help himself by reorganizing the executive branch in accordance with these canons.

Slightly more than a decade after the Brownlow group completed its work, the first Hoover commission continued the classicists' effort to rationalize the executive branch. Hoover I originated in a generally sensed need to rethink the outlines of a federal organization that had grown in size and influence through the Depression and World War II. Republican Representative Clarence Brown of Ohio, who drew the commission's terms of reference, sensed a need for a comprehensive look at government organization (perhaps the basis for the current interest in "reinventing"?), particularly in light of the widespread expectation that the Democratic hegemony would end in 1948 with the defeat of President Truman. (Truman himself, of course, had not gotten the message. Not only did he expect his own reelection in defiance of the conventional wisdom, but he insisted that reorganization was a presidential prerogative. Truman's preferred approach—not inconsistent with the premises of the classical tradition—was to submit executive branch reorganization plans for congressional rubber stamping.)

Hoover worked virtually full time, often personally editing or even drafting study group documents. The commission's reports generally supported moves toward a more centralized executive branch with presidential authority unified in clarified lines of command. They recommended that where possible, these lines should run through cabinet secretaries directly responsible to the president; the cabinet officers in turn were to be responsible for administering policies through functionally organized departments.

A Sea Change in Political Culture

The publication of the report of the first Hoover commission marked a point of discontinuity of sorts in American administrative history. Close readers of this history have discerned evidence of a shift in the underlying intellectual mood.[25] An inflection occurred in the attitude of most Americans—apparently, including even most presidents—toward bureaucracy. Classical public administration fell "out of synch" with both popular and elite attitudes.

Classical administrative theory, as discussed above, had been premised on the twin beliefs that state capacity in the form of bureaucracy needed to be developed, and that such capacity could be reconciled with control. The latter optimistic belief began to wane early in the postwar period among the members of the second series of landmark commissions, who seem to have been increasingly preoccupied with the challenge of control. They were by no means confident that they would find the way to bring a large, unwieldy, and putatively unresponsive bureaucracy to heel. What changes had occurred, what experiences had intervened, to account for the sea change in American political culture?

A kind of "intellectual deracination" of classical public administration (for want of a better term) occurred during the two decades or so following the end of World War II. Donald F. Kettl has written, with apparent admiration and approval, of the Washington invasion of public administrators during the war: "From one end of town to the other, they managed key positions in the war effort."[26] It would never occur to any informed observer of the governmental scene today that the nation's leaders would turn in a major way to public administrators in a time of crisis. Whatever special knowledge (and special intellectual cachet) practitioners and scholars of public administration were once thought to possess has been lost during the years since Brownlow and Hoover I.

Zeitgeist-type explanations can take historians only so far. But they do sometimes provide insights into broad if subtle changes in intellectual climate. The ascent of behavioralism among the panjandrums of social science, many of whom affected scorn for the "formal-legal approach" to political study, contributed to the diminution in the intellectual stature of classical public administration. The rise of economists and the (perhaps meretricious) allure of the style, both empirical and theoretical, that they brought to the corridors of power also helped in the displacement of public administrators. And as Curtis Ventriss has persuasively argued, the rise of policy science has somehow had the effect of relegating many public administrators to the less glamorous roles of follower-uppers, detail-handlers, and "implementers."[27] Members of the faculties of the most prestigious public policy schools have been zealously complicitous in this process.

Keepers of the original flame such as Ronald Moe bemoan the NPR authors' rejection of the classical tradition. But for many members of the president's and vice president's generation, in fact probably for Americans generally, bureaucracy as a concept and certainly as an institution means something different than it did to the informed public of a century or so ago, when the Progressives began constructing the modern American administrative state. The rationalized, unified structures that the Brownlow and Hoover I task force members extolled had, certainly by 1960, ceased to be widely regarded as potentially effective instruments of executive policy. In his account of the Kennedy presidency, Arthur Schlesinger, Jr., captured the changed mood. President Kennedy, Schlesinger wrote,

> had to get the government moving. He came to the White House at a time when the ability of the President to do this had suffered steady constriction. The cliches about the 'most powerful office on earth' had concealed the extent to which the mid-century Presidents had much less freedom of action than, say, Jackson or Lincoln or even Franklin Roosevelt. No doubt the mid-century Presidents could blow up the world, but at the same time they were increasingly hemmed in by the growing power of the executive bureaucracy and of Congress.[28]

Furthermore, the changing nature of the chief executive's job itself forced presidents to economize on their energies by devoting themselves selectively to the principal challenges of the job. Members of a new postwar generation of commentators, such as Stephen Hess, argued that these challenges had to center not on administration and management but on politics and policy. Presidents could and should delegate the more prosaic managerial functions to staff aides in the central agencies, especially the Office of Management and Budget, or devolve them on the proven administrators in the "managerial slots" within the departments and agencies.[29] Hess's point—that presidents must first of all serve as political leaders, and as top managers only as a kind of afterthought—was made in 1976.[30] In more recent years, one finds echoes of Hess's contention in the writings of a leading commentator on presidential reorganizational efforts, Peri E. Arnold, and most recently of the columnist David Broder.[31] The elevation of the president's political and policy roles over his managerial functions can, it appears, be taken to be something like a *leitmotiv* of contemporary American political science.

Closely related to Hess's point are two themes from perhaps the most influential American student of the presidency in recent years (at least among professional academics), Richard E. Neustadt.[32] The first is Neustadt's famous stressing of the nature of presidential power as "the power to persuade" rather than the kind of mandatory authority that the hierarchical model of bureaucratic governance implies. This emphasis on the power to persuade in a system of informal relationships helped undermine classical public administration, with its emphasis on public law and formal organizational or jurisdictional arrangements. Neustadt also seems to imply that presidents tend to identify organizations with the individual appointees with whom they deal. At the high policy levels, at least, a new sense of the primacy of the person over the position resulted in a further tipping of administrative thought away from the organizational emphasis of classical theory.

During roughly the same time period, Congress began a reclamation of power that continues to this day. Typical episodes of congressional reassertiveness include the War Powers Resolution of 1973 and the Congressional Budget Impoundment and Control Act of 1974. Members of the lawmaking branch have displayed a determination to redress a constitutional balance that had gotten badly out of kilter. The collapse of the Soviet Union and the ending of the cold war have reinforced this trend. There have been suggestions—for example, in Donald Kettl's analysis of the Gore report in chapter 1 of this volume—that the NPR calls for a transfer of power from the legislature to the executive. If so, it may be that the Gore team has espoused a position at odds with the natural and rightful direction of change in the post–cold war era—that is, toward a recovery of legislative power, arguably more in keeping with the Framers' original design. The point is by no means trivial or unrelated to the question of what may reasonably be expected from the NPR in the way of actual change. Battling against the mainstream of history is rarely a formula for institutional success. Nor does it bode to be in the case of the National Performance Review.

The Second Series: Legitimizing Bureaucracy Bashing

It was against this backdrop of intellectual and institutional unsettlement between the end of World War II and the end of the cold war that a second series of major reformist studies got under way.

The issue on which the post-1950 second series of studies focused was less the role of the president vis-à-vis Congress than that of the chief executive *versus* the bureaucracy—the very federal bureaucracy that the earlier study teams had actually done much to strengthen. Alas, the fact that the premises of the first series had been rejected did not necessarily imply the existence of a new set of core concepts to take the place of the classical principles. On the contrary, unlike the studies in the first series, which had shared a common vision of capacity and control, the second-series efforts add up to a spectacle of dissensus.

The members of Hoover II (1955) commenced work with a broad charter: they were to consider policy as well as managerial issues.[33] However, they lacked a compelling administrative model and strong support from President Eisenhower.[34] Ike was uncongenial to the idea of a reconstituted Hoover commission kibitzing from an independent base. He appointed several competing advisory panels of his own (the Rockefeller and Kestnbaum groups) and apparently relied on their work far more heavily than he did on the studies that the Hoover II groups produced. Furthermore, the members of the second Hoover commission had themselves apparently lost faith in the old administrative nostrums. For example, they were willing to concede the need for a sprawling, rather disorganized constellation of federal agencies.[35] This was in stark contrast with the insistence by the members of the Brownlow committee and the Hoover I task force on the need for executive unity.

The years between the two Hoover commissions had seen the completion of the arduous effort to reconstitute the nation's security apparatus.[36] This process, which had involved some of the finest minds and most influential figures in the country, produced the framework of agencies that included the Department of Defense (with a weak secretary and four semi-independent fiefdoms: the Joint Chiefs of Staff and the three military departments), the Central Intelligence Agency, the Atomic Energy Commission, and the National Security Council. No enterprise in institution building filled the minds of American decisionmakers more fully than did the only partly successful effort to create a unified, rationalized "Brownlow-type" defense establishment. The lessons of the effort to rationalize a defense system riven with contending interests and brimming with functional and intellectual complexity, perhaps as much as any other single factor, chastened the members of the second Hoover commission.

The members of Lyndon Johnson's two major reorganizational task forces (1964, 1967), headed respectively by Harvard dean Don K. Price and Chicago businessman Benjamin W. Heineman, suggested policy analysis as a unifying intellectual approach to governance and also as a method by which a strong chief executive could reclaim control of an increasingly unruly bureaucracy.[37]

Then under President Nixon came the attempt of the early 1970s to revise the basis of executive leadership through presidential politicization of the federal bureaucracy: the Ash council recommendations

(1971).[38] This marked the beginning of what Richard Nathan called the "administrative presidency." Based on their perception that (in Nathan's words) "operations is policy," the Nixon inner group determined to seize full control over the bureaucracy by inserting loyalists into line positions within the key domestic agencies. By directly controlling departmental operations, they would indirectly—but automatically and inevitably—reclaim control over policy from a disloyal bureaucracy. Nathan characterizes the Nixon moves toward the administrative presidency as a way out of the dilemma presented by the "idea that individual citizens through their representatives should make governmental decisions" and "a system in which, increasingly, decisions about public policy are made on the basis of technical knowledge"—in other words, by those bureaucratic possessors of neutral competence.[39]

Structurally, the imagery of the administrative presidency strikingly resembles what would be expected if the classical canons of the administrative mangers and first Hoover commission were carried to the completion of their form: a pyramidal executive branch with a strong president exerting control over a bureaucracy rationally organized along functional lines and through a narrow-span set of subordinates. Much of the problem in this arrangement as Nixon developed it no doubt derived from the fact that it was set up by indirection.

President Carter's advisers, also placing their faith in the potentialities of rational analysis, adopted the synoptic approach.[40] Candidate Carter's extravagant (and rather naive) promise to consolidate 1,900 federal agencies into 200, reminiscent of the Brownlow committee recommendations for executive unification, quickly became an embarrassment.[41] But in any case, the Carterites' structural predilections seem to have been less powerful than their methodological prepossessions. The members of the Carter circle believed in technique rather than in any one set of organizational principles, such as the classical theorists' "canons of efficiency."

The report of the Grace commission (1984) during Ronald Reagan's presidency represented the most combative (and credulous) espousal to date of private-sector managerial techniques in government.[42] However, ideas on the public-private relationship similar to those that dominated the Grace commission seem to have been well represented among both the principals and the staff members of the second Hoover commission, as well as the Ash council.[43] To public administrators who had been brought up on Wallace Sayre's apothegm about the public and private sectors' similarity "in all unimportant respects," the Grace commission approach must have represented the most extreme form of rejection of the classical traditions.[44]

The NPR, State Capacity, and the Problem of Control

Now comes the spokesman for the Clinton administration's contribution to this farrago, Vice President Al Gore, with a grab bag of bromides and panaceas such as organizational culture, empowerment, and incentive-driven (rather than rule- or order-driven) organization. Following the president's explicit cue, the Gore researchers have rejected precisely what the main contributors to the Keep, Taft, Brownlow, and first Hoover study groups celebrated—namely, bureaucracy. According to the Gore report,

> The problem is not lazy or incompetent people; it is red tape and regulation so suffocating that they stifle every ounce of creativity. . . . Washington is filled with organizations designed for an environment that no longer exists. . . . In today's world of rapid change, lightning-quick information technologies, tough global competition, and demanding customers, large, top-down bureaucracies—public or private—don't work very well. . . . We must change the underlying culture of government . . . by introducing market dynamics, sharing savings from cuts with agencies, exposing unnecessary programs to the spotlight of annual performance measures, and giving customers the power to reject what they do not need.[45]

The NPR is mainly about governmental capacity—to the point, indeed, of carelessness about the value of control. The Gore researchers' theory of human capacity in turn is based on a belief in the productive potential of an individual, even a bureaucrat, who is released from undue restrictions and is (as economists might put it) "properly incentivized."

As Laurence E. Lynn, Jr., has suggested, to the extent that the NPR has an intellectual pedigree, it traces back not through the landmark commissions—and, as emphasized, certainly not through the first series—but rather through what might be thought of as the arational countertradition in twentieth century management theory.[46] This countertradition extends from Osborne and Gaebler and Peters and Waterman back to the contributions of the human relationists (McGregor and Maslow) and thence in a strange and rather oblique way to the scientific managers' appreciation of the "integral of small efficiencies."[47] Ultimately it leads to the idea that individual human creativity, if released and somehow institutionally supported by appropriate public actions, can more or less automatically generate the continuing stream of innovations on which a prosperous future depends. James Willard Hurst's influential essay on the early American political culture, "The Release of Energy," perhaps best expresses this viewpoint.[48] State capacity in the public sector, as in the private, originates in human energy, creativity, and motivation.

As a corollary of the "release of energy" approach, much of the point of the NPR is to undo—or at least to moderate—the instruments of bureaucratic control that Americans have inherited from the scientific managers and administrative lawyers. This raises some questions about capacity and control that might evolve if the NPR were to be played out to its full conclusions.

Federal Work Force Quality

First, can the existing federal work force validate the high expectations that the NPR authors have for their creativity, diligence, motivation, and staying power? The civil service in the second half of the 1990s is largely the product of recruitment efforts completed during years when a popular president, Ronald Reagan, was denigrating government service and bashing public-sector bureaucrats. During a portion of this period, the president's Office of Personnel Management director, Donald Devine, was stressing the "competence"—*not* the excellence—of civil servants in a way reminiscent of Andrew Jackson's undemanding estimate of the skills needed by American public servants.[49]

It would be surprising indeed if more than a decade of bureaucrat bashing from the White House itself had passed without negative effects on the quality of the federal work force. Responsible observers from both without and within the Washington bureaucracy have voiced doubts about the ability and willingness of government employees to accept the challenge implicit in the Gore report.[50] "The real problem," an experienced U.S. Department of Education employee wrote in a letter to a *Washington Post* columnist, "is that the ideology of reinventing government pretends that these people are suddenly going to change 20 years of bad habits and become productive."[51] The doubters' concerns on this score, if justified, could prove decisive for the future of the "reinventing" movement, which its proponents quite explicitly hinge on the capacity of administrators far more than on the organization of administration.

Decentralization and the Organizational Culture Approach

Second, if the federal work force as it is currently constituted may not be up to the job, can the attitudinal transformation that Vice President Gore promised refurbish it intellectually and emotionally for the task?[52] Can the organizational culture approach be relied upon to inspire the kinds of mental and behavioral vigor in the work force that the NPR program requires?

Cultural transformation is an approach consistent with the decentralization that the NPR researchers claim to be a touchstone of their thinking. The point of classical organizational theory was that a properly designed bureaucracy—one with an intact structure of hierarchical controls—could indeed be directed from the top. Based on this essentially Weberian organizational model, the would-be architects of executive leadership who crafted the Brownlow and first Hoover (and even the Ash) recommendations sought a few structural changes that could ensure presidential leverage over a large and complex organization, the federal bureaucracy. By contrast, there is in the culturalist imagery no parsimonious set of levers to be wielded from the fulcrum of the presidency. There are instead only hundreds of thousands of individual actors engaging in literally millions of discrete actions. With the kind of cultural transformation that Gore professes to envisage, thousands of innovations by members of an energized federal work force would integrate to create constructive change across the bureaucracy at large.[53] Reculturation in a group of any size, however, takes time and enormous effort. The active forces of change are diffuse and individually minute. Their aggregated impulse needs to be sustained long enough, and broadly enough, for altered attitudes to translate into fundamentally modified work habits across the federal work force.

The Problem of Control—Revisited

Third, does the aspiration of the reinventers to release federal bureaucrats from many (if not, indeed, from most) of the administrative controls that have been developed over the years threaten to undo an admittedly cumbersome but relatively effective system of democratic accountability? It is arguable that the Gore changes, if pushed beyond some threshold, would fail to meet the second criterion of any acceptable reform, the maintenance of an adequate system of controls on the administrative apparatus of government. (But given the robustness of the existing system of controls, one may doubt that Clinton, Gore, or any other knowledgeable leader can possibly be serious in suggesting that the reinvention effort could ever be pushed very far, just as one may question the candor of those who suggest the possibility of a relatively quick and easy transformation of the federal work culture.)

The Jacksonians and the Progressives sought to satisfy the criterion of control in very different ways, based on contrasting conceptions of the governance process; but nevertheless they did meet it, at least in theory. Can one say quite as much for the NPR? The Clinton-Gore advisers' espousal of bottom-up discipline for the bureaucracy can surely be regarded as an essay in control theory. Having conceded the existence of a theory, however, the question of its applicability, both normative and empirical, remains. George Frederickson has argued that the "citizens-as-customers" orientation is normatively wrongheaded in that it undermines the very concept of citizenship. As such, Frederickson argues, it offers no stable long-term basis for a reform of governance that simultaneously meets the philosophical requirements of democracy.[54]

The case for the customer-oriented approach to federal bureaucratic restructuring may be as empirically weak as critics charge it is normatively. Donald Kettl has described the evolution of the national government's role as a transition from retail to wholesale governance. Well into the twentieth century, federal officials provided direct—often face-to-face—services. But such "retail" functions constitute a diminishing share of the activities of federal bureaucrats. Although federal spending has mushroomed, the federal civilian labor force is now about the same size as it was in the 1950s. Increasingly, Kettl has documented, federal workers act as check writers, service packagers, and program overseers. Federal employees "wholesale" programs to a vast network of state and local officials or private contractors: the retailers, as Kettl terms them, who actually deliver the products or programs that the federal government funds. The authors of the NPR fail to explain how customers are going to influence federal bureaucrats, most of whose activities they experience only as mediated by multiple layers of intervening state, local, and frequently private actors working on contract.[55]

Any theory of control requires showing that the lines of accountability are intact. Thus the practice of rotationary patronage appointments of loyal subordinates under the Jacksonian theory and the invocation of hierarchical authority under the Progressives' bureaucratic approach posited lines of control to complete their theories. The case seems much weaker in the NPR. Vis-à-vis state, local, and private-sector retailers, federal bureaucrats are mainly supervisors—not service providers. Vis-à-vis many of those whom the proponents of the bottom-up theory describe as "customers," federal bureaucrats have no direct relationship at all.

The basic problem may not lie, as Ronald Moe fears, in the prospect of old organizational solutions offered for modern situations, but in the danger that, after rejecting the classical tradition, the implementers of the NPR will prove unable to solve the classical problem of control.[56]

Philosophy, Program, and Administrative Aspiration

The final question is whether the reinvention initiative bodes, in the end, to contradict the larger philosophical and programmatic purposes of the Clinton presidency.

As Erwin Hargrove and Michael Nelson have pointed out, inherent in the aspiration for a "presidency of achievement" is the tendency to generate legislative initiatives of such scope, and so riddled with political compromises and support-purchasing payoffs, as to make management and implementation problems virtually inevitable down the line.[57] Take, for example, President Clinton's hopes for health care reform. It seems clear that health reform, if there is to be any, will be hammered out in congressional subcommittees, with very substantial political inputs. The authors of a recent volume on health reform have urged anticipatory attention to issues of administrative feasibility.[58] A nice thought, that. But it is unlikely that administrative foresight or managerial concerns will figure as major factors in this essentially—and necessarily—political process. Similar questions can be raised about the prospects for welfare reform, not to mention implementation of the North American Free Trade Act or that of any military actions in which the United States could easily become involved.

President Clinton purports to want to effect, through the NPR, changes that are inherently managerial. The theme of "cut red tape, reduce costs, and improve efficiency" runs like a skein through the Gore report. Alas, however, a leader whose political life has been based on his skill at having it both ways may now have to choose: Either retreat to a policy agenda that does not threaten to overtax the administrative and managerial capacities of the federal government, or else—if Clinton persists in his expansive programmatic ambitions—devote requisite energies to organizational development, personnel upgrading, and managerial improvement throughout a bureaucracy that will have to manage the new programs. The key figures in that bureaucracy hardly need to have its "reinvention" as the primary claim on their brainpower and energies.

What, then, is really "inside the NPR"? In the unlikely event that the president can replicate his budgetary and NAFTA successes in the arenas of health reform and welfare reform, these will represent developments of historic significance in domestic public policy—ironically, a kind of unintended validation of the Hess-Arnold-Broder thesis about the proper focus of a presidency. But there will probably be some meretricious claims and politically cynical anecdotes in the near-term account that the Clinton-Gore followers will give of the achievements of the NPR. It is still more likely that the mismatch between policy aspirations and managerial attainment in the early 1990s will lead, in the longer run, to some of the implementation problems that are well remembered by those who followed the story of the last would-be president of achievement, Lyndon Johnson, to its inglorious end.[59]

As it gradually becomes clear how much less there is in the NPR than meets the eye, the Gore effort bodes to become not the fundamental transformation that the "reinventing" tag promises, but a modest move toward better public management, based on some welcome applications of common sense.[60] It will also be a commendable effort to identify and eliminate gross procedural aberrations in the administrative process.[61] That is not what the hyperbolic press releases and advertising puffery promise. But in the context of politics as usual, neither would it be an achievement to be scorned.

4 ||| Varieties of Reinvention: Six NPR "Success Stories"

Beryl A. Radin

MOST OF WHAT is understood to be the National Performance Review (NPR) has come from speeches, reports, and analyses released by the vice president's office, the White House, and the independent office established to implement the NPR. These efforts have focused on governmentwide strategies for change as well as specific recommendations for particular departments and agencies. As other chapters in this volume suggest, these activities express a set of values and strategies articulated by or at least indicated to be a part of the Clinton presidency. In chapter 2, Donald Kettl characterized the goals of the NPR as an admixture of entrepreneurial government, changing bureaucratic culture, and shrinking the bureaucracy.

The NPR resembled a political campaign: fast, intense, and controlled by generalists. It utilized direct communication with citizens, face-to-face exchanges with career bureaucrats, and a series of teams of experienced federal employees who examined agencies and crosscutting issues. A parallel set of activities took place in each of the federal departments and agencies. The NPR report noted that "the President also asked all cabinet members to create Reinvention Teams to lead transformations at their departments, and Reinvention Laboratories, to begin experimenting with new ways of doing business."[1]

Some of the new "experiments" described in the report actually predate the NPR process; indeed, in several cases the agenda for change for a federal agency or department was devised before the advent of the Clinton administration. Other activities were originally conceptualized as a part of the policy or management agenda of the organization's chief executive (either cabinet secretary or agency head). And other undertakings were developed in response to the vice president's directives and closely followed the approach defined by the NPR.

The executive departments and agencies were given the difficult job. Not only did they have responsibility for implementing the crosscutting goals and the specific agency recommendations in the NPR report, but they also were held responsible for carrying out their own agendas. Although the NPR continued to play a role in the process—some would call it a "cheerleading" role—the management of the details was left to the departments and agencies.

This chapter provides an analysis of four areas: the relationships between the management and policy agendas found within the departments or agencies, the levels and methods of involving career and political actors, the role and influence of approaches borrowed from the private sector, and the strategies employed to implement the NPR. It focuses on the question: is there a central tendency or sense of direction that can be discerned by examining six organizations that have, according to the NPR's own leaders, taken the NPR seriously? And, if there is a central tendency, can it be attributed to the guidance provided by Gore and the NPR office, or is it due to attributes and strategies within the department or agency? To what extent has the NPR become an all-purpose cloak for an agency head or cabinet secretary's own policy and management agenda?

There are at least six types of departmental or agency activity relevant to the NPR: changing policies, reorganizing structure, reducing the budget, empowering line managers, improving customer service, and changing decision systems.

—Some of the NPR activity and recommendations involve substantive changes in the design of policies or programs. In most cases, these changes require action by Congress as well as the support of the White House.

—The organizational structure of the implementing department or agency was sometimes a target of the reinvention effort. Thus proposals for changes in organizational structure (both in headquarters and in the field) emerged as NPR initiatives. Many of these proposals require congressional action.

—A major assumption of the NPR activity is that reinvention processes will produce budget savings or new sources of revenue for agencies or departments. Reductions in the size of the work force are expected to be a major element in achieving budget savings.

—Bureaucratic cultures based on a command and control approach are believed to be major contributors to ineffective government performance. Decentralizing decisionmaking to lower levels of the organization, devising new accountability mechanisms, and improving the quality of the work situation are viewed as important components to an alternative approach.

—The NPR strategy builds on the private sector's emphasis on customer service and attempts to improve the ways government services are delivered. This includes an emphasis on customer surveys, competition, and other attempts to simulate a market situation.

—Slow, unresponsive and inefficient bureaucracies are the target of NPR efforts to change decision systems. Recommended changes involve new ways of developing the budget, personnel, procurement, regulations, intergovernmental relations, and inspection processes.

The NPR: Six Works in Progress

This chapter focuses on the process of implementing the NPR by examining the early experience of six departments or agencies: the Departments of Agriculture, Health and Human Services, Housing and Urban Development, Interior and Labor, and the Agency for International Development. Each of these federal organizations was identified as a major "success story" in interviews with NPR leaders. They were held up as examples of public agencies that have taken the reinvention task most seriously. But as this chapter explains, even these "successes" illustrate significant variability in both the process and the substantive response to the NPR inside the federal bureaucracy. There is wide variation in the pace and content of the change achieved. At the same time, there is much going on within the federal government in the name of the NPR that may have little or nothing to do with the administration's "reinvention" plans or priorities.

Department of Agriculture

The U.S. Department of Agriculture (USDA) is one of the largest, most dispersed federal agencies: it has more than 11,000 field offices, more than 110,000 employees, and the fourth largest federal budget, with outlays of more than $60 billion. Its organizational structure has included forty-three agencies and staff offices.[2] Over the 1980s, despite dramatic changes in the extent and nature of the American agricultural sector, attempts to restructure and redefine the mission of USDA had been stymied, largely because of political pressures from constituents and interest groups. An effort at the end of the Bush administration to close down a large number of field offices did not move beyond the proposal stage.

From the beginning of Agriculture Secretary Mike Espy's term, change, restructuring, and reinvention were his central goals. Indeed, during his confirmation hearings, Espy promised that USDA would restructure the headquarters staff and streamline the field structure.[3] On March 3, 1993—the day that Vice President Gore announced the creation of the National Performance Review—USDA had scheduled a conference of all the department's human resource professionals in the Washington area. This meeting, the Personnel Leadership Forum, introduced the reinvention concept, and reinvention guru David Osborne spoke to the group.[4] Before this, efforts had been ongoing within the department, largely staffed by the personnel office, to focus on modernizing administrative processes.

Through the Personnel Leadership Forum as well as other activities, members of the personnel community were asked to identify personnel, procurement, and other administrative practices in the department—a "stupid things list"—that participants in the forum believed should be stopped. They were categorized in terms of the types of changes needed (such as whether regulations or rules had to be changed or training was required) as well as the time frame required for change.

As the NPR activity developed, sixty USDA employees drawn from different agencies within the department and at different levels were assigned to work on the effort; thirty went to the Gore team while the others worked within the department. The internal effort had two elements. One, led by the deputy secretary and the assistant and under secretaries, focused on the structure of the department and budget issues. The second was largely composed of career staff who identified issue areas, developed a questionnaire, and scheduled employee forums. The NPR liaison was a career staffer from the department's Office of Personnel.

Employees were given the opportunity to articulate their issues at meetings. The internal department group received more than 8,000 written responses and so many phone calls that they lost track of them. Many of the comments criticized inefficiencies of the procurement system, the complexity of the budget process, and a rigid and rule-bound human resources system. USDA's thirteen reinvention laboratories emerged from suggestions by employees who, in order to get approval for their idea, were required to get an endorsement from their agency leadership.

On September 7, 1993—the day the Gore report was released—USDA also announced its reinvention agenda.[5] Foremost in the proposal was a reorganization plan, structured along six mission lines, that reflected both a redefinition of USDA's role and the department's response to the downsizing (called "rightsizing") imperatives of the Clinton administration. It emphasized rural development as well as the traditional agricultural issues such as conservation programs and food, nutrition, and consumer services. The plan articulated four principles: improvement of the delivery of services to the department's customers; consistency with the mandated missions of USDA; establishment of the agency as a better place for employees; and saving taxpayers' money.

The Gore report had seven recommendations for USDA that also included a reorganization proposal as well as several other management suggestions.[6] In addition, the recommendations emphasized specific policy changes (such as ending the subsidies for wool, mohair, and honey). Although there was significant support for these recommendations, some critics—such as the General Accounting Office—were concerned that the proposals did not recognize that "Congress and the administration need to develop a consensus on USDA's missions" and that the policy recommendations are "judgments that Congress will have to address."[7]

Following the issuance of the two reports, the efforts moved along a dual track. The reorganization proposals required legislation and largely involved the Espy political team. The other efforts were centered in the personnel staff and became integrated into the existing human resources processes. By the summer of 1994, more than one hundred pages of the department's personnel manual had been eliminated, plans were in place to move away from use of the standard federal personnel application form (form SF-171), and efforts were being made to create a less rigid merit promotion system. Recommendations involving other internal processes were assigned to existing mechanisms and structures (for example, changes in the regulation development process were assigned to the Office of Budget and Program Analysis). By early 1994 the USDA NPR group had effectively disbanded; it had meetings only when issues emerged that were directly related to the NPR report. The Office for Modernization of Administrative Processes was given responsibility to coordinate the residual NPR activities.

The two-track approach to the reinvention activity within USDA reflected very different approaches to management change. The reorganization and "rightsizing" activities were top-down efforts, driven by both political and budget realities. By contrast, the other element of USDA's activity was defined by a bottom-up, organizational development approach that attempted to empower line managers and provide opportunities for career staffers to voice problems and solutions. However, even as the department is asking employees what they would like to do, its leaders acknowledge that they are operating in an environment that will demand reductions in staff. Despite efforts to continue face-to-face meetings (including training, seminars, and workshops) with a range of career staffers, some participants in the process are concerned about employees' cynicism as the department attempts to implement NPR and the restructuring proposals.

The pattern that can be discerned from these activities suggests clear separation between the agenda of the careerists and that of the political appointees in the Department of Agriculture. The careerists emphasized activities that empowered line managers and attempted to change decision systems. By contrast, the political agenda accentuated policy change, reorganization, and budget reductions (largely through downsizing).

Department of the Interior

The U.S. Department of the Interior, with approximately 77,000 full-time employees located at more than 700 U.S. sites,[8] has often been characterized as a holding company. Its program elements are diverse, many have strong and independent constituencies, and most parts of the department do not provide direct services to the public. Over the past few decades, because of conflicts between environmentalists and advocates of private development, the programs of the department have been increasingly subject to controversy. Well-established relationships between the department and its long-time constituencies have been challenged by the newer environmental groups. In addition, the organization has been viewed as insular and fragmented, with minimal coordination across the program units. The Clinton administration's efforts to change this department reflect a commitment to improve the quality of the management of natural resources yet to do so with fewer staff and resources.

The activity within Interior that was parallel to the White House–led NPR activity emphasized the participation of career staffers. During the summer of 1993, the secretary's office organized eleven teams to identify areas in which change could take place.[9] These teams focused on more than one hundred individual recommendations, eleven of which were identified as "quick fixes" that were easy to implement.[10] Among these were recommendations to eliminate government driver's licenses, institute paperless time and attendance systems, and initiate a government credit card application process for Interior staff members. The department's reinvention laboratories also emerged from the "bottom-up" internal process.

In contrast to these micromanagement suggestions, the fourteen recommendations for Interior in the NPR report emphasized policy changes (such as creating a new mission for the Bureau of Reclamation and redefining federal oversight of coal mine regulations) and broader management concerns (for example, shifts in the way the department manages and acquires federal lands).[11] These recommendations emerged from the NPR Natural Resources Team (which covered Agriculture, Interior, and the Environmental Protection Agency). Three of the fourteen recommendations came directly from the department.

In October 1993, the leader of the NPR Natural Resources Team (a career appointee in another agency) came to Interior to head up the process within the department. The NPR office was located within the office of the chief of staff, who has responsibility for the day-to-day management of the department. When the team leader arrived in Interior, she found that the coordinating group for the eleven departmental teams was not operating effectively enough to implement the NPR changes.

The Interior effort involved three levels. The first emerged from the activity based on the management consulting model (executive orders from the White House, the performance agreement Secretary Bruce Babbitt signed with President Clinton, implementation of specific recommendations from the NPR, the reinvention laboratories, and the internal activity within the department). The second involved communications activities both internal to and external to the department. A newsletter, *Solutions*, was published to communicate the NPR activity. The third involved the Secretary's Operating Council, a group composed of deputy assistant secretaries, deputy bureau heads, and directors of offices. Its membership was 60 percent political appointees and 40 percent career officials. This council was conceptualized as the accountability mechanism that would be responsible for implementing the various NPR proposals. A coordinating group of the leaders from the eleven internal teams was established by the department's chief of staff to serve as an implementation team to utilize the efforts of managers and employees across the department. [12]

Much of the activity within the Department of Interior has taken place at the agency level. Both the Bureau of Land Management and the Bureau of Reclamation have attempted to change their mission focus and work toward goals of improving customer service, empowering employees, and streamlining decision processes. The Bureau of Reclamation has given "risk" coupons to its managers, inviting them to use them when they have a good idea that is somewhat risky. They are asked to take two "risks" a year. At this writing, no risk coupons have been used, and the process for carrying out the concept has not been defined. The National Park Service has attempted to reorganize and reduce headquarters staff. This approach responds to the dispersed nature of the department and a strategy that attempts to find ways for the NPR effort to permeate the agencies.

In March 1994 the secretary of Interior signed a performance agreement with the president that set forward seven goals: to establish a national biological survey; to reform land management; to reinvent the Bureau of Reclamation; to strengthen the commitment of the national park system to employees and the American public; to act as a partner with American Indian tribes; to make the Endangered Species Act work; and to champion collaboration and performance in the department. [13]

The strategy that has been employed with Interior, like that in other departments, is derivative of a private-sector, management consulting approach that emphasizes employee participation and culture change. The department has established a goal of reducing its staff by 50 percent, but calls this process "rightsizing," the assignment of staff to meet organizational priorities, not "downsizing." Efforts have been made to identify career staff to be spokespeople for the NPR activities and approach. The diffuse nature of the department has made it difficult to distribute the newsletter that was developed to communicate the NPR-related activity.

Department of Interior staff emphasize the importance of continuing leadership from the White House, particularly the vice president, to maintain the energy for the changes. They note that there is tremendous cynicism within the department and that better training and communication are required to minimize the effects of that cynicism.

In sum, the Department of Interior has emphasized three types of activities under the NPR rubric. Both careerists and political appointees have been involved in efforts to empower line managers. The other two predominant activities—policy change and budget reduction—have largely been the agenda of the political appointees.

Agency for International Development

Since the Agency for International Development (AID) was created in 1961, much has changed in terms of U.S. policy regarding its role in international development. The roughly 2,000 employees in Washington and 1,700 overseas staff face an international landscape that is very different than it was more than thirty years ago.[14] The original two purposes of the agency—responding to the threat of communism and helping poorer nations develop and progress—were achieved to some degree. The end of the cold war shifted the challenge of development, and a number of nations experienced economic growth. At the same time, serious threats remain: continuing poverty, limited literacy, poor health, environmental damage, and the absence of democracy.

The National Performance Review activity was not the first to focus on the challenge of redefining AID. Even before the advent of the Clinton administration, GAO and other agencies released a series of reviews that suggested the agency did not have a clearly articulated mission or a management plan that could respond to changing world circumstances. The appointment of Administrator J. Brian Atwood, who had management experience on Capitol Hill as well as the State Department, heralded a major shift in approach. The administrator charged the policy office of the agency with the lead role in the effort to revitalize the organization, acknowledging that the strategy had to cross a range of activities within the agency and involve rewriting the Foreign Assistance Act as well as other initiatives. The lead individual was a career foreign service staffer. A quality council was established in the summer of 1993 with a cross section of agency employees as members; it was designed to be a sounding board or clearinghouse, not an operational body.

From the beginning of the NPR activity, the AID goal was to harness the White House activity so as to support the organization's existing reform agenda. An arrangement was devised with the NPR foreign policy team that both allowed the NPR group to maintain its sense of independence and provided a way for the AID staff to harmonize the recommendations with the administrator's own direction. The NPR team chose to have many small meetings with staff rather than a few large meetings.

The Gore report contained seven recommendations for AID: a redefinition and refocus of the agency's mission and priorities; a reduction in funding, spending and reporting micromanaging; an overhaul of the personnel system; an attempt to manage AID employees and consultants as a unified work force; establishment of an innovative capital fund; reengineering the management of AID projects and programs; and consolidation or closing of AID overseas missions. [15]

The recommendations reflected not only the agency's priorities but also a sense within Congress that this was an appropriate route for change. These activities coincided with congressional development of the new foreign assistance act, the Peace, Prosperity and Democracy Act of 1994. During the development of this legislation, Congress stipulated that the NPR recommendations must be implemented by March 31, 1994, or AID would not be able to utilize its 1994 funding. Even before the Gore report was released, it was clear to the administrator that missions would have to be closed or phased out because of programmatic reasons as well as budget constraints. Criteria were drafted for closeout decisions. To indicate the seriousness of the commitment to change, the entire AID organization was defined as a reinvention laboratory.

At this point in the process, it appeared that most changes that were demanded involved management issues. As a result, the primary responsibility for implementing the NPR was moved from the policy office to the management staff. The lead person for that effort was a career Foreign Service staffer who had been a long-time critic of existing AID decision systems. She established a six-person temporary office to coordinate all the NPR efforts (including reengineering, cultural change, experimental missions, and customer service). The quality council continued to operate, and a reengineering reference group (a group of twenty-eight individuals drawn from across the agency) was set up from it. This group was asked to identify a vision for recreating AID. An intensive reengineering team was established, made up of mid-level staff who were identified as being budding or potential leaders, unafraid of change, and able to work in teams. Both these groups interviewed individuals within and outside AID to uncover problems and requirements and to test new ideas. The two unions that represent AID staff were involved and a union-management partnership council office was formed (see chapter 5 for a description of these councils). A professional resources council of AID contractors was convened and informed about the NPR-related activities.

The strategists for the changes within the agency have based their efforts on a recent book about corporate change.[16] At the same time, AID staff acknowledge the differences between the public and private sectors—particularly the role of Congress, the inability of AID beneficiaries to make demands on the system, and limitations on choices about use of resources.

AID officials report their reinvention accomplishments in eight areas: procurement reform, financial management reform, streamlined organization, results-oriented government, reform of the personnel system, regulatory management, information policy and technology, and customer service improvements.[17]

Efforts are also under way to identify approximately ten experimental missions. Once chosen, these missions will receive training in teamwork and coaching skills and will be asked to do customer surveys (customers are defined as participants in AID activities in host countries) and keep in good communication with headquarters.

When the activity within the agency began, there were some "negative rumblings"; people were not sure how seriously to take this effort since they had experienced previous management reform initiatives. As the process unfolded, however, its proponents believe that the staff has grasped the enormity of the change. What is called NPR activity in the agency is an encompassing umbrella for change that is much broader than the Gore report's original seven recommendations and includes decentralization, client orientation, reorganization, and reengineering. Staff members became more aware that this approach would require different rewards, incentives, policies, and procedures. Some were energized by this effort; others found it tiring, bewildering, and a lot of work.[18]

AID staff believe that the involvement of the vice president's office is an important source of legitimacy and authority. Discussions of the appropriate configuration of the audit function, for example, have called on input from the Gore staff. Interest groups that are fighting for earmarking of funds are reminded that the focus on results comes from the White House as well as the agency. Attempts are being made to minimize the congressional predilection to micromanage the agency; this is being done by focusing on performance objectives in broader program areas rather than specific projects.

AID is the only organization included in this analysis that has engaged in major activities in all six of the approaches suggested: policy change, reorganization, budget reductions, empowering line managers, improving customer service, and changing decision systems. In addition, AID alone has involved both career and political staff in all these predominant activities.

Department of Health and Human Services

The U.S. Department of Health and Human Services (HHS) is the largest domestic cabinet organization, with a staff of 127,000, 250 separate program units, and a budget of $673 billion.[19] Since its creation in 1953 as the Department of Health, Education and Welfare, the department has undergone several major reorganizations and has been the focal point for a series of social policy controversies related to race, income, and gender. Its components range from the all-federal Social Security Administration (where staffers actually deliver the services to citizens) to agencies, such as the Health Care Financing Administration, that deliver dollars and regulations to others (largely state and local governments) who provide the services.

Despite management reform efforts over a period of several decades, HHS has been viewed by many both inside and outside the department as an organization that is difficult, if not impossible, to manage. Its size and diversity make it difficult for talk about a centralized strategy to become more than lip service. More important, however, the policy environment in which the department operates creates a sense of instability and uncertainty about both the substance and the processes of program implementation. During the 1980s, proposals for management reform were closely entwined with a policy agenda that sought to diminish a federal role in social policy. As a result, some perceive management changes as a vehicle for a conservative agenda.

When HHS Secretary Donna Shalala assumed office in January 1993 there were several management reform efforts already under way that had sought to separate "good management" from policy change. Career staffers had developed both a continuous improvement process and a total quality management (TQM) effort. A decision was made not to replace these efforts but rather to bring them into the orbit of the new administration. An advisory group was created, composed of career staff drawn from throughout the department, that in its early phases was parallel to the NPR activity.

Although a steering committee composed of senior political appointees was formed in the spring of 1993, many of the new Clinton appointees were not personally invested in its operation since they were focused on major policy initiatives that involved the department. Both the health care reform and welfare reform efforts took center stage and consumed the time, interest, and energy of the newcomers. As a result, few political appointees became directly involved with the management reform efforts.

The fourteen recommendations for HHS in the September 1993 Gore report included a range of policy, programmatic, process, and management issues. However, they were prefaced by the following statement: "Two primary concerns of the Department of Health and Human Services are the delivery of health and welfare services to individuals. Since the Administration has special, ongoing efforts dealing with these areas, they are not covered by the National Performance Review."[20] The recommendations included policy changes (such as a call for integrated service delivery and reconfiguration of support for health professions education). Five items focused on the Social Security Administration (improvement of disability claims, investment of trust funds, information collection, collection of outstanding debts, and redesign of technology). They also called for strengthening departmentwide management and a review of the field and regional office structure.[21]

The department's internal process began in September 1993; it operated out of the Office of the Deputy Secretary and was managed by a senior career staffer. It was named the secretary's continuous improvement program and involved over 300 HHS employees working through six work groups, all chaired by career staffers. These groups were established to respond to "the more than 3,000 ideas which have been submitted to the Secretary, and to the recommendations from the Vice President's National Performance Review."[22] The employee suggestions emphasized leadership and management, program operations changes, customer services, and personnel management. More than half the recommendations focused on the operation of the Social Security Administration.[23]

Several principles were a part of the continuous improvement program design: it should compliment, not duplicate, the health care and welfare reform efforts; employee, customer, and partner participation is critical; and it should be built on the secretary's three themes (fostering independence, emphasizing prevention, and improving customer service). The common thread in all of the work groups was described by officials in the secretary's office as "decontrol—that is, removing unnecessary layers of review and delegating authority to the operating level so that those who do the work have the tools they need to succeed."[24] The organization of the effort was devised so that a new organizational structure would not be created. No one was detailed to the work groups full time; rather, the decision was made to use existing staff and program structures, to avoid the creation of an elite team of reinventors, and to describe the effort as a "self-audit" by employees of the department.

The strategic planning work group is attempting to develop plans and budget figures that both respond to the work force streamlining requirements established by the administration and provide a way of focusing on the administration's crosscutting policy goals. However, HHS's five reinvention labs tend to emphasize agency-specific changes. In April 1994, a crosscutting laboratory was added by defining as a reinvention laboratory the Georgia Common Access Project, a multi-agency application demonstration effort in Atlanta involving former President Jimmy Carter.

Although there is some indication that the NPR efforts are improving the culture of career staffers, there are many forces affecting the process that push against change. As one individual described it, "We are dealing with an environment, structures and systems that are not amenable to change. Career staffers have a sense of insecurity that has resulted from years of bureaucrat bashing and underinvestment in people and skills." In addition, there is some cynicism expressed by political officials who see the NPR activity as an exercise in management processes that does not focus on substantive policy change.

Overall, the activity within HHS has involved three of the varieties of NPR activities: policy change, empowering line managers, and changing decision systems. This activity has moved along two quite separate tracks. Many of the political appointees have focused on policy change, but on changes that are not included under the NPR umbrella. By contrast, the careerists (largely through the continuous improvement program) have emphasized activities that empower line managers and change decision systems.

Department of Labor

The U.S. Department of Labor (DOL), created in 1913, has approximately 18,000 employees located in 440 offices across the United States. Thirty-eight cities have DOL offices with 50 or more employees;

seventeen cities have offices with 100 or more employees.[25] The department's work is largely done through ten agencies that operate autono-
mously in specialized areas (such as the Employment and Training
Administration, the Occupational Safety and Health Administration,
the Bureau of Labor Statistics, and the Mine Safety and Health Administration).

Labor's reinvention activity began early in the Clinton administration
as a result of the interest and background of Secretary Robert Reich and
Deputy Secretary Thomas Glynn. Both were committed to changing
the image of the department from that of a tired, old second-class
organization to one that was more relevant and modern. Glynn already
had experience in public management, concern about customer service,
and a commitment to make changes in the way the department operated. The DOL activities began in April 1993 with an address by
management expert Tom Peters, who challenged the participants to find
ways to reengineer their organization.[26] In June 1993 a three-day reinvention seminar was held that provided the opportunity to define problems, develop recommendations to address the problems, present the
recommendations to the secretary, and receive a response directly from
the secretary either approving or disapproving the recommendations.
Most of the issues identified involved personnel, procurement and
budget. Approximately 120 managers participated, drawn from both
career and political ranks. Because a number of political positions were
still unfilled, a larger number of careerists attended than might otherwise have been anticipated. The participants were chosen by the deputy
secretary and the agency heads and included representatives from the
department's trade unions.

Before the release of the Gore report, a seventeen-member departmental leadership team was created to provide general direction and
policy for the effort. In addition, every one of the department's ten
agencies organized an agency reinvention team. These teams were empowered to make decisions about restructuring the department and
changing the culture and the way work is performed.[27] These teams are
viewed as the location of the "seat of reinvention power" and are described as entities that institutionalize the union-management partnership; agency heads pick their members and unions pick theirs. In
addition, the effort integrated some of the TQM activity that had been
under way in the department before the change of administration.

The twenty-one recommendations for the DOL in the Gore report
contained a mixture of policy and management suggestions.[28] Policy

changes included new approaches for occupationally disabled federal workers, new worker adjustment strategies, and shifts in strategies to achieve workplace safety. Several recommendations called for changes in rulemaking (including expanded use of alternative dispute resolution), financial reporting, and competitive contracting for some programs. Although the GAO agreed with some of the suggestions made in the Gore report, it noted that several areas of congressional concern had not been included or were not addressed by well-developed recommendations (such as problems with the Pension Benefit Guaranty Corporation and the Occupational Safety and Health Administration).[29]

By December 1993 a management consultant in the private sector was brought in to head the Office of Reinvention, which provides resources, such as expertise and time, to agencies that want assistance. The approach emphasizes coordination possibilities rather than control and seeks to encourage some crosscutting efforts across the units within the department. Meetings and workshops have been provided a mechanism for agencies to share experiences. Efforts have been made to provide regular evaluations of the progress and descriptions of the approaches taken by the department's three reinvention laboratories.

The office has collected success stories, called "reinvention one-pagers," to provide recognition to agencies and staffers willing to try something new. Examples have included new forms of union-management partnership, efficiencies in regulation development, and streamlined information and decisionmaking processes. In one case, an agency reduced its inspection manual from 400 pages to 91 pages. In addition, the Office of Reinvention provides tracking data on the status of decisions already made. The reinvention activity within DOL is integrated into the substantive agenda of the department. Secretary Reich identified four goals in his 1994 performance agreement with President Clinton; one of them was called "Reinventing DOL" (to help meet the first three goals by measuring and improving customer service, reinventing administrative systems and producing savings, providing better information, increasing ethnic and gender diversity, and making DOL a high-performance workplace).[30]

The DOL effort is constructed on the recognition that the Office of Reinvention does not have many levers to use in attempting to make change. The office does not have control over the budget or an extensive staff; however, it can influence the decisionmaking process. Although DOL staff believe that the office has made some progress in changing the culture of the organization, there continues to be a lot of skepticism that much of what has been done is simply public relations or the repackaging of existing practice.

In addition, staff members note that it is difficult to get all the appropriate participants lined up because of the complexity of relationships within the public sector. At the same time that managers are being asked to have courage, to give up control, one staff member said, "We are telling middle managers that they are superfluous and what they did in the past is not valid. We are telling them that not only do they have no future, but they have no past."

Taken as an entity, the Department of Labor has engaged in three predominant activities related to the NPR: empowering line managers, improving customer service, and changing decision systems. In all three cases, both political appointees and career staff have worked together.

Department of Housing and Urban Development

Few federal agencies were as demoralized at the start of the Clinton administration as the U.S. Department of Housing and Urban Development (HUD). The organization had lost its sense of mission, overwhelmed by the growing urban crisis and the recognition that existing federal programs and policies did not effectively address these problems. The new administration found a sense of hopelessness and a pervasive cynicism about the possibility of change among the HUD staff. The department's more than 13,000 employees, located in regional, state and area offices (there are eighty-one HUD field offices),[31] were dispersed in four major program areas that had minimal relationship to one another.

Secretary Henry Cisneros came into the department with a clear vision of change. During his confirmation hearings he emphasized the tragedy of a society characterized by the loss of an entire generation of young people, divisions by race, and the reality of violence. Within a few months after assuming office, he articulated a vision for the organization that committed it to the development of communities that provide opportunities for all citizens, regardless of class or race. Staff were asked to come up with quantifiable goals to measure progress.

By March 1993 HUD had embarked on its reinvention process with a two-day secretary's retreat. More than eighty HUD staffers participated in the session, joining Vice President Gore and the secretary in a discussion of HUD's role, guiding values and principles, and problems. The retreat identified ten overarching goals for the department: the context for community, economic development, self-sufficiency, human capital, the spectrum of housing need, the necessity of urban amenity, housing and employment choice, inclusive decisionmaking, HUD as enabler, and national urban leadership.

Following this March retreat, a decision was made to offer a similar experience to every HUD employee. Staff members were chosen from all parts of the department to serve as facilitators for the sessions. Each meeting played a videotaped message from the secretary and provided structured sessions that provided discussion of the ten departmental goals and principles of service. The sessions were available day after day both in the headquarters and in field offices. Between 7,000 and 9,000 individuals participated in the meetings.

As these sessions were taking place, the secretary announced that a Reinventing HUD Task Force would be established to collect and review recommendations emanating from the work sessions, conduct a comprehensive review of HUD's operations, develop ways to put the department's goals and principles into action, and work with Gore's task force. The task force was formally established in May 1993 with people assigned to work on two teams: a management excellence team (to focus on budgeting, personnel, procurement, training, and other administrative issues, led by the assistant secretary of administration) and a policy redesign project (to analyze policy and program issues, led by the assistant secretary for policy development and research). Twenty-seven people (including several union representatives) were assigned to the teams, based on their expertise and interests.[32]

The task force's mission primarily involved receiving feedback from the departmental sessions, developing recommendations to correct adverse workplace conditions, proposing "quick fix" solutions, identifying longer-term solutions, and assisting in the department's business process reengineering effort. As the process unfolded, the task force held retreats in various parts of the department, had meetings in more than fifteen cities, and sought recommendations from outside organizations.

The task force received approximately 7,000 suggestions from staff comments, which became the primary basis for preparing two reports: one on workplace conditions and one on internal management improvements to be implemented within six months (called the "quick fix" report). The workplace report was reviewed by the top departmental staff, union officials, and several members of the NPR task force. It was transmitted to all HUD employees in early August. The recommendations in the "quick fix" report were also presented to the secretary;

approximately 80 percent of the recommendations either are in the process of being implemented or are planned to be implemented.

The ten HUD-related recommendations in the Gore report focused almost entirely on policy changes or management changes that would require or provoke congressional concern.[33] One called for a streamlining of HUD field operations, and several others suggested major changes in the ways loans and real estate were managed by the department. Among the major policy recommendations were suggestions to reinvent public housing and to create new ways to administer housing support programs.

The effort culminated in the development of the document that became the presidential performance agreement with HUD.[34] It emphasized five community empowerment principles: a commitment to community; a commitment to support families; a commitment to economic "lift"; a commitment to reciprocity and to balancing individual rights with responsibilities; and a commitment to reduce separations by race and income in American life.

By the time this agreement was signed, all members of the HUD reinvention teams had returned to their jobs. The work that had been developed by the teams was integrated into the new day-to-day operating procedures of the department, an approach that was perceived to be the secretary's original intention. The special assistant who had been assigned to work with the effort continued to be the liaison to the Gore effort but was not at all involved in any of the details of the initiatives. By the spring of 1994, it was difficult to identify an individual or office within the department that could provide an overview of the NPR-related activities.

HUD activities have involved four types of NPR activities: policy change, empowering line managers, improving customer service and changing decision systems. In all four areas, both career and political staff have been involved.

Some Preliminary Patterns

These six cases indicate the great variation among federal departments and agencies in their response to the NPR activity. Much of what has occurred follows past patterns of management reform, reflecting the authority structure of the organization, the level of autonomy of subunits within the organization, and both positive and negative past experiences. In three cases—AID, HUD, and Labor—

Table 4-1. National Performance Review Activities in Six Federal Agencies, by Type of Staff Involved

Activity	Type of staff					
	USDA	Interior	AID	HHS	DOL	HUD
Policy change	P	P	B	P	. . .	B
Reorganize structure	P	. . .	B	. . .	. . .	. . .
Budget reductions	P	P	B	. . .	. . .	. . .
Empower line managers	C	B	B	C	B	B
Improve customer service	. . .	. . .	B	. . .	B	B
Change decision systems	C	. . .	B	C	B	B

P = Political appointees predominant.
C = Career staff predominant.
B = Both political and career staff predominant.

there was a general perception both within and outside the organization that change was needed. And in AID and HUD, there was some match between the internal agenda and the expectations of Congress and other external players. As table 4-1 indicates, all the activities that were predominant in those organizations involved both political appointees and career staff.

At the same time, however, other organizations fell into the trap of separating the management agenda from efforts at substantive policy change. This occurred both because of the types of officials involved (career or political appointees) as well as the strategy employed (top-down or bottom-up). While organizations were often creative in the ways career officials were involved in the process, these efforts tended to exclude external actors. In the case of HHS, the separation of the two agendas occurred at the White House, not in the department. Other departments or agencies were able to use Gore's interest and the White House aura as a window of opportunity to give their own proposals attention and a source of legitimacy.

The six organizations employed both permanent and temporary strategies. Several of the departments created NPR offices that were transformed into ongoing institutional structures charged with orchestrating continuing efforts at change. Others, by contrast, behaved as matrix organizations—short-term task forces that spun off assignments and activities to the institutionalized units and processes within the organization.

The substantive range of the proposals for change was extremely wide. The six organizations engaged in a total of twenty-four significant activities: fourteen of them involved both career and staffers, six involved only political actors, and four involved careerists. Only one agency, AID, developed significant activities in all six areas, suggesting that it is possible to find a way to develop a single strategy that encompasses multiple approaches. Others, by contrast, picked and chose among activity types.

As table 4-1 indicates, all six agencies engaged in activities to empower line managers; in two cases these activities predominantly involved career staff, while both political and career staff were involved in the other four. Five of the six organizations engaged in policy change; these activities were the agenda of the political appointees in three of the organizations, while both political and career people were involved in policy changes in two. Five of the organizations also changed decision systems; in three cases both political and career staff were involved and in two only career staff were predominant.

Activities to improve customer service were found in three agencies as a result of both political and career involvement. Budget reduction activities, also found in three agencies, were the agenda of political appointees in two and joint efforts by both career and political staff in one. Finally, reorganization activities were found in two situations; in one department they were the result of political appointee involvement and in another the result of joint activity.

Although some of the recommendations that emerged from the Gore report and from internal processes were far-reaching in scope, some of the proposals identified by career staff members involved micromanagement questions that sometimes appeared trivial to political appointees and those outside the organization. However, both the careerists and political appointees were influenced by concepts and literatures borrowed from the private sector. Work by Osborne, Peters, and Hammer and Champy clearly influenced the internal processes. The language of TQM was pervasive, particularly concerning the need for an emphasis on customer service. These examples also indicate that the management concept of reengineering found its way into the public sector.

As other chapters in this book have indicated, there is a dark side to the NPR activity. All the organizations examined have confronted widespread cynicism among the career staff as they have embarked on their NPR activities. To some degree this reflects a sense of burnout and a perception that the NPR is simply one more of a series of management reforms that have been unsuccessfully advanced by political figures over the past several decades. However, much of the cynicism can also be attributed to the linkage within the NPR between personnel cuts and the other aspects of management change (see chapter 5 for a discussion of these issues).

Conclusions

What, then, can be learned about the NPR in practice from the evidence gleaned from these six profiles? Even given the variation in organizational settings, are there any central tendencies that can be ascertained from the early experience to this point?

Separation of Management and Policy

The organizations that tied management reform to processes and agendas dealing with policy issues did so because of attributes at the departmental or agency level, not because of directives or even guidance from a central NPR office. The link between policy and management reform in Labor emerged as a result of the strategy of the top leadership. In AID, it came both from the top leadership and from external pressure from Congress to change. Similarly, the HUD approach reflected a belief by both top leadership and external actors that change was dramatically needed. The cases of failure to link policy and management also occurred as a result of both past and current forces within specific organizations. HHS was preoccupied with policy change and also had historical problems with management reform. Reorganization efforts within the Department of Agriculture took top billing for time and interest.

Emphasis on Executive Power

All six of the agencies examined borrowed concepts, models, and expertise from private-sector management. In some cases, the individuals who played the major strategy role for the activity came directly from the private sector. Even when career officials played a leadership role, they relied on private-sector experience as their model. This tended to emphasize internal aspects of change, using the concept of a chief executive officer as the focal point. Although informants in all the organizations studied did emphasize the relationship between their efforts and those of the NPR writ large, they tended to view that relationship as one that legitimated their own internal activities. In effect, the NPR and the White House provided a useful "cover" for the change that was desired within the agency and leverage for top officials to shake up their organizations.

Conflict Avoidance

Some of the organizations invested in a bottom-up process, reaching out to career staff with a message that "we're all in this together." In several instances, these processes did not produce approaches that fit the agenda of top leadership; thus it was difficult to meld the two together. As table 4-1 indicates, however, four of the six organizations were able to develop activities that empowered line managers through involvement of both career and political staff. However, it was more difficult to find ways to deal with budget reductions and downsizing through collaborative action.

The NPR itself tended to avoid politics and the conflict that occurs as a result of dealing with Congress and interest groups. Three of the organizations studied, however, did reach out to acknowledge the diverse perspectives of Congress and external groups, suggesting that they did not perceive themselves to be constrained by the guidance provided by the NPR.

Accountability Mechanisms

At the present time, it is difficult to ascertain whether the agencies examined have been able to create bureaucratic, legal, professional, or political accountability mechanisms that represent the new approaches. Much of the rhetoric about accountability involves promises related to the measurement and assessment of performance through the requirements of the Government Performance and Results Act (GPRA). In the NPR's first year, however, GPRA was still a promise, not a reality. Although expectations about change are pervasive, it is not clear what is being asked of career public servants that will transcend this administration. For what and how will they be held accountable? The widespread cynicism reported among career staffers suggests that they, too, are unclear about their future role and the durability of current initiatives. Similarly, although the GAO provided support for some of the specific recommendations made by the Gore report, it clearly will continue its independent assessment of management progress within the federal government.

It appears that these organizations have engaged in serious activity. However, the pace and substance of these efforts varies even in the organizations that are viewed as the success stories. The agencies that have moved quickly have done so because cabinet secretaries or agency heads have used the NPR as a window of opportunity to legitimize their own agendas for change. The NPR has been aggressively pursued only when it seems to help promote an agency head or cabinet secretary's management and policy mission.

Although there is no governmentwide, lockstep march toward change, some departments and agencies have taken up the White House challenge to "reinvent" themselves. Some Clinton appointees have been willing to engage in the difficult and detailed implementation task within their own organizations, utilizing the resources of both political appointees and career staff in the process, orchestrating and responding to both internally and externally defined desires for change. Other appointees, by contrast, have not.

It is not easy to link policy and management agendas. Many different forces work against the development of this linkage: complex decision processes, congressional pressure, baggage from past experience, career or political conflicts, and crowded policy and management agendas. This analysis shows that some organizations are able to overcome these forces and carry out both policy and management change. It is not yet clear how—or if—these efforts will be sustained. It is still very early in the process and the jury is still out.

5 ||| Unions, Management, and the NPR

Carolyn Ban

AS DONALD F. KETTL notes in chapter 2, the NPR envisions a move away from the traditional adversarial, legalistic approach to labor-management relations toward a cooperative, problem-solving approach based on labor-management partnerships. To understand the radical nature of the proposed changes, it is useful to begin with a brief discussion of the status quo ante in federal labor relations.

From the perspective of both labor and management, federal unions and the labor-management process faced serious problems in the period leading up to the NPR. Although some federal unions (particularly for postal employees) have existed since the late nineteenth century, the modern era of active employee unions dates only to the 1960s, when President John F. Kennedy, in an executive order, officially recognized the right of employee organizations, such as unions and professional societies, to represent employee interests and to negotiate on at least some aspects of working conditions.[1] Title VII of the Civil Service Reform Act of 1978 (CSRA) first codified in law the right to union representation and the scope of bargaining, that is, the range of issues over which unions and management could negotiate. Although statutory coverage was an important gain from the union perspective, the law left much to be desired.

In particular, the scope of bargaining under title VII was severely limited. Many of the issues that were most important for unions were made nonnegotiable, including pay and benefits. Further, the law set up a complex, three-tiered system. Prohibited (nonnegotiable) issues were those considered core management rights, including determining the mission, budget, organization, and number of employees, as well as operational matters, such as hiring, firing and layoff decisions, assigning work, and making decisions concerning contracting out.[2] Mandatory topics for negotiation included what is generally referred to as "implementation and impact" of the agency's decisions. This includes, specifically, "appropriate arrangements for employees adversely affected by the exercise of any authority under this section by such management officials."[3] The problem this poses is the difficulty in drawing the line between the exercise of a management authority (such as the decision to conduct a reduction in force), which is nonnegotiable, and the impact of that decision on affected employees, which is negotiable. A third set of issues was made nonmandatory or permissive (negotiable at the option of management), including the number or grades of employees assigned to specific units or projects and the technology or methods of performing work.[4] Not surprisingly, given their choice, management has mostly chosen not to negotiate on the latter set of issues.

In fact, the distinctions drawn by the law between the three categories are far from clear. In part, that was a result of the political compromises needed to pass the law, which allowed both labor and management to claim victory.[5] Conflicts over whether an issue is negotiable are resolved by the Federal Labor Relations Authority (FLRA), which does so only on a case-by-case basis. Such disputes are common, expensive, and slow to resolve. Indeed, a recent General Accounting Office (GAO) report found that "more than two-thirds of the experts we interviewed thought the negotiability appeal process was working poorly and was a major obstacle to effective bargaining." A major source of their discontent was FLRA decisions that were "inconsistent, unclear, and untimely." In fact, twenty-eight of thirty people the GAO interviewed "found it difficult to understand what was negotiable and not negotiable even though FLRA has issued hundreds of negotiability appeals decisions."[6]

Federal unions have been perceived as relatively weak, both because of the severe limitations on the scope of bargaining and because of the statutory prohibition on strikes. During the Reagan-Bush years, the political clout of federal unions was weakened further. The tone was set early in the Reagan years, when Reagan chose to enforce the prohibition on strikes as dramatically as possible. When air traffic controllers struck for higher wages, Reagan mobilized military air traffic controllers to keep planes flying and broke the strike by firing the strikers, arresting the union leadership, and decertifying the union.[7]

The number of federal workers represented by unions grew rapidly following the 1962 executive order, from 12 percent in 1964 to a high of 62 percent in 1987 (see figure 5-1). As figure 5-1 also makes clear,

Figure 5-1. Federal Union Representation, by Type of Worker, 1964–92[a]

Percent

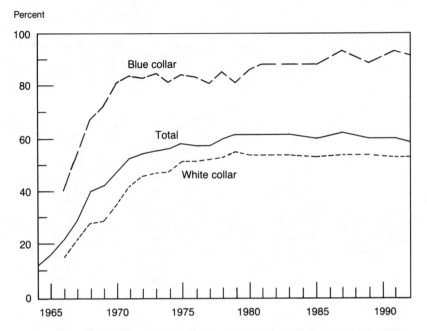

Source: Office of Personnel Management, *Union Recognition in the Federal Government* (December 1992).
a. Data for 1964 and 1965 not broken down by type of worker.

blue-collar workers are consistently represented at a much higher rate than white-collar workers (91 percent compared with 53 percent in 1992). In part this reflects the fact that supervisors and managers are not normally represented by unions. But in addition, support for unions has traditionally been strongest in such "industrial" settings as navy shipyards, which employ large numbers of blue-collar workers.

The level of unionization differs markedly from agency to agency (see table 5-1). For example, only about one-quarter of white-collar employees at the Department of Agriculture (USDA) are represented by unions, compared with more than three-quarters at the Department of Housing and Urban Development (HUD) and the Department of Treasury. Thus, although the NPR anticipates development of labor-management partnerships, in many agencies relatively few employees are currently represented by unions.

Representation does not, however, equal membership. Under the terms of the current labor-management statute, unions are required to operate as "open shops," that is, they must represent all members of

Table 5-1.   Federal Union Representation, by Department or Agency, 1992[a]

Department or agency	Total federal workforce		Blue-collar workers		White-collar workers	
	Number	Percent	Number	Percent	Number	Percent
Departments						
Agriculture	34,878	27	1,950	1	32,928	26
Commerce	15,796	42	957	3	14,839	39
Defense						
Office of Secretary	10,846	37	562	2	10,284	35
Air Force	131,658	75	52,688	30	78,970	45
Army	192,498	68	59,931	21	132,567	47
Navy	193,346	62	101,156	33	92,190	30
Defense Logistics Agency	47,663	74	15,353	24	32,310	50
National Guard	37,609	71	23,175	44	14,434	27
Other[b]	14,286	42	761	*	12,525	*
Education	3,065	59	8	*	3,057	59
Energy	8,570	44	1,554	8	7,016	36
Health and Human Services	71,801	56	2,562	2	69,239	54
Housing and Urban Development	10,368	77	19	*	10,349	77
Interior	28,693	35	6,915	9	21,778	27
Justice	37,028	51	3,231	5	33,797	47
Labor	12,644	73	47	*	12,597	72
State	795	*	*	*	795	*
Transportation	34,257	49	2,810	4	31,447	45
Treasury	127,091	78	4,075	3	123,016	76
Veterans Administration	172,870	65	32,967	13	139,903	53

the bargaining unit, even those who chose not to join the union and to pay dues. Not surprisingly, this creates an enormous free-rider problem. Thus, although the level of union representation has dropped off only slightly (see figure 5-1), holding on to dues-paying members appears to be a problem for several federal unions.

Membership in the largest federal union, the American Federation of Government Employees (AFGE) has declined precipitously, dropping by almost 50 percent from a high of 301,000 in the late 1960s to 156,000 in 1990.[8] This was less than one-quarter of the 642,000 people represented by AFGE bargaining units.[9] The membership of the second largest union, the National Federation of Federal Employees (NFFE), is only about 40,000, slightly more than one-quarter of the 148,000 people represented. Only the National Treasury Employees Union (NTEU) has a nearly 50 percent membership rate (65,000 members out of 138,000 represented.) Declining membership means declining

Table 5-1   (continued)

Department or agency	Total federal workforce		Blue-collar workers		White-collar workers	
	Number	Percent	Number	Percent	Number	Percent
Agencies						
Agency for International Development	1,304	*	4	*	1,310	*
Environmental Protection Agency	7,094	38	39	*	7,055	38
Equal Employment Opportunity Commission	1,998	*	4	*	1,994	*
Federal Communications Commission	1,256	*	158	*	858	*
Federal Deposit Insurance Corporation	9,501	63	46	*	9,455	63
Federal Emergency Management Agency	1,016	*	158	*	858	*
General Services Administration	11,348	55	3,864	19	7,484	36
National Aeronautics and Space Administration	12,425	48	554	2	11,871	46
Office of Personnel Management	3,106	45	38	1	3,068	44
U.S. Information Agency	2,299	*	199	*	2,100	*

Source: Office of Personnel Management, *Union Recognition in the Federal Government* (December 1992).

a. Percentages shown are based on total agency employment, which includes employees excluded from union coverage under 5 USC 71. These percentages are not indicative of the proportion of representation among eligible federal employees, nor of union membership.

*Less than 1 percent or fewer than 2,600 employees.

b. Includes Defense Financial and Accounting Service, Defense Contract Audit Service, Defense Information Service, Defense Mapping Agency, and Defense Nuclear Agency.

revenues, and the federal unions have not been well funded. AFGE, in particular, faced serious financial troubles in the late 1980s, when it came close to bankruptcy and had to be bailed out with a $1.5 million loan from the AFL-CIO.[10]

Relations between the unions and management have also often been adversarial and legalistic. Rather than trying to resolve conflicts constructively, both sides (but particularly unions) have been likely to take disputes, even over minor issues, to third parties or to the courts, where they often went unresolved for years.[11]

In sum, the problems with the current system of labor relations in the federal government are so severe that neither labor nor management feels the system is working well or serving its needs. The GAO report on labor relations reported pervasive discontent with the current system and concluded that "the problems in the federal labor-management relations program appear to be so widespread and systemic that piece-meal technical revisions would not be a workable solution." The GAO recommended establishment of "a panel of nationally recognized experts in labor-management relations and participants in the federal program to develop a proposal for comprehensive reform."[12]

The Impetus for Reform: Partnership and Politics

There were probably mixed motives for the NPR's decision to involve the unions in the reform process. Some observers have described the motive as frankly political, based on the need for the unions' support of the NPR as a whole. According to this school of thought, once the decision was made that the NPR recommendations should stress not only management improvement but also significant cuts in the work force, the need to head off political opposition by the Democrats in Congress became obvious. Although federal unions are relatively weak, they do have political clout, and their influence is likely to increase in the future, now that most parts of the Hatch Act limiting political activity by federal employees have been repealed. Heading off union opposition to the NPR was critical.[13] One decision that may reflect the desire for union support was to focus the cuts on managers, who are not represented by the unions.

But senior people both at the NPR and in the unions told me that there was also an awareness on both sides of the need for change. As a senior union official told me, "I think there was a genuine recognition on the part of everyone that the systems were broken and they had to be fixed. . . . It was not just the need for political cover that brought the parties together. I believe it was much more sincere and deeper than that."

The broad direction of reform in labor-management direction was spelled out in an executive order issued shortly after the NPR report.[14] The order established the National Partnership Council (NPC) to develop proposals for labor law reform. It also immediately broadened the scope of bargaining, directing agencies to negotiate over items that previously were nonmandatory. Finally, it directed agency heads to create labor-management partnerships "at appropriate levels" within the agencies and to "involve employees and their union representatives as full partners with management representatives to identify problems and craft solutions to better serve the agency's customers and mission." Each of these three changes is potentially significant.

The National Partnership Council

The National Partnership Council is composed of representatives from the highest levels of labor, management, and organizations charged with resolving labor-management disputes. It includes the heads of the three largest federal unions, the AFGE, NTEU, and NFFE, and a representative of the Public Employee Department of the AFL-CIO. Management members include the director of the Office of Personnel Management, as well as the assistant secretaries of Treasury and Defense, the deputy secretaries of Labor and Health and Human Services and the deputy director of the Office of Management and Budget. Neutral members include the chairman of the Federal Labor Relations Authority and the director of the Federal Mediation and Conciliation Service. Members of the NPC are appointed to two-year terms, which can be extended by the president. In short, the composition of the NPC is very close to that recommended by the GAO as a body for drafting labor-management reform proposals.

The NPC is important both substantively and procedurally. Its proposals for labor law reform may shape future legislation. And the process of creating it was an attempt to model labor-management partnership and interest-based bargaining at the highest level. That process was not without difficulty. This was a new way of working for most of the group members, and the problems were exacerbated by a very tight deadline. (The NPC was created in October 1993 and charged with proposing statutory changes to the president by January 1994.) In order to develop substantive proposals, the NPC established a planning group and five ad hoc working groups, in the areas of labor law, staffing, classification and compensation, performance management, and phasing out the Federal Personnel Manual.[15] The internal politics within the planning and working groups was complex. As one working group member, on the management side, described it to me:

The unions had an agenda. The FLRA had an agenda. It was quite an experience. [We] were supposed to engage in the interest-based approach. The time frame was too short. [We] had 30 people, all advocates and litigators, trying to reach consensus.

For those representing management, the task was complicated by the fact that, as this person told me:

We knew the unions had met with the vice president, and if you've looked at the organization chart, he's somewhere above me. There was no feedback from above on whether there was a deal. There was not much guidance from the people we work for directly. I've never been in a more untenable position in my life. I had no idea what my principals needed.

The NPC process required labor and management leaders to try to work together collaboratively, not an easy task for either side. And it also required that labor unions find common ground with each other, also not an easy task since in some cases there had been bitter rivalry between them.[16]

Although there was some disagreement reflected in the National Partnership Council report, particularly on the scope of bargaining (discussed below), the report still reflects substantial agreement on a wide range of issues, such as recommendations for improved and streamlined dispute resolution processes, including mediation and impasse procedures, and on the need to train all parties (including neutrals) in alternative dispute resolution techniques. In other human resources areas, the report generally supported the NPR recommendations for decentralization and deregulation, with the proviso that such issues as additional hiring flexibility, a revamped classification system, and agency programs for performance management should be subject to collective bargaining.

One important area unresolved by the NPC was what the group termed "union effectiveness," that is, ensuring the financial health of the unions by addressing the free-rider problems all federal unions face. Significantly, the NPC report acknowledged that "union effectiveness requires strong, professional, financially secure unions that are able to operate as full partners with agencies."[17] But the members of the NPC failed to reach consensus on how to meet this goal and, indeed, presented four options:

—The status quo (no fee for nonmembers) would be preserved.

—Nonmembers would be required to either join or pay a fee for any bargaining unit in which voluntary membership reached 60 percent.

—Parties would negotiate a fair-share service fee and a fee for individualized services, with the option of including a provision permitting individual employees to decline in writing to pay the fee.

—There would be a statutory requirement that employees pay for individualized services, and parties would be permitted to negotiate a fair-share service fee.[18]

Although the NPC was an effective vehicle for involving the unions in the NPR process and developing initial proposals for reform, it is too early to say with certainty what its ongoing role will be, or whether the reforms it proposed will be acceptable to Congress. Before the 1994 elections, some union officials were optimistic about the eventual possibility of legislative action, while others recognized it would take a major educational effort to change congressional perceptions. Republican control of Congress changed the political environment dramatically. Louis Jasmine, the new president of the NFFE, was quoted as saying that "it was 'unlikely' that unions would win the right to charge fees for services to nonunion workers covered by bargaining agreements."[19]

One important continuing role for the NPC will be to provide guidance and support for partnership efforts within agencies. Indeed, its plans for the future focus on fostering and supporting the formation and development of agency partnerships and sharing information about successful partnerships. This includes promoting training for partnership throughout the federal government.

Changing the Scope of Bargaining: Redefining the Boundaries

Expanding unions' involvement in operational issues is controversial because it raises a question about the appropriate role for unions. The issue, simply, is whether unions will espouse positions that are good for the agency as a whole, or whether, when the chips are down, they will fight for what benefits their members directly. The NPC attempted to address that question by recommending a "good government" substantive bargaining standard that obligates both parties to "pursue solutions that promote increased quality and productivity, customer service, mission accomplishment, efficiency, quality of work life, employee empowerment, [and] organizational performance . . . while considering the legitimate interests of both parties."[20]

Nonetheless, some managers doubt whether the good government standard is viable and see it as papering over fundamental differences of interests between unions and management. The argument against expanding the unions' role was made to me by a manager who had reviewed the NPC report. As he put it:

To suggest that the core management rights, such as to assign work, should be put on the table [is] going too far and being naive. . . .

Is it realistic to expect unions to go along with a decision to cut workers? That's too much to expect. That's not the role of the union. They are *not* responsible for effective operation of the agency. [21]

Further, managers who have been promised more discretion as a result of deregulation are often less than enthusiastic about the effects of a broader union role. Managers I talked to expressed their concern about expanding the scope of bargaining; several told me that they feared that managers would be hamstrung if the 10,000-page Federal Personnel Manual were replaced by 10,000-page collective bargaining agreements.

The disagreement over the proper boundaries for union involvement in agency operations is at the heart of the debate that took place within the NPC itself. Lack of consensus over the scope of bargaining is reflected in the presentation of three different options in the NPC report. Option 1, which was a management proposal, envisions relatively minor change: it called for codifying the changes made in the executive order requiring agencies to bargain on previously permissive subjects. "Core and operational matters would remain reserved to agency management, but bargaining would be required on proposals that did not substantially interfere with such rights." A key issue here, for some management representatives, was preventing bargaining over hiring. Option 3, on the other hand, called for immediate negotiation over operational matters, such as hiring, firing, or layoffs. This is close to a private-sector model. As one union person involved in the process told me, this was "the typical union point of view, that, short of mission and budget, everything should be negotiable."

Option 2 was an attempt to craft a compromise position. It calls for moving to bargaining over operational matters gradually, in a three-phased process. The report concludes that "the Council believes Option 2 provides a workable conceptual framework for legislation but recognizes it raises a central issue: whether the transition from one stage to the next would occur automatically or be subject to some discretion."[22] Indeed, there remains considerable confusion over how Option 2 would work in practice. One of the participants in the process on the management side told me, "I keep hoping I don't have to explain Option 2. It is clouded. . . . Option 2 is a compromise developed by the Planning Group and the NPC itself. And it split the baby. In my estimation, you ended up with parts of a dead baby."

According to a union person involved in the process, managers have raised several concerns about Option 2. Some have stressed the need for some discretion in the timing of movement through the three stages, based on progress in developing partnerships. Further, "management wants the ability to pull out if it doesn't work, and go back to mean-spirited bargaining. It's usually from people who tell war stories about being raked over the coals by some grizzly union people."

Resolution of this conflict will await the process of attempting to craft a bill that both labor and management (and a majority in Congress) can support. Meanwhile, the changes outlined in the executive order are being implemented. It is too early to see much effect: few contracts are now being negotiated, so there have been no major disagreements yet. But one often overlooked effect of deregulation of the civil service system is an indirect expansion of the scope of bargaining. Areas that are covered by regulations are not subject to collective bargaining; thus deregulation (including elimination of the Federal Personnel Manual and of agency regulations) automatically opens up new subjects for negotiation. One such case has already been heard by the FLRA, in which the army argued that an issue was nonnegotiable because it was covered by the Federal Personnel Manual, chapter 630, which covers procedures for granting excused absences.[23] The relevant chapter had been eliminated, so the issue was ruled negotiable.

In sum, directly or indirectly, the scope of bargaining already has changed as a result of the NPR-NPC process. How unions use that expanded scope will depend, in large part, on the success of partnership at the agency level.

Learning to Work Together

The executive order calls for agencies to establish partnership councils. This process faces a number of challenges. First, there has been very little guidance, so the agencies that are out in front are feeling their way. As one of the management people involved in the NPC told me, "As far as partnering at the local level, we can't write a regulation saying, 'You will partner, and this is how to do it.' First, no one knows what it is. It's a trendy word." But he and others agreed that partnership entailed using alternative dispute resolution approaches, or what has been termed "win-win" bargaining or "interest-based bargaining," rather than the traditional adversarial collective bargaining model. Several agencies have already moved in that direction in recent years, most notably the Department of Labor and the Internal Revenue Service, where the union and management have been reasonably successful at working past the accumulated distrust engendered by years of conflict to develop positive, cooperative relationships.[24]

According to an informant at the Office of Personnel Management, which is tracking partnership agreements, almost all agencies that have bargaining-unit employees have negotiated partnership agreements. Typically, agencies sign a national agreement, which has a steering function, with one or more unions. The critical agreements are between unions and management at what are called "units of recognition" in the federal government (that is, at the level where bargaining agreements are negotiated). These are typically at a regional or facility level, depending on the structure of the agency. Many such agreements have already been signed, covering well over 50 percent of employees represented by unions.

Even getting to the point of a national partnership agreement is a significant accomplishment. As one union official put it, "Certainly at the agency level, they're getting off the ground, meaning they were able to sign a paper without strangling each other." This frank recognition of the distance both sides must come was mirrored by the NPR staff member who told me, "We're finding it's all relative depending on what the history of the agency was. In some places, they think it's partnership if they are just talking to each other, because the relationship was so hostile in the past." In short, both sides recognize that this will be a long, incremental process, with ups and downs.

Signing an agreement is just the first step. Implementing partnership throughout an agency poses several technical and logistical problems, which most agencies are just beginning to address. Who should sit at the table is not always clear. For example, as will be discussed below, groups other than unions are asking to be represented. Another potential dilemma is coordination of national and local activities and oversight by the union. When I asked a union official who serves as head of the national council of AFGE locals in her agency how they would decide which issues would go to the agency's national partnership council and which to local partnerships, she told me, "That's a good question, and we haven't really resolved that." A national official in a different union raised a similar concern about what might happen if decisions made by local partnerships are not in the interest of the union:

We have to monitor what's going on in the groups, and, before the group makes a final decision, we need to circulate the recommendations and get feedback through our normal channels. . . . The agency may suffer if they invest time in this, and then the committee comes out with a recommendation and the union trashes it.

Further, partnership places heavy demands on union resources. For example, if there are partnerships at every work site, who will represent the unions? As one union official told me,

It puts a strain on us, because if we keep putting chapter leaders on these teams, we are in trouble running the chapter. The alternative is to get members, stewards or others, to do this. . . . But the problem is they don't have the experience of how to think unionwide, and you see some pettiness—some "that's ok if it's done in my shop." So it's creating a lot of pressure to rethink how we service members.

Further, union leaders, as well as managers, need extensive training in order to handle this new role. The larger unions have the capacity to provide training and are already starting to do so, and the Public Employee Department of the AFL-CIO is putting together a training package for smaller unions, designed for labor-management pairs to be trained together. But getting the training down to the lower levels may be difficult.

The new demands on the unions will continue to push them toward a more professionalized style of management. For example, the AFGE is now going through an internal debate about whether to restructure. A key question is whether its fifteen districts should continue to be headed by elected national vice presidents, or whether professional staff should handle the actual administration of the districts, with vice presidents responsible only for policymaking. A leader of the group proposing movement to a more professionalized management model expressed concern that "the 15 districts sometimes seem like separate unions which makes it hard to have national programs."[25] This proposal is far from universally supported, but reinventing government may also require reinventing federal unions.

In fact, changing the unions, both structurally and psychologically, may be at least as difficult as changing management. Many union leaders have learned their jobs in an adversarial environment and are not convinced that partnership is to their benefit or that they can trust management. Partnership does not replace the traditional collective bargaining process, which will continue; this raises the question of which issues should go to which venue. Further, the need to be able to move back and forth between the two approaches creates role conflicts that are uncomfortable for union officials. Indeed, one senior union official told me that his union had been training its local people in interest-based bargaining for a while, with mixed success. As he put it, "They are saying, 'It's hard to represent someone who's being screwed in the morning, and then flip the switch and be buddies with management in the afternoon, when we are still angry.'"

The conflict between the traditional union role of employee advocate and the new role of partner with management has led, in some agencies, to a dual structure, with two types of union stewards: partnership stewards and grievance stewards.

> Partnership stewards are usually responsible for talking with and negotiating agreements with management (or individual managers) on workforce issues and sometimes individual cases. . . . Meanwhile, the grievances stewards continue to play the traditional role of representing individual employees who believe that a current procedure or action (whether agreed to by the union or not) adversely affects them.[26]

The possibilities for confusion and conflict created by such a dual structure are obvious.

In fact, several observers (both managers and heads of professional associations) expressed the concern that union leaders are too far out in front of their members. The leaders are on board, but where the rank and file will come down is still uncertain; if lack of support by the rank and file is widespread, it could derail partnership efforts. Those implementing the NPR on the management side cannot control the internal political process in the unions, although they may try to sway it. For example, Vice President Al Gore's appearance at an AFGE Partnership Training Conference demonstrated his close relationship with John Sturdivant, the president of the AFGE.[27] Sturdivant faced a serious challenge in his bid for reelection in August 1994. Although he survived, partnership was a serious issue in that race. Sheila Velazco, president of the NFFE, recently lost her bid for reelection to Louis Jasmine. Although partnership was not the central issue in that race, rank-and-file support for partnership remains problematic. If the top leadership cannot sell the new union to their members, managers may end up facing unions that are still adversarial but over an even wider range of issues.

The low levels of actual membership in most unions contribute to resource problems and also to the charge that unions do not really represent all the employees. Active membership is sometimes drawn primarily from certain units or levels, more typically lower-level blue-collar or pink-collar workers rather than professional employees. There is some early indication, however, that partnership may attract new members who want in on the action. Indeed, an AFGE official confirmed that and reported that their membership was up in 1994. As he put it, "We see it. People are excited, they are coming forward as partnership evolves in the workplace, and they see that there is a role for them to play as participants." But if those new members come from different units or levels in the organization, their interests may differ from those of the older members. If they also are more supportive of partnership, conflict between older and newer members is at least possible.

The early stages of partnership in agencies have sometimes been rocky. In one agency with a partnership agreement in place, a union official told me that management—without even notifying, let alone consulting with, the union—commissioned a major outside study to recommend how large parts of the organization should be restructured. Further, union officials at the agency level, like their national counterparts, now have to learn to work not only with management but with each other. As the same agency-level union official told me, "Unions have never worked together in the past. At least at the national headquarters, locals have always been highly competitive. . . . There's always been internal fighting for a piece of the pie among unions." In this agency, four separate unions have a seat in the partnership council. The large defense installations may have even more unions represented.

In short, unions as well as management will need to make significant changes to adapt to the new environment. While some unions are already well along in that process, others are still facing internal resistance. The chronic lack of resources unions face because of their free-rider problem will only make the necessary adjustments more difficult.

Who Speaks for Managers?

In talking about partnership, both at the national level and within agencies, I have focused thus far on the role of unions. The usual presumption in the private sector is that management speaks with one voice and that top management can adequately reflect the interests of all levels of management in making policy for the organization and negotiating with unions. But in the public sector, management is hardly so unified; supervisors, mid-level managers, and even senior executives have formed organizations to represent their interests and views, which are sometimes quite different from those of top management, who are usually short-term political appointees.

Although the NPR staff recognized the importance of involving the unions in the process of reinvention, they chose not to reach out in similar fashion to the management organizations or to involve them in the NPC. Thus, although many individual managers were involved in designing the NPR report, such managers' organizations as the Senior Executives Association, the Federal Executive Institute Alumni Association, and the Professional Managers Association were not involved or consulted. It is unclear whether this was an oversight (as one NPR staff person described it) or a conscious decision, based on an incorrect assessment that these organizations could safely be ignored. The head of one such organization termed the failure to involve the professional associations the result of applying a private-sector model and thus "disregarding stakeholders in the public sector that don't exist in the private-sector model."

This may have been a political miscalculation, a failure to recognize the clout of organizations representing federal managers. Further, managers felt they were bearing the brunt of the NPR cuts. As the informant cited above explained:

They never reached out to any management organization. There was inclusion of the unions and exclusion of the management organizations. There was the perception of managers as the enemy. They cut managers rather than looking at programs and priorities and how you adequately staff and fund them. Instead they chopped away in an arbitrary way at management.

The reaction of these organizations to their exclusion from the process was a "strength in numbers" strategy, the formation of a managers' group called the Coalition for Effective Change. One of its leaders explained:

The CEC grew out of our frustrations because they weren't listening to us earlier. So we banded together and said, "Now we represent about half the federal work force. Will you talk to us now?" They are all stakeholders and have to have a voice. The CEC's role is one of coordination and information sharing, rather than advocacy.

Although the CEC is so diverse that it hardly speaks with one voice, it has the ear of the NPR staff, has met with Vice-President Gore, and is serving as an informal advisory committee to the President's Management Council.

Another important issue concerns the role of professional organizations, particularly those representing first-line and midlevel managers, in the partnership councils. Although they were not invited to join the National Partnership Council, they are pushing hard to take a formal role in the partnership councils being established in individual agencies. As the head of one such organization told me:

> You see the management organizations playing a role at the agency and especially at the facility level. After all, we're talking about trust. You do that by bringing people together who have to work together. You have to bring in the first-level supervisors, or you won't have a true establishment of trust. We're encouraging our chapters to get out at the facilities and try to get . . . official representation of [our organization] . . . at the agency level, and maybe representation at the department level.

When I questioned whether this meant that his organization was acting more like a union, he replied, "If you broadly define a union as an employee organization that represents our members, then we are a union, in the broadest sense." The movement of professional associations to a quasi-union role and their formal inclusion at the table raise a number of difficult problems. What happens when several management organizations request representation? What happens when the interests of different management levels do not coincide? Such questions may be hard to resolve, given the fact that there is no formal process, akin to union elections, by which managers can explicitly choose who speaks for them. Further, proposals for delayering and reducing the number of supervisors create potential conflicts of interest for both unions and management groups if people who are acting, at least to some extent, as first-level supervisors can potentially belong to both a union and a professional association.

Participative Management: Mixed Messages

At the same time that the NPR is asking managers to take on broader responsibilities, to be entrepreneurial, and to share power with their employees (via total quality management) and with the unions (via partnership), it is giving a strong negative signal that many supervisors and managers are superfluous. Midlevel managers are the primary target of the NPR's 272,900-person work force reduction. The language of the NPR report here is quite loaded. It talks about "shedding the power to make decisions from the sedimentary layers of management and giving it to the people on the ground who do the work," and "pruning layer upon layer of managerial overgrowth."[28]

Both the timing of the cuts and the way they are being made undermine the credibility of the NPR effort for many managers. Making the cuts first, before introducing the deregulation and new management approaches that were the ostensible justification for the cuts, opens the NPR to a charge that it was just an elaborate smoke screen for reaping political credit by slashing the bureaucracy. That perception is further intensified by the use of across-the-board cutback strategies rather than careful case-by-case analyses of program needs as the basis for reengineering organizational structures and staffing patterns.[29]

Vice President Gore exhorts managers to empower their employees and talks about reinvention permission slips, but managers who are at risk of losing their jobs are cautious about giving up control, since they know they will be held accountable for their subordinates' mistakes. When I asked a senior NPR staff member about the effects of downsizing on implementing quality, he told me that he felt the downsizing would actually drive the needed culture change, but admitted that "we are having a difficult time with our message on this." But a senior federal manager who has been tracking the NPR process told me about speaking to a group of federal managers whose main concern was how to manage during a reduction in force (RIF). As he put it, "Forget about reinvention and creativity for a year or two. A RIF is a destructive process."

Conclusions

Changing the role of unions and their relationship to management could end up being one of the most significant accomplishments to come out of the NPR process. Even without further legislation, broadening the scope of bargaining through the executive order and indirectly through deregulation gives unions a considerably greater range of issues to negotiate. And the creation of partnership councils at both the national and agency levels, and potentially down to each workplace within the government, provides at the minimum an avenue for discussion outside the traditional adversarial collective bargaining process.

As implementation of these reforms continues, there are four potential problems that all those involved need to be aware of: leadership, capacity, oversight and evaluation, and credibility.

The Leadership Problem

Long-term culture change requires long-term leadership commitment. This means leaders must be willing to devote the resources needed, to model partnerships in their own relationships, and to send strong messages down through the ranks that their commitment is real and that they will hold their subordinates responsible for acting on it. Instability of leadership among unions or top management could threaten the success of partnership. It is unclear what effect the recent change in leadership in the NFFE will have on that union's commitment to partnership, although Sturdivant's victory ensures continued support by the AFGE. But one must also be concerned here about the usual rapid turnover among top political appointees, as well as the effects of the next presidential election. Those involved in implementing the reforms put in place by President Carter's Civil Service Reform Act of 1978 remember all too well the difficulty of maintaining momentum after the election of 1980. The 1994 elections, in which Republicans gained control of Congress, may cause similar problems. Union leaders were reported to be feeling "estranged" because the administration dropped labor law reform from the draft civil service reform bill.[30]

The Capacity Problem

Managers at all levels and union leaders will take on new responsibilities while being asked to change their whole approach to their jobs. Both groups will need extensive training, not just on the new culture and values but on the specific skills needed to do their jobs. Current training plans appear to stress the former and give short shrift to the latter. Further, allocating sufficient resources to training in a time of cutback is always problematic. Indeed, one potential weakness in the NPR was the failure to recommend that agencies set aside a specific amount for training, since training is often the first thing cut when budgets are tight.[31] The unions also may have trouble meeting the resource demands, both for training and for staffing partnerships, without a change in the dues structure. This is a serious risk for the unions. As one union person put it, "If the administration puts added responsibility on the unions to be competent partners, there needs to be support, or it will be the weak link in the chain. If it isn't a true equal partnership, it just won't work."

The Measurement and Evaluation Problem

The NPR can be seen as a huge experiment, introducing new approaches that, in theory, should improve government performance. But can one tell if it is working? Without good performance measures, it is hard to assess the effect of the changes. The Government Performance and Results Act (GPRA) requires agencies to develop performance measures, but that will take several years. Given the considerable costs of implementing the NPR, it may be hard to sustain support without being able to prove its worth. The administration is focusing on publicizing individual success stories, but there is no systematic evaluation planned. The National Partnership Council's assignment of outreach and evaluation of its efforts to the same committee certainly does not give the impression that there will be any independent assessment of its efforts.

Serious evaluation requires a vehicle for collecting systematic information, not just anecdotal success stories. The NPR is on the horns of a dilemma here. On the one hand, it calls for eliminating oversight and control functions. On the other hand, it needs to use the oversight mechanisms it has maligned in order to manage the NPR process and to tell what is working.

The Credibility Problem

Credibility is an issue in two ways. First, both credibility and trust are necessary for creation of genuine labor-management partnerships. Unions need to know that management's promises of cooperation are not just lip service, and that they will not find themselves cut out of the tough decisions, while management needs assurance that unions will use their new power responsibly. It will require time, patience, and goodwill on both sides to move away from the traditional adversarial relationship.

Second, there is the problem of establishing the NPR's credibility with career civil servants, and particularly with managers, who are still poorly informed about the NPR and who are most threatened by its emphasis on cutbacks and delayering.[32]

How such problems are handled will determine how successful the proponents of reinvention will be at overcoming the ingrained skepticism of career civil servants and managers who have seen wave after wave of reform come and go. Although some federal employees, managers, and union members are enthusiastically embracing the NPR reforms, probably the more common attitude is more cautious. Overcoming that skepticism requires showing by action that the agenda is not merely, once again, making political capital by scapegoating federal workers and cutting the size of the federal work force, and that the commitment to improving management in the federal government is genuine and enduring.

6 ||| Reinventing Politics? The NPR Meets Congress

Christopher H. Foreman, Jr.

FOR THE National Performance Review's administrative revolution to succeed, Congress must cooperate. And to hear the Clinton administration tell it, Congress—even in its Republican incarnation—should certainly want to. If the Gore-Clinton vision of an entrepreneurial state prevails, its proponents claim, federal agencies will be more attentive to their various citizen "customers" while behaving more economically themselves, especially as procurement customers. Senior agency managers will delegate more authority to lower ones, who will do the same for their own subordinates. Persons at the bottom of the organizational hierarchy will find a new respect for their good ideas. Some jobs and field offices will vanish as operations are vigorously streamlined, but remaining organizational components can pursue both customer satisfaction and superior program results through competition, rigorous program evaluation, and the latest information technology. The system will stress accountability but without unnecessary rules or bureaucrat bashing. Ideally, all of this will produce a leaner administrative architecture, a transformed administrative culture, and substantial savings—some $108 billion over five years, according to the NPR.[1]

As Donald Kettl observes in chapter 2 of this volume, the NPR is a complex and demanding endeavor that largely sidesteps important questions about the role of Congress. To what extent will Congress embrace and sustain not only the NPR's many details but also its long-term vision, some of which may be politically unpalatable or incompatible with the way Congress currently functions? Congress has been recasting the NPR while allowing the White House to claim many accomplishments. This was the near certain outcome of legislative-executive interaction on a set of proposals as vast and varied as those promoted by the White House.

Continuing congressional investment in the NPR's guiding spirit will be essential, even though, as the administration boasted, many reforms can be initiated without legislation. But such cooperation implies significant institutional change, about which the NPR offers little more than exhortation. In particular, urging that Congress refrain from micromanaging the bureaucracy will come to little unless Congress and its executive branch relations are reinvented at least modestly.

Ideally, members of Congress should hold some combination of the following three perceptions of reinvention. First, reinvention's salient effects must appear generally positive, or at least not particularly harmful. Compelling and well-publicized anecdotes, along with systematic data indicating constituent satisfaction, should considerably help the administration's cause inside Congress. Second, the political benefits to be derived from supporting reinvention (such as favorable media coverage, interest group support, and affirmation and favors from party leaders) should exceed the political costs of doing so. Third, members should ideally perceive the political benefits of opposing reinvention to be small compared with the costs. In short, Congress must believe that interests it holds dear will be served as well as, or better than, they are currently served. How the administration might prod Congress in this direction is the great unanswered (and largely unasked) question of the NPR, a question made even more pertinent by the Republican sweep of 1994.

The Nature of Congress

The Madisonian fundamentals include a bicameral and highly constituent-sensitive Congress that presidents must negotiate with, not dictate to, even when one party controls both legislative and executive branches. Members also stand individually for election under a system of weaker party discipline than tends to prevail among parliamentary democracies.[2] Members may challenge the executive on legislation or administration from perches within a specialized and decentralized committee system, usually without fear of serious repercussions.[3] Each member's ability and motivation to do so stems from a unique mix of factors (including personal preferences, institutional forces, and actual or potential constituency judgments).[4] Congress therefore reflects a vast potpourri of wants and needs, many of which conflict and have little to do with efficiency (however one defines the term) or pursuit of a presidential agenda, regardless of who is president.

Distributive and equity concerns often carry more weight in Congress than the efficient pursuit of goals. This affects how Congress perceives and reacts to the NPR. To be sure, many members of Congress exhibit a strong desire to make good public policy (that is, to advance the national interest as they see it). This inclination is reflected in preferred committee assignments, legislative activity, and oversight of program implementation.[5] But Congress's idealism about formal policy *ends* cannot easily be separated from its various preferences, commitments, and fears relating to *means*; the latter impinge on congressional constituencies and coalitions in ways that may deflect attention from the former. Ends and means are both important to Congress because both yield politically relevant results. Over time this will challenge the ability of Congress and the administration to forge mutually satisfactory understandings about which program results (and therefore which NPR results) are most desirable and significant. This will be true regardless of whether one party controls both branches or there is divided party control.

Although the NPR aims to improve program management, Congress is often both indifferent to considerations of administrative capacity and slow to grapple effectively with even manifest administrative problems.[6] This is not to suggest that Congress remains indifferent to administration. Congress has an insatiable appetite for administrative details, a strong interest in comprehending their political implications, and a willingness to intervene. But for a number of reasons congressional interest is selectively piqued. Time is short, and the government is vast and engaged mostly in unremarkable or routine activities that defy even an approximation of comprehensive monitoring. Members' electoral incentives and prior political and policy agendas may incline them to focus on relatively narrow or micro-level concerns instead of broad program results. They often display constituent-sensitive and scandal-focused responses to "fire alarms" rather than a more rational or comprehensive "police patrol" style of oversight.[7]

The congressional attributes described thus far assured that both the NPR and reforms fashioned in its wake would receive an uneven reception on Capitol Hill, where customer organizations and other interest groups could seek to avoid the pain associated with reinvention, and where some legislators (such as notoriously aggressive Texas Democrat Jack Brooks) might not share the reinventors' basic premises.[8] Even

Republican members of Congress tend to think of a program's customers as any persons presently or potentially affected by it, especially if these persons are organized and vocal. Federal education policy's customers, for example, would include not only students but also parents, teachers, school administrators, and taxpayers. Members sense that they must attend to the interests and views of this diverse audience and maintain winning coalitions through broadly distributed benefits, even when ostensibly concentrating on the "bottom line" of student performance.[9]

The Character of the NPR

Important keys to the congressional fate of reform lie in the character of the NPR itself. A crucial attribute is sheer scope. The NPR report lists over 250 "major recommendations by agency" and another 130 "major recommendations affecting governmental systems" that concern virtually the entire federal government.[10] Leaving few administrative stones unturned, the NPR opens a host of matters on which legislative assent is ultimately crucial (agency structures and cultures, budgeting, staffing, acquisitions, inspections, regulations, and information management). So far-reaching and varied are these recommendations—ranging from a sweeping reform like biennial budgeting to the relative minutiae of fewer diplomatic missions and Marine Guard detachments—that the administration was certain to identify points of both resistance and opportunity.[11] Some matters (facility closures, service cuts, and assaults on the dreaded micromanagement) particularly risked treading on congressional sensitivities. And yet genuine political opportunity beckoned a Congress squeezed by spending constraints, hungry (within Democratic party ranks) for a successful presidency, and anxious about voters' desire for change.

At the same time, the NPR largely avoided the obvious political pitfall of major bureau relocations and terminations. To be sure, the report advised closure of the Uniformed Services University of the Health Sciences (the military medical school), the consolidation of field offices in the Departments of Housing and Urban Development and Agriculture, the sale of the Alaska Power Administration, and other structural changes.[12] But the Clinton administration should be spared the sort of explosive disagreements that erupted when Franklin Roosevelt contemplated transferring the Forest Service from Agriculture to Interior and reorganizing veterans' programs in a proposed Department of Welfare.[13] Proposals like these arouse the opposition of organized clienteles and threaten disruption of congressional committee jurisdictions. The relative lack of structural reshuffling may reflect partly the administration's grasp of political realities, partly the way the NPR was crafted (the advice of federal government workers was enthusiastically sought), and partly the NPR's guiding philosophy of agency entrepreneurship. The Clinton administration is presumably content to see a reinvented Forest Service remain where it is.

For this reason, it is harder for Congress to brand the NPR a harbinger of dictatorial intent by the president, even though greater bureaucratic discretion could obviously challenge congressional interests in particular instances. Indeed, the NPR's aims are quite different from, and arguably even inconsistent with, the traditional goal of increased White House management capacity. Presidents as otherwise different as Franklin Roosevelt and Richard Nixon pursued reorganization mainly to enhance executive leadership.[14] Similarly, the first Hoover commission (1947–49) recommended strengthening the presidential staff, pulling discretionary authority away from bureau chiefs for redistribution to political appointees, and grouping agencies more assiduously within mission-focused departments.[15] By contrast, President Clinton's primary aims are not so much strengthening presidential power as empowering low-level officials, saving money, and deflecting antigovernment sentiment.[16]

Even though the NPR does not hinge significantly on structural reconfiguration of the executive branch, its proposals in this regard have proved politically problematic. A merging of both the Bureau of Alcohol, Tobacco and Firearms and the Drug Enforcement Administration into the Federal Bureau of Investigation was declared dead within three months of the NPR's release, partly due to congressional indifference and opposition.[17] A proposal to move meat and poultry inspection from Agriculture to the Food and Drug Administration within Health and Human Services met a frosty reception from the Democratic chairman of the House Agriculture Committee, who favored consolidation, if at all, only within Agriculture.[18] Within the cabinet itself, both Attorney General Janet Reno and Agriculture Secretary Mike Espy concluded that these transfers of authority were unnecessary for their respective departments.[19] The military medical school (and the nearly 700 civilian jobs it sustained in suburban Maryland) soon developed ardent champions, including members of the Maryland congressional delegation and the chairman of the Senate Appropriations subcommittee on defense.[20]

Opposition by key members of Congress stalled the shift of federal air traffic control responsibilities from the Federal Aviation Administration to a new government corporation.[21]

But like a rich diamond mine, the NPR promises to yield political gems that might outshine whatever rubble is displaced to harvest them. With so many proposed reforms pursued at the same time in so many agencies and programs, the administration was certain to uncover either success stories it could trumpet or more examples of things apparently worth fixing. Critics decry the NPR's focus on "anecdotes," but it is precisely the striking concrete example, not dull generalities about management, that politicians, reporters, and voters find most riveting. Congressional hearings about administrative performance usually abound with anecdotes and are sometimes grounded in little else. And while the NPR might propose to reinvent government, it would not have to invent from whole cloth all of its themes and proposals. The closure and consolidation of agency field offices are perennial and bipartisan rationalizing maneuvers (albeit suspect among those directly affected). In some areas (such as user fees, procurement reform, result-based performance measures, and marketlike approaches to pollution control) the administration would unabashedly preach to the converted, or at least the demonstrably interested, since Congress had shown interest through laws proposed or enacted.

An important element assisting the NPR in Congress is the plan's divisibility. The NPR is a huge and heterogeneous plan, but it avoids the potential vulnerability that could have unhinged an effort built entirely around a single piece of omnibus reform legislation. Recall that in 1938 more than one hundred House Democrats deserted Franklin Roosevelt, narrowly killing his executive reorganization bill after weeks of acrimonious debate, in the kind of major defeat that no president relishes.[22] But no such problem need bedevil the NPR. This divisibility initially distressed reform advocates, like Senator William V. Roth, Jr., Republican of Delaware, who believed that forcing a single up-or-down vote could, to the administration's advantage, position congressional opponents as reinvention obstructionists.[23] On the other hand, a more disaggregated strategy left the administration free to set priorities among those portions of the NPR that will require congressional assent, to calculate the evolving political costs and benefits associated with each portion, and to bundle items when feasible. Such diverse matters as procurement, personnel, and budgeting are, in political terms at least, separable pieces of the grand reinvention. Whether the pieces that survive Congress add up to a coherent and workable whole is another matter.

A final element giving the NPR momentum is its overall political status. Clearly enjoying the president's confidence, a vice president with an appetite for policy detail (amply demonstrated during a sixteen-year congressional career) plunged energetically into the project, discounting advice that doing so would be an unwise career move. What is more, six months after releasing his report, Vice President Gore's attention appeared still engaged.[24] The NPR's themes also offer potent ammunition for a president courting the political center (and Ross Perot's crucial 19 million voters) while reassuring the Democratic core.[25] The NPR's broad centrist appeal also makes it a likely stage for cooperation between President Clinton and a Republican Congress.

The Clinton White House could not cast the federal government as the injurious meddler portrayed by Reaganite demonology.[26] Instead, the focus had to be on making talented and benevolent Uncle Sam, grown befuddled and disorganized with age, once again energetic and productive, "a government as good as our people are," as Jimmy Carter liked to say. One should not underestimate the broad symbolic appeal of the effort, both inside Congress and beyond. Release of the report brought an overwhelmingly positive public response, especially among crucial political and policy elites. One of these was Congress's primary oversight staff agency, the General Accounting Office, which took a favorable first cut at the NPR.[27]

Inevitably, the NPR is also a creature of deficit politics. Both the document and its presentation reflect pressure for significant savings that would attack the deficit or yield money for other worthy endeavors, such as crime control. Presidential rhetoric predictably embraces all these goals, temporarily suppressing if not vanquishing the tensions among them:

> We can and will cut the deficit. We can and will run a government that works better and costs less. We can and will turn those savings to helping America, including helping more Americans be safer in their homes and on their streets.[28]

But soon after these presidential remarks, the Congressional Budget Office (CBO) released an analysis showing budget savings dramatically lower than the administration claimed from enactment of the proposed

Government Reform and Savings Act of 1993, a key legislative pillar of reinvention.[29] This was just one early example of an analytic independence that amplifies Congress's structural separation from the executive branch. The episode highlighted how essential it would be for the NPR to grapple effectively with Congress, arguably its most important customer.

Lawmaking and the NPR

No matter how energetically the White House might have tried, a reform plan as multifaceted and ambitious as the NPR could not have avoided the legislative process entirely. One NPR feature that generated early legislative momentum was its targeting of reform in areas either where significant (if partly latent) congressional support already existed or where Congress was inclined to perceive little concrete threat and considerable symbolic appeal.

Government Performance and Results Act

The Government Performance and Results Act (GPRA), enacted while the NPR was in gestation, is a good example of a proposal that posed little threat and had great symbolic appeal. The Democratic Congress passed the GPRA, which claims to refocus managerial and political attention toward results rather than inputs, in June 1993 with a remarkable absence of rancor or floor debate, especially considering how profoundly the law's advocates hope federal program management will change in its wake. Since its introduction in an earlier incarnation in October 1990, the GPRA's most ardent champion had been a Republican, Senator Roth, whose frustration with government's focus on inputs rather than results meshed with a new Democratic administration's desire for significant administrative reform that did not simply gut programs.

In pursuit of a shifted emphasis, the GPRA requires that agencies prepare "strategic plans" that "shall cover a period of not less than five years forward from the fiscal year in which [they are] submitted, and shall be updated and revised at least every three years" and an annual "performance plan" anchored to the extent possible in measurable progress toward program goals. By the year 2000 and each year following, federal agencies will submit to the president and to Congress annual "program performance reports" describing both the relevant "performance indicators" and the "actual program performance achieved compared with the performance goals expressed in the [performance] plan for that fiscal year."[30]

The failure of these legislative provisions to ignite major controversy is not surprising. Unlike structural reorganization, the GPRA was unlikely to mobilize any organized or readily organizable opposition. In the abstract, who could be against such apparently sensible management reforms as these, especially given that implementation will occur incrementally through pilot programs? Indeed, many members of Congress who voted for the GPRA probably had little familiarity with it. And while doubts about outcome-based management and performance budgeting abound, federal reformers have no monopoly on the idea. Numerous states are moving toward "benchmarking" in management, a development that can only help propel interest at the federal level.[31]

But the absence of troublesome legislative controversy does not spell the end of skepticism or a lack of implementation hurdles. Concerning the federal GPRA and similar mechanisms in the states, skepticism is high and as easy to comprehend as the political appeal of the GPRA concept. The landscape of management reform is, after all, littered with abandoned and discredited rationalizing mechanisms. Such past innovations as planning-programming-budgeting systems (PPBS), zero-base budgeting (ZBB), and management by objectives (MBO) are all familiar failures that give students of public administration ample reason for doubt.[32] Donald F. Kettl has hopefully noted advantages held by the GPRA over these earlier efforts: its overt legislative endorsement, its cautiously incremental implementation, and its demonstrable support within the bureaucracy.[33]

From a congressional perspective, perhaps the major question the GPRA raises is whether an undeniable fondness for its motivating idea can translate into sustained comfort, among both politicians and managers, with the kinds of information such an exercise yields about particular programs. Can Congress use the forthcoming performance plans and reports to give agencies better guidance? Will it even want to? Or will a combination of measurement hurdles and political incentives prove insurmountable? The legislative history of the GPRA clearly indicates a desire that the planning process become an instrument of congressional oversight.[34] In the past, however, oversight has often been more deeply political than neutral terms like *outcome* and *performance* might suggest, and the return of divided government makes this far more likely. Oversight of administration regularly acquires partisan and political overtones. The process often flows from unsettled questions of legislative intent, from a desire for ammunition to hurl against one's opponents, and from a hunger for media attention, not from a dispassionate interest in guiding agencies toward higher levels of technical proficiency. Much oversight has also concentrated energetically on inputs rather than ultimate policy goals.[35] Indeed, agencies attend so assiduously to inputs not only because goals are often conceptually problematic but also because Congress demands that agencies behave in this way.

The Federal Workforce Restructuring Act

Within weeks of the release of the NPR's report, Congress found itself once again focused on inputs, this time jobs and budget constraints. How could the federal government, with the least pain and unfairness to government workers, achieve a 12 percent reduction in the civilian nonpostal work force over five years?[36] Candidate Clinton had promised to pare the federal work force by 100,000 positions, a figure boosted to 252,000 by the vice president's review and increased late in the game by Congress to some 272,900 positions by the end of fiscal year 1999.[37] With the task complicated by a slowing in work force attrition rates, the administration pushed for a "buyout" plan to stimulate retirements and thus avoid disruptive and costly layoffs (known in government jargon as reductions in force or RIFs). A major advantage of buyouts for the administration lay not only in the alleged management efficiencies they would permit but also in giving a largely white and male management corps incentive to leave government early, reducing the federal payroll and making room for minorities and women who might rise to replace them. RIFs, on the other hand, would slash heavily at persons recently hired or promoted, affecting minorities and women more adversely.

Under the buyout proposal, a federal worker taking early retirement could receive up to $25,000. But late in 1993 the legislative authority for the administration's plan was temporarily stalled by Congressional Budget Office projections that, whatever their long-term payoff, buyouts would impose near-term costs—some $519 million over five years. Although the delay may have been, as District of Columbia congressional delegate Eleanor Holmes Norton put it, "a bad case of short-sighted, penny-wise and pound foolishness," it reflected the deficit-dominated political environment in which Congress currently operates.[38]

Buyout legislation cleared the House 391 to 17 in early February 1994, but two controversial Roth-backed provisions in the Senate version—one would have used work force savings to finance a contemplated increase in local police forces—slowed progress again, as House Democrats objected to mingling the crime and buyout issues.[39] Meanwhile, the lack of buyout authority meant that agencies throughout the government edged closer to the less appealing RIF option. Less than a week after the House vote, the Office of Personnel Management announced the elimination of 523 jobs, the first nondefense RIF of the Clinton administration.[40] In mid-March, a House-Senate conference agreed on a buyout bill that dropped the Senate crime provision, prompting Republican threats of a filibuster. It materialized and was quickly broken, the final hurdle before passage of the Federal Workforce Restructuring Act after months of struggle.[41]

The buyout saga displays the significance for both Congress and the White House of short-term considerations, politically relevant inputs, and policy goals beyond enhanced managerial performance, notwithstanding the recent enactment of the GPRA. And in the cash-poor political environment of the 1990s, proposals for personnel cuts prove politically far easier to sell than the buyout funding needed to achieve them.

Government Management Reform Act

The buyout proposal had originally been part of a larger reinvention bill, a proposed Government Reform and Savings Act. Referred to seventeen standing House committees as H.R. 3400, the bill contained a plethora of provisions (such as the closure of the military medical school) that together constituted a major section of the blueprint for a government that works better and costs less. Although individual committees successfully blocked some changes (such as reforming the federal helium program and requiring cadets at the United States Merchant Marine Academy to pay tuition), H.R. 3400 as passed by the House 429 to 1 at the end of the 1993 session would have fully implemented thirty-six NPR recommendations.[42] But the resistance of committee chairmen stalled the legislation in the Senate, which took ten months to pass a far less ambitious bill.[43] Retitled the Government Management

Reform Act, the Senate legislation focused mainly on financial management reforms (including the encouragement of electronic funds transfers to pay government employees and retirees) and the consolidation of agency reports to Congress.[44] The House quickly passed the Senate version, which the president signed on October 13, 1994.[45] By then the administration was resigned to putting the best possible face on a legislative disappointment.

Federal Acquisition Streamlining Act

The administration made significant progress toward procurement reform in the months after the NPR's report. Indeed, the administration-backed procurement reform bill passed Congress in September 1994.[46] One reason for this administration success was the bipartisan appeal of the issue inside Congress even before Clinton's election. However, Congress had created or long tolerated many conditions that reform was supposed to address.[47] For many years, critics inside and outside government had assailed irrationalities in federal procurement, including the widespread resistance to evaluating contract proposals in light of vendors' past performance.[48] In the fiscal year 1991 defense authorization legislation, Congress had created an advisory body (the "section 800 panel") whose report helped set the stage for a new reform attempt by Congress in tandem with a new administration.[49]

Introducing the procurement reform bill (S. 1587) on the Senate floor in October 1993, John Glenn, Democrat of Ohio, made clear that the bill would enjoy close cooperation between the Committee on Governmental Affairs, which he chaired, and the Armed Services Committee, and also between the relevant congressional committees and the NPR staff.[50] As with the GPRA, the bill's main principles of simplification and economy were, by themselves, hard to challenge. Major proposals included a significantly increased threshold (from $25,000 to $100,000) for simplified procedures for small purchases and increased governmental reliance on "off-the-shelf" commercial products, a departure from more costly and cumbersome government-only specifications. Glenn noted that the bill was directly responsive to a number of specific NPR recommendations.

From the outset, though, reformers recognized that major political hurdles lay in the broader social goals embedded in procurement and in Congress's fondness for procedural safeguards against fraud, waste, and abuse. Congress may want simpler and more economical purchasing, but it also cherishes using the procurement process to serve nonprocurement goals: the advancement of minority, disadvantaged, and small business contractors; affirmative action by prime contractors; "buy America" content provisions; and the protection of local wage rates. The administration could hardly abandon these objectives as superfluous. In fact, it urged that the Defense Department's technical assistance program for minorities be expanded to civilian agencies.[51] Defense sought waivers of certain affirmative action requirements for small and commercial purchases, but the White House declined to endorse them.[52] On the local wage protections of the Davis-Bacon Act, the administration moved to strike a deal with labor and business, hoping the former would accept reductions in enforcement paperwork and the latter, worker lawsuits in defense of prevailing wages.[53] Some in Congress were also reluctant to see an increased risk of contractor fraud and waste as an acceptable price to pay for the promise of greater procurement flexibility.[54] In the end, however, the bill's substantive and political merits proved irresistible. Unlike the watered-down Government Management Reform Act signed the same day, the Federal Acquisition Streamlining Act marked a significant legislative triumph for the administration.

The NPR in the 103d Congress

Overall, the NPR found Congress receptive to broad ideas for change but anxious and resistant on a plethora of details and particular cases. Not surprisingly, many of the same frustrations and ideas that found their way into the NPR had made their way to Capitol Hill as well. Perhaps most conspicuously among federal departments, the Department of Agriculture was ripe for serious administrative surgery. Edward Madigan, the Bush administration's agriculture secretary, had earlier developed tough proposals for headquarters reorganization and field office closures.[55] The 98-to-1 Senate endorsement of Secretary Mike Espy's reorganization plan in April 1994 has a history that, like that of procurement reform, predates the Clinton presidency.[56] And, like procurement reform, the reorganization of agriculture programs provided President Clinton with a legislative victory.[57] In all, the 103d Congress would pass, and President Clinton would sign, thirty laws containing NPR recommendations.[58]

But even with the end of divided government in 1993 and the

Clinton-Gore administration's willingness to make the NPR a high priority, reform faced unavoidable limits. The version of the Government Reform and Savings Act that passed the House contained the kinds of compromises and omissions one would expect.[59] The chairman of the House Veterans Affairs Committee mobilized to exempt the veterans' health program from personnel cuts, a move that the administration viewed as a potentially destructive precedent.[60] Congress also shielded the Treasury Department's law enforcement activities from the work force restructuring act's personnel knife.[61] The reinvention effort was sufficiently large and diverse to allow the administration some victories, but the fate of each component hinged on its presentation in immediately favorable political terms.

One of the least favored, and probably least defensible, major legislative recommendations aims squarely at Congress itself: the NPR's call for a two-year congressional budget cycle. Supporters of biennial budgeting have argued that it would promote longer-range thinking and predictability while diminishing "busy work" in the budget process. The NPR report opines that in the twenty states using it, "governors and legislatures have much more time to evaluate programs and develop longer-term plans."[62] But knowledgeable critics have pointed to serious weaknesses in the case for biennial budgeting. Louis Fisher and Albert J. Kliman argue that the NPR badly misinterprets the state experience and point out that the state-level trend since 1940 is actually away from biennial budgeting.[63]

The Republican Future

Although the Republican sweep in the 1994 congressional elections has complicated life for the Clinton White House, reinvention's future may be brighter than before. President Clinton's political stake in reinvention is now far higher; it may be one of the few arenas where he and the new Republican congressional majority can cooperate. And it is in the Republican party's interest to enter the 1996 elections with at least part of the credit for having tamed, if not slain, the bureaucratic dragon. Reinvention allows the Republicans to do this while claiming that they have reached out and found significant common ground with Clinton.

The entrance of so many new members and the ascent of a completely new roster of committee and subcommittee chairmen automatically disrupts settled alliances and replaces old policy preferences with new ones. For example, legislated personnel floors, opposed by the NPR but favored by many Democrats fearful of agency staffing cuts, should be easier to set aside. Crusty Texas Democrat Jack Brooks, strident skeptic of reinvention, has been sent packing back to Beaumont. Energy and Commerce Chairman John Dingell, among the most ardent and feared micromanagers in Congress, has been stripped of his institutional power base. Ironically, the theme of change that propelled Clinton into the White House may, in the case of the NPR, be given momentum by the ascendancy of his opposition. Indeed, Clinton's task now will be to contain the zeal of his new and unwanted congressional partners. Although Republican control of Congress pushed the administration toward finding programs to trim and consolidate, Clinton will constantly have to remind both congressional Republicans and the voters that reinvention is not synonymous with elimination.

President Clinton and the new Republican congressional majority must also deal with a number of tensions implicit in the NPR itself. If the bureaucracy takes the NPR's charge to middle- and low-level entrepreneurs seriously, both policy integration and accountability could suffer. Greater discretion for managers may conflict with attempts to bridge gaps across agencies and departments in the interest of policy consistency. It may also require Congress to relinquish certain kinds of control over programs. Shortly after the NPR's release, more than one commentator noted that authority experimentally delegated to Forest Service field offices had been terminated, suggesting that this might prove a tough sell.[64] And though some may not care to stress it for the present, achieving program results and producing budget savings are two different and potentially opposing objectives. Congressional deficit hawks who support the GPRA may face choices between results and savings when higher spending might yield beneficial effects. By the same token, congressional liberals will have to balance concerns about economy and efficiency against their interest in social justice. The NPR's high-profile and active support by an energetic president does not overcome these tensions.

Long-term congressional oversight of administration, always an uncertain component of reinvention, becomes even more uncertain in the wake of the Republican sweep. Congress must supervise and at least tacitly support even reforms that it did not formally approve. The Reagan-Bush era ought to have shown that high-profile domestic policy initiatives by the executive invite political struggle, and that neither the executive nor the judicial branch can keep Congress at bay with high-minded admonitions to know its place and stay there.[65] Vice

President Gore, a self-described "recovering legislator" who established a reputation in the House for challenging the bureaucracy, is well aware of the role that Congress must play.[66]

When well-intended uses of entrepreneurial discretion turn out badly, will Republicans react by administering their own harmful doses of micromanagement? After all, the parties may have changed but certain institutional fundamentals have not. The news media is unlikely to contain its appetite for scandal, and astute politicians of both parties still face incentives to discover and trumpet administrative misdeeds. How will Republican support for reinvention fare when it competes with generalized hostility to bureaucracy and the inevitable temptation to use agency performance to bludgeon a "Democrat president" through the oversight process?

The NPR must actively and continually cultivate congressional support, now more than ever. Republican oversight committees must become at least moderately faithful converts to the reinvention religion; otherwise they will scramble to condemn administrative sacrileges in their hearing rooms. The NPR staff has discussed giving individual members of Congress a stake in reinvention by finding ways for them to share public credit for savings and efficiencies in their districts and states, a kind of reverse pork barrel. That clever, and perhaps fanciful, idea will necessitate creativity and sustained energy to work. Ideally, the executive will also negotiate many small and mostly informal bargains, including perhaps de facto committee vetoes, to keep reinvention working smoothly. As Louis Fisher has pointed out, the legislative veto device that the Supreme Court assailed (but failed to stamp out) in *Immigration and Naturalization Service* v. *Chadha* originated in the effort to allow greater freedom to the *executive* while also preserving congressional prerogatives.[67]

The NPR pleads for Congress to minimize restrictions and to allow agencies to consolidate and simplify the mountain of reports submitted. But Congress must see such devices as unnecessary. When congressional committee chairs can informally and effectively convey their desire that certain kinds of information be made available in the future without prompting, or that a particular category of administrative action be cleared with their committees in advance, formal requirements and restrictions recede in importance. Such understandings would have to proliferate, and to be adhered to over time, for micromanagement to decline. But are they sustainable in the new political environment? The return of divided government, which enables the parties to displace blame onto one another more aggressively, may have placed such understandings beyond reach.

In short, the combination of an energetic presidential initiative and creative uses of administrative discretion is insufficient to nourish the NPR politically. As both lawmaker and overseer, Congress is a crucial player. Any administration that hopes to successfully promote pervasive and lasting administrative reform has little choice but to confront the incentives and interests at work in Congress, even when the primary objective is citizen satisfaction, not presidential power.

Notes

Chapter One

1. Todd S. Purdham, "Clinton Turns to Gore's Proposal for Faster, Cheaper Government," *New York Times*, December 19, 1994, pp. A1, B10.

2. Ibid, p. A1.

3. National Performance Review, *From Red Tape to Results: Creating a Government that Works Better and Costs Less* (Government Printing Office, 1993).

4. Stephen Barr, "Bureaucracy Review Opens with a Rally," *Washington Post*, April 16, 1993, p. A23; and Mike Mills, "Clinton and Gore Hit the Road to Build a Better Bureaucracy," *Congressional Quarterly Weekly Report*, September 11, 1993, pp. 2381–89.

5. Mills, "Clinton and Gore Hit the Road," p. 2385.

6. Richard Benedetto, "Key to Gaining Ground Is Sticking to Basics," *USA Today*, September 27, 1993, p. A1.

7. David Osborne and Ted Gaebler, *Reinventing Government: How the Entrepreneurial Spirit Is Transforming the Public Sector* (Reading, Mass.: Addison-Wesley, 1992); David Osborne, "Government That Means Business," *New York Times Sunday Magazine*, March 1, 1992, pp. 20–28; and David Osborne, "Reinventing Government: Creating an Entrepreneurial Federal Establishment," in Will Marshall and Martin Schram, *Mandate for Change* (New York: Berkley Books, 1993).

8. For example, see Republican Senator Charles E. Grassley, "Reinventing Government, The Final Verdict," *Vital Speeches of the Day*, vol. 60 (January 1, 1994), pp. 167–70.

9. William V. Roth, Jr., "Reinventing Government: Maintaining the Momentum," *Public Manager*, vol. 22 (Winter 1993–94), pp. 15–17. At that time, Roth

was the ranking minority member of the Senate Committee on Governmental Affairs.

10. General Accounting Office, *Management Reform: GAO's Comments on the National Performance Review's Recommendations*, OCG-94-1 (December 1993).

11. Alliance for Redesigning Government, "Rego, for Real?" *Public Innovator*, no. 1 (December 1993), p. 4.

12. David S. Broder, "Reinvention Dissenters," *Washington Post*, March 16, 1994, p. A19.

13. B. Guy Peters and Donald J. Savoie, *Reinventing Osborne and Gaebler: Lessons from the Gore Commission* (Ottawa: Canadian Centre for Management Development, November 1993).

14. Laurence E. Lynn, Jr., "Government Lite," *American Prospect*, no. 16 (Winter 1994), p. 144.

15. Herbert N. Jasper and Anita F. Alpern, "National Performance Review: The Good, the Bad, the Indifferent," *Public Manager*, vol. 23 (Spring 1994), p. 27.

16. Louis Fisher and Albert J. Kliman, "The Gore Report on Budgeting," *Public Manager*, vol. 22 (Winter 1993-94), p. 19-22.

17. Stephen Barr, "On Capitol Hill, 'Reinventing Government' Is Off to a Crawling Start," *Washington Post*, November 24, 1993, p. A15.

18. Guy Gugliotta, "Look for the New Titles from Reinvention Press," *Washington Post*, February 1, 1994, p. A19.

19. See Tom Shoop, "Targeting Middle Management," *Government Executive*, vol. 26 (January 1994), p. 11; and Stephen Barr, "Senators Uneasy about 'Buyout' for Bureaucrats," *Washington Post*, October 20, 1993, p. A27.

20. For a small but representative sample of critical commentary on the "reinvention movement" and the NPR, see Ronald C. Moe, "Let's Rediscover Government, Not Reinvent It," *Government Executive*, vol. 25 (June 1993), pp. 46–48, 60; John J. DiIulio, Jr., "Mothers of Reinvention: Why Gore's Red-Tape Reformers Won't Save Money," *Washington Post*, August 22, 1993, p. C1; Charles T. Goodsell, "Did NPR Reinvent Government Reform?" *Public Manager*, vol. 22 (Fall 1993), pp. 7–10; Paul Glastris, "Whose Government Is Gored?" *New Republic*, October 11, 1993, pp. 33–34; David Segal, "What's Wrong with the Gore Report," *Washington Monthly*, November 1993, pp. 18–23; David H. Rosenbloom, "Editorial: Have An Administrative Rx? Don't Forget the Politics!" *Public Administration Review*, vol. 53 (November–December 1993), pp. 503–07; Paul A. Volcker and others, "An Open Letter on the Report of the National Performance Review," National Commission on the Public Service, Washington, February 14, 1994; Ronald C. Moe, "The 'Reinventing Government' Exercise: Misinterpreting the Problem, Misjudging the Consequences," *Public Administration Review*, vol. 54

(March–April 1994), pp. 125–36; and Peri E. Arnold, "Reform's Changing Role: the National Performance Review in Historical Context," paper prepared for the Woodrow Wilson International Center for Scholars, April 12, 1994.

21. Donald F. Kettl, *Reinventing Government? Appraising the National Performance Review*, A Report of the Brookings Institution's Center for Public Management, CPM 94-2 (Brookings, August 1994).

22. Transcript 362 of *Prime Time Live*, ABC News, August 11, 1994, p. 9.

23. National Performance Review, *Human Resource Management: Accompanying Report* (GPO, 1993), p. 1; and James Q. Wilson and John J. DiIulio, Jr., *American Government: Institutions and Policies*, 6th ed. (Lexington, Mass.: D.C. Heath, 1994), p. 393.

Chapter Two

1. The term *National Performance Review* has taken on three different meanings: the six-month survey of federal management, conducted by hundreds of federal managers during the middle of 1993; the report that survey produced, National Performance Review, *From Red Tape to Results: Creating a Government That Works Better and Costs Less* (Government Printing Office, 1993); and the effort that followed to put the report's recommendations into effect. I will follow the convention and use "NPR" to refer to all these pieces of the NPR. The meaning will be clear from the context.

For other surveys of the NPR's progress, see National Performance Review, *Creating a Government That Works Better and Costs Less: Status Report* (GPO, 1994); letter from William M. Hunt, U.S. General Accounting Office, to Senator John Glenn, Senator William V. Roth, Representative John Conyers, Representative William F. Clinger, and Representative John R. Kasich, GGD-94-203R (September 1994); and Tom Shoop, "True Believer," *Government Executive*, vol. 26 (September 1994), pp. 16–23.

2. Before the waivers, OMB required that all government forms, including surveys, be cleared before use. The result frequently was a months-long delay before surveys could be used, which prevented government officials from gaining timely information about citizens' views.

3. NPR, *From Red Tape to Results*, p. 89.

4. The passage of the "buyout" bill in March 1994, which is discussed below.

5. According to the NPR's electronic network, "A Reinvention Lab is a place that cuts through 'red tape,' exceeds customer expectations, and unleashes innovations for improvement from its employees. Depending on the priorities of an agency, a lab may focus upon programs, processes, administrative structures, or a combination of all three. A lab provides a focus for reinvention efforts, diminishes

the fear of failure that accompanies risk, and provides opportunities to highlight the successes of reinvention and to recognize the people responsible for those successes."

6. National Performance Review, *Reinvention Roundtable*, no. 2 (May 6, 1994), p. 1.

7. Interview with Public Health Service officials, May 18, 1994.

8. See, for example, Eliza Newlin Carney, "Still Trying to Reinvent Government," *National Journal*, June 18, 1994, pp. 1442-44.

9. R. Kent Weaver explores these traps in "Reinventing Government or Rearranging the Deck Chairs? The Politics of Institutional Reform in the United States," paper prepared for the Fulbright Symposium on Public Sector Reform, Brisbane, Australia, June 23-24, 1994.

10. David Osborne and Ted Gaebler, *Reinventing Government: How The Entrepreneurial Spirit Is Transforming the Public Sector* (Reading, Mass.: Addison-Wesley, 1992), p. 25.

11. For a broader view of the history of administrative reform, see chapter 3 by Gerald Garvey.

12. This, in fact, was the basis of the argument that management reform depends far more on evolution than invention. See John J. DiIulio, Jr., Gerald Garvey, and Donald F. Kettl, *Improving Government Performance: An Owner's Manual* (Brookings, 1993), pp. 1-3.

13. The count comes from the General Accounting Office, *Management Reform: GAO's Comments on the National Performance Review's Recommendations*, OCG-94-1 (December 1993), p. 1.

14. National Performance Review, "Reinventing Government: Six Month Status Report," March 3, 1994.

15. NPR, *From Red Tape to Results*, pp. iii-iv.

16. NPR, *Creating a Government That Works Better and Costs Less: Status Report*, p. 121.

17. The work force reduction calculations were complex. When he first took office, Bill Clinton promised to reduce federal civilian employment by 100,000 workers. The NPR increased the number by 152,000, for a total of 252,000, and used the number of employees at the beginning of fiscal year 1993 as the baseline. When Congress acted in March 1994 on the bill to make the reductions possible, it used the actual fiscal year 1993 employment level, which produced a baseline 20,900 higher than the NPR figure. That resulted in a downsizing target of 272,900 employees.

18. Quoted in Tom Shoop, "Targeting Middle Managers," *Government Executive*, vol. 26 (January 1994), pp. 11-12.

19. Ibid., p. 13.

20. For an analysis of the buyout, see Tom Shoop, "Exodus," *Government Executive*, vol. 26 (June 1994), pp. 43–47.

21. General Accounting Office, *Federal Employment: The Results to Date of the Fiscal Year 1994 Buyouts at Non-Defense Agencies*, T-GGD-94-214 (September 1994), pp. 4–5.

22. Paul C. Light, *Thickening Government: Federal Hierarchy and the Diffusion of Accountability* (Brookings and Governance Institute, 1995).

23. For an analysis of the economics of federal downsizing, see Congressional Budget Office, *Reducing the Size of the Federal Civilian Work Force* (December 1993).

24. Letter from CBO Director Robert D. Reischauer to Representative John Joseph Moakley, November 19, 1993; and Steven Greenhouse, "Savings Vastly Overestimated in Streamlining Plan, Agency Reports," *New York Times*, November 17, 1993, p. A22.

25. Administration officials estimated that regular turnover alone would not be enough to hit the target. They calculated, therefore, that they would have to offer inducements for federal employees to take early retirement and devised a $25,000 one-time payment for employees who resigned or retired early. Stephen Barr, "US Budget May Force Layoffs," *Washington Post*, January 30, 1994, p. A1.

26. Interview with the author.

27. Interview with the author.

28. See chapter 4 by Beryl Radin for descriptions of how different departments and agencies managed the task.

29. Charles H. Levine and Rosslyn S. Kleeman, "The Quiet Crisis of the Civil Service: The Federal Personnel System at the Crossroads," in Patricia W. Ingraham and Donald F. Kettl, eds., *Agenda for Excellence: Public Service in America* (Chatham, N.J.: Chatham House, 1992), p. 208.

30. National Commission on the Public Service, *Leadership for America: Rebuilding the Public Service* (Washington, 1989), p. 4. See also Mark L. Goldstein, *America's Hollow Government: How Washington Has Failed the People* (Homewood, Ill.: Business One Irwin, 1992).

31. NPR, *From Red Tape to Results*, pp. 87–88.

32. For a more detailed discussion of government employee unions under the NPR, see chapter 5 by Carolyn Ban.

33. *National Partnership Council: A New Vision for Labor-Management Relations* (GPO, 1994), p. i.

34. Stephen Barr, "OPM Turns Over 10,000 New Leaves," *Washington Post*, January 28, 1994, p. A21.

35. Stephen Barr, "Adieu, SF-171," *Washington Post*, May 9, 1994, p. A15.

36. For a description, see Tom Shoop, "Swing Your Partner," *Government Executive*, vol. 26 (March 1994), p. 34.

37. See National Performance Review, *Reinventing Human Resource Management* (GPO, 1993), p. 93. Recommendation HRM05.1 said: "Reduce by half the time required to terminate federal managers and employees for cause. Make other improvements in the systems for dealing with poor performers."

38. The OPM runs the Federal Executive Institute in Charlottesville, Virginia, as a training center for senior career civil servants about to enter the Senior Executive Service (SES). The Senior Executives Association represents members of the SES.

39. Quoted in Shoop, "Swing Your Partner," p. 33.

40. Allan J. Kam and G. Jerry Shaw, "Managers and Top Professionals Band Together," *Public Manager*, vol. 22 (Winter 1993–94), p. 8. The article also contains a history of the development of the Coalition for Effective Change (pp. 9–10).

41. Coalition for Effective Change, "Comments on NPC Report," March 1, 1994, pp. 3–4.

42. Office of Personnel Management, *Union Recognition in the Federal Government* (December 1992), pt. 1, p. 2.

43. Ibid., pp. 1–2.

44. Stephen Barr, "Unions, Clinton at Odds on Civil Service Reform," *Washington Post*, December 15, 1994, p. A25.

45. "Gored!!!" *FedNews* (National Association of Government Employees), January 1994, p. 1; and "From Rowing to Steering to Abandoning Ship," *Government Training News*, vol. 17 (November 1993), p. 1.

46. "Execs Eye Reinvention Warily," *Government Executive*, vol. 26 (July 1994), p. 6.

47. Interview with the author, June 3, 1994.

48. Quoted in Shoop, "Targeting Middle Managers," p. 13.

49. "Gore on the Future of the Federal Executive," *Government Executive*, vol. 26 (May 1994), pp. 52, 54.

50. Interviews with the author. See also James E. Colvard, "In Defense of Middle Management," *Government Executive*, vol. 26 (May 1994), pp. 57–58.

51. Levine and Kleeman, "The Quiet Crisis in the American Public Service," pp. 261–63.

52. An important step in this direction is the accompanying report to the NPR, *Reinventing Human Resources Management*.

53. Al Gore, "The New Job of the Federal Executive," *Public Administration Review*, vol. 54 (July–August 1994), pp. 317–31.

54. "Gore on the Future of the Federal Executive." The NPR explored some of these issues in greater depth. See National Performance Review, *Creating Quality Leadership and Management* (GPO, 1993). For a much more extensive and extremely

thoughtful analysis of the problem, see National Academy of Public Administration, *Leading People in Change: Empowerment, Commitment, Accountability* (Washington, June 1993).

55. Denis Ives, "After Managerialism: The Emerging APS [Australian Public Service]," paper prepared for delivery at the Fulbright Symposium on Public Sector Reform, Brisbane, Australia, June 24, 1994, p. 9.

56. For example, the Federal Quality Institute has assembled a "basic training" guide for those who conduct such exercises throughout the federal work force. See *Creating A Customer-Driven Government* (Washington: Federal Quality Institute, 1994).

57. Public Service Commission, *A Framework for Human Resource Management in the Australian Public Service* (Canberra: Public Service Commission, 1992), p. 73.

58. Derived from Office of Personnel Management, *Human Resource Development in the Federal Service: Fiscal Year 1991* (1993), p. 2.

59. Interviews with the author.

60. For one very useful view, see Paul Light, "Do We Still Need an OPM?" *Government Executive*, vol. 26 (March 1994), p. 51.

61. National Performance Review, *Office of Personnel Management* (GPO, 1993), p. 1.

62. Osborne and Gaebler, *Reinventing Government*; Thomas J. Peters and Robert H. Waterman, Jr., *In Search of Excellence: Lessons from America's Best-Run Companies* (Harper and Row, 1982); and Peter F. Drucker, *Innovation and Entrepreneurship: Practice and Principles* (Harper and Row, 1985).

63. See the transcript of the discussions that Vice President Gore held with business leaders, government officials, and academics in Philadelphia. National Performance Review, "Reinventing Government Summit," Philadelphia, June 25, 1993.

64. For better or worse, a reasonably well-articulated philosophy of managerialism and consumerism, for example, has driven reforms in Great Britain, Australia, and New Zealand. Among many sources, see Christopher Hood and Michael Jackson, *Administrative Argument* (Aldershot, England: Dartmouth, 1991); Christopher Pollitt, *Managerialism and the Public Services: The Anglo-American Experience* (Oxford, England: Basil Blackwell, 1990); Jenny Potter, "Consumerism and the Public Sector: How Well Does the Coat Fit?" *Public Administration*, vol. 66 (Summer 1988), pp. 149–64; Robin Hambleton, "Consumerism, Decentralization and Local Democracy," *Public Administration*, vol. 66 (Summer 1988), pp. 125–47; John Stewart and Kieron Walsh, "Change in the Management of Public Services," *Public Administration*, vol. 70 (Winter 1992), pp. 499–518; Task Force on Management Improvement, *The Australian Public Service Reformed: An Evaluation of A*

Decade of Management Reform (Canberra: Australian Government Publishing Service, 1992); State Services Commission, *New Zealand's Reformed State Sector* (Wellington: State Services Commission, 1994). For a survey of management reform in industrialized nations, see Organization for Economic Cooperation and Development, *Public Management Developments: Survey 1993* (Paris: OECD, 1993).

65. For just two examples, see first the exchange between H. George Frederickson, "Painting Bull's Eyes around Bullet Holes," *Governing*, vol. 6 (October 1992), p. 13; and David Osborne, "The Power of Outdated Ideas," *Governing*, vol. 6 (December 1992), p. 61. Then see the exchange between Ronald C. Moe, "Let's Rediscover Government, Not Reinvent It," *Government Executive*, vol. 25 (June 1993), pp. 46–48, 60; and David Osborne, "Reinvention Revisited," *Government Executive*, vol. 25 (July 1993), p. 56. See also David H. Rosenbloom, "Have an Administrative Rx? Don't Forget the Politics!" *Public Administration Review*, vol. 53 (November–December 1993), pp. 503–07.

66. *The Federalist*, no. 70 (New York: Modern Library, 1937), p. 455.

67. For an excellent history, see Francis E. Rourke, "Whose Bureaucracy Is This, Anyway? Congress, the President and Public Administration," *PS: Political Science and Politics*, vol. 26 (December 1993), pp. 687–92. See also Laurence E. Lynn, Jr., "Government Lite," *American Prospect*, no. 16 (Winter 1994), p. 138.

68. Harold Seidman and Robert Gilmour, *Politics, Position, and Power: From the Positive to the Regulatory State*, 4th ed. (New York: Oxford University Press, 1986).

69. See Ronald C. Moe, "The 'Reinventing Government' Exercise: Misinterpreting the Problem, Misjudging the Consequences," *Public Administration Review*, vol. 54 (March–April 1994), pp. 111–22.

70. The importance of these theories is explained in DiIulio, Garvey, and Kettl, *Improving Government Performance*, pp. 24–28.

71. See, for example, R. H. Coase, "The Nature of the Firm," *Economica*, n.s., vol. 4 (November 1937), pp. 386–405; Armen A. Alchian and Harold Demsetz, "Production, Information Costs, and Economic Organization," *American Economic Review*, vol. 62 (December 1972), pp. 777–95; Michael Jensen and William Meckling, "Theory of the Firm: Managerial Behavior, Agency Costs, and Ownership Structure," *Journal of Financial Economics*, vol. 3 (October 1976), pp. 305–60; and Terry M. Moe, "The New Economics of Organization," *American Journal of Political Science*, vol. 28 (November 1984), pp. 739–75. Excellent analyses of the theory are Charles Perrow, *Complex Organizations: A Critical Essay*, 3d ed. (Random House, 1986), chap. 7; Gary J. Miller, *Managerial Dilemmas: The Political Economy of Hierarchy* (Cambridge: Cambridge University Press, 1992); and Gerald Garvey, *Facing the Bureaucracy: Living and Dying in a Public Agency* (San Francisco: Jossey-Bass, 1993).

72. The leading student of transaction costs is Oliver E. Williamson. See *The Economic Institutions of Capitalism* (Free Press, 1985).

73. Jonathan Boston, "Origins and Destinations: New Zealand's Model of Public Management and the International Transfer of Ideas," paper prepared for the Fulbright Symposium on Public Sector Reform, Brisbane, Australia, June 23–24, 1994; and Jonathan Boston and others, eds., *Reshaping the State: New Zealand's Bureaucratic Revolution* (Oxford: Oxford University Press, 1991).

74. Interview with the author.

75. The OMB, furthermore, has mandated greater attention to customer service in its 1994 revision of Circular A-11, the federal government's basic budget preparation guidance.

76. The original version of this section was prepared for delivery at the Fulbright Symposium on Public Sector Reform, "New Ideas, Better Government," Brisbane, Australia, June 23–23, 1994. I am grateful to the Fulbright Symposium for its generous support and to the symposium organizers, Glyn Davis and Patrick Weller, for their comments and permission to reuse the revised material here.

77. Roy Bahl, *Financing State and Local Government in the 1980s* (New York: Oxford University Press, 1984), pp. 184–85.

78. Irene S. Rubin, *The Politics of Public Budgeting: Getting and Spending, Borrowing and Balancing* (Chatham, N.J.: Chatham House, 1993), pp. 51–52.; and J. Richard Aronson and John L. Hilley, *Financing State and Local Governments*, 4th ed. (Brookings, 1986), pp. 223–24.

79. Bahl, *Financing State and Local Government in the 1980s*, p. 185.

80. E. S. Savas, *Privatizing the Public Sector: How to Shrink Government* (Chatham, N.J.: Chatham House, 1982), pp. 160– 17.

81. Grace Commission (President's Private Sector Survey on Cost Control), *A Report to the President* (GPO, 1984), p. II-1.

82. Charles Goodsell, "The Grace Commission: Seeking Efficiency for the Whole People?" *Public Administration Review*, vol. 44 (May–June 1984), pp. 196–204.

83. Jack W. Germond and Jules Witcover, "A Political Elixir for the President?" *National Journal*, September 11, 1993, p. 2211.

84. Donald F. Kettl, *Sharing Power: Public Governance and Private Markets* (Brookings, 1993).

85. Michael Hammer and James Champy, *Reengineering the Corporation* (New York: HarperBusiness, 1993).

86. Jerry Mechling, "Reengineering: Part of Your Game Plan? A Guide for Public Managers," *Governing*, vol. 7 (February 1994), pp. 41–52.

87. Hammer and Champy, *Reengineering the Corporation*, pp. 2–3.

88. Ibid., pp. 47–49.

89. Mechling, "Reengineering," p. 44.

90. General Accounting Office, *Management Reforms: Examples of Public and Private Innovations to Improve Service Delivery*, AIMD/GGD-94-90BR (February 1994), pp. 37–38.

91. Frederick Winslow Taylor, *Principles of Scientific Management* (Harper and Brothers, 1911).

92. Henri Fayol, *General and Industrial Management* (London: Pitman, 1949); and Luther Gulick, "Notes on the Theory of Organization," in Luther Gulick and Lyndahl Urwick, eds., *Papers on the Science of Administration* (New York: Institute of Public Administration, 1937), p. 25.

93. James Q. Wilson, *Bureaucracy* (Basic Books, 1989), p. 163.

94. Hammer and Champy, *Reengineering the Corporation*, p. 6.

95. NPR, *From Red Tape to Results*, p. 94.

96. Mechling, "Reengineering," p. 50.

97. W. Edwards Deming , *Out of the Crisis* (Cambridge: Institute of Technology Center for Advanced Engineering Study, 1982).

98. Rafael Aguayo, *Dr. Deming: The American Who Taught the Japanese about Quality* (New York: Lyle Stewart, 1990), p. 19.

99. Bill Creech, *The Five Pillars of TQM: How To Make Total Quality Management Work for You* (Dutton, 1994), pp. 27, 54; and Steven Cohen and Ronald Brand, *Total Quality Management in Government: A Practical Guide for the Real World* (San Francisco: Jossey-Bass, 1993).

100. Creech, *Five Pillars of TQM*, esp. pp. 6–7.

101. Cohen and Brand, *Total Quality Management in Government*, pp. 175–97.

102. Peter M. Senge, *The Fifth Discipline: The Art and Practice of the Learning Organization* (Doubleday, 1990); and Donald F. Kettl, "Managing on the Frontiers of Knowledge: The Learning Organization," in Patricia W. Ingraham and Barbara Romzek, eds., *New Paradigms for Government* (San Francisco: Jossey-Bass, 1994), pp. 19–40.

103. Henry C. Metcalf and Lyndahl Urwick, *Dynamic Administration: The Collected Papers of Mary Parker Follett* (Harper, 1941); and Abraham H. Maslow, "A Theory of Human Motivation," *Psychological Review*, vol. 50 (July 1943), pp. 370–96.

104. See Graham T. Allison, "Public and Private Management: Are They Fundamentally Alike in All Unimportant Respects?" in Richard J. Stillman II, ed., *Public Administration* (Houghton Mifflin, 1992), pp. 282–98. Allison, in turn, built on Paul H. Appleby, *Big Democracy* (Knopf, 1945).

105. Frederickson, "Painting Bull's Eyes around Bullet Holes," p. 13.

106. Ronald C. Moe and others, "Analysis of the Budget and Management

Proposals in the Report of the National Performance Review" (Washington: Congressional Research Service, September 21, 1993), p. 4.

107. Moe, "Let's Rediscover Government," p. 47.

108. Moe, "The 'Reinventing Government' Exercise," p. 117.

109. See DiIulio, Garvey, and Kettl, *Improving Government Performance*. We have also recommended reduction in middle management, but as part of a broader strategy for rethinking supervision and information in the federal government. For another view, see Shoop, "Targeting Middle Managers."

110. Frederickson, "Painting Bull's Eyes around Bullet Holes," p. 13; and Moe, "The 'Reinventing Government' Exercise," p. 117.

111. Frederickson, "Painting Bull's Eyes around Bullet Holes," p. 13; and Moe, "The 'Reinventing Government' Exercise," pp. 117–18.

112. Lynn, "Government Lite," pp. 141, 143.

113. Osborne and Gaebler, *Reinventing Government*, pp. 76–80.

114. See William A. Niskanen, Jr., *Bureaucracy and Representative Government* (Chicago: Aldine-Atherton, 1971); Allan H. Meltzer and Scott F. Richard, "Why Government Grows (And Grows) in a Democracy," *The Public Interest*, no. 52 (Summer 1978), pp. 111–18; and E. S. Savas, *Privatization: The Key to Better Government* (Chatham, N.J.: Chatham House, 1987).

115. Kettl, *Sharing Power*.

116. The General Accounting Office struggled, with only modest success, to define what an "inherently governmental function" is. See *Government Contractors: Are Service Contractors Performing Inherently Governmental Functions?* GGD-92-11 (November 1991), esp. pp. 4–5.

117. See Osborne and Gaebler, *Reinventing Government*, esp. chaps. 3, 7; and NPR, *From Red Tape to Results*, pp. 62–64.

118. Leonard D. White, *Introduction to the Study of Public Administration*, 3d ed. (Macmillan, 1948), p. 8 (emphasis in original).

119. See Marver H. Bernstein, *The Job of the Federal Executive* (Brookings, 1958).

120. See Frederick C. Mosher, *Democracy and the Public Service*, 2d ed. (New York: Oxford University Press, 1982).

121. On the last point, see Charles O. Jones, *The Presidency in a Separated System* (Brookings, 1994).

122. Interview with the author, July 7, 1994.

123. NPR, *From Red Tape to Results*, p. 44, (emphasis in original).

124. National Performance Review, *Improving Customer Service* (GPO, 1993).

125. Ibid., p. 5. For a discussion, see Tom Shoop, "From Citizens to Customers," *Government Executive*, vol. 26 (May 1994), pp. 27–30.

126. General Accounting Office, *Veterans Benefits: Status of Claims Processing Initiative in VA's New York Regional Office*, HEHS-94-183BR (June 1994).

127. Frederickson, "Painting Bull's Eyes around Bullet Holes."

128. For an expansion of the argument that follows, see DiIulio, Garvey, and Kettl, *Improving Government Performance*, pp. 48–54.

129. The Clinton administration decided to reintroduce the wolves against the strenuous objections of the ranchers. See Dirk Johnson, "Yellowstone Will Shelter Wolves Again," *New York Times*, June 17, 1994, p. A12.

130. Donald F. Kettl, *Government by Proxy: (Mis?)Managing Federal Programs* (Washington: Congressional Quarterly Press, 1988).

131. For a sweeping examination of these problems, see American Society for Public Administration, *Improving Management and Performance in the Federal-State-Local System*, Recommendations of the Symposium on Public Administration (September 1993).

132. *The Oregon Option: A Proposed Model for Results-Driven Intergovernmental Service Delivery*, July 25, 1994, p. 1.

133. Oregon Progress Board, *Oregon Benchmarks: Standards for Measuring Statewide Progress and Government Performance* (Salem: Oregon Progress Board, December 1992). See also Neal R. Peirce, "Marking Progress Oregon-Style," *Oregonian*, April 11, 1994, p. B7.

134. *The Oregon Option*, p. 18.

135. David S. Broder, "Federalism in a State of Ferment," *Washington Post*, December 11, 1994, p. C7.

136. George Frederickson, "George and the Case of the Government Reinventors," *PA Times*, vol. 17 (January 1, 1994), p. 9.

137. See Jonathan Rauch, *Demosclerosis: The Silent Killer of American Government* (New York: Times Books, 1994).

138. See Hambleton, "Consumerism, Decentralization and Local Democracy"; Potter, "Consumerism and the Public Sector"; Mary Seneviratne and Sarah Cracknell, "Consumer Complaints in Public Sector Services," *Public Administration*, vol. 66 (Summer 1988), pp. 181–93; Stewart and Walsh, "Change in the Management of Public Services"; and Peter Aucoin, "Administrative Reform in Public Management: Paradigms, Principles, Paradoxes and Pendulums," *Governance*, vol. 3 (April 1990), pp. 115–37.

139. A public good is one for which an individual's consumption does not diminish another individual's ability to consume.

140. Potter, "Consumerism and the Public Sector," p. 159.

141. Panetta later became President Clinton's chief of staff, and Rivlin replaced Panetta as OMB director.

142. Statutory management responsibilities would continue to remain under

the supervision of separate offices: the Office of Federal Management, the Office of Federal Procurement Policy, and the Office of Information and Regulatory Affairs.

143. Office of Management and Budget Office Memorandum No. 94-16 (March 1, 1994), p. 8.

144. Ibid, p. 12.

145. See Alan Dean, Dwight Ink, and Harold Seidman, "OMB's 'M': Fading Away," *Government Executive*, vol. 26 (June 1994), pp. 62–64.

146. OMB Director Leon Panetta, who issued the order launching the OMB 2000 reorganization, ironically had introduced a bill while chairman of the House Budget Committee to create a separate office of federal management.

147. P.L. 103-62, sec. 2(b)(1).

148. Office of Management and Budget, "Evaluation Framework for Assessing Implementation of GPRA," February 1, 1994; and interview with author, August 3, 1994.

149. See the 1994 revision of Circular A-11.

150. For a review of the issues, see several General Accounting Office reports: *Performance Measurement: An Important Tool in Managing for Results*, GGD-92-35 (May 1992); *Program Performance Measures: Federal Agency Collection and Use of Performance Data*, GGD-92-65 (May 1992); and *Performance Budgeting: State Experiences and Implications for the Federal Government*, AFMD-93-41 (February 1993). See also Joseph S. Wholey, *Evaluation and Effective Public Management* (Little, Brown, 1983); James E. Swiss, *Public Management Systems: Monitoring and Managing Government Performance* (Prentice-Hall, 1991); Congressional Budget Office, *Using Performance Measures in the Federal Budget Process* (July 1993); and John J. DiIulio, Jr. and others, *Performance Measures for the Criminal Justice System* (GPO, 1993).

151. See CBO, *Using Performance Measures in the Federal Budget Process*, and GAO, *Performance Budgeting*. For a discussion of both methods and background issues, see Swiss, *Public Management Systems*.

152. CBO, *Using Performance Measures in the Federal Budget Process*, p. xiii.

153. A useful approach to understanding these distinctions is Robert N. Anthony and David W. Young, *Management Control in Nonprofit Organizations*, 5th ed. (Burr Ridge, Ill.: Irwin, 1994).

154. Matthew D. McCubbins and Thomas Schwartz, "Congressional Oversight Overlooked: Police Patrols Versus Fire Alarms," *American Journal of Political Science*, vol. 28 (Fall 1984), pp. 169, 172.

155. NPR, *From Red Tape to Results*, esp. pp. 110–19.

156. For a careful analysis of the NPR's congressional strategy, see chapter 6 by Christopher Foreman.

157. Christina Del Valle, "The Job-Training Squabbles: Is This Any Way to Reinvent Government?" *Business Week*, August 1, 1994, p. 37.

158. See Carney, "Still Trying to Reinvent Government," p. 1444, for an analysis of the critical role of congressional support in following through on the NPR.

159. Ann Devroy and Stephen Barr, "Clinton Offers Cuts in Five Agencies," *Washington Post*, December 20, 1994, p. A1.

160. See Executive Office of the President, *Budget of the United States Government: Analytical Perspectives, Fiscal Year 1994* (GPO, 1994), pp. 275–98. See also two General Accounting Office reports, *Improving Government Performance: Actions Needed to Sustain and Enhance Management Reforms*, T-OCG-94-1 (January 1994), and *OMB's High-Risk Program: Comments on the Status Reported in the President's Fiscal Year 1995 Budget*, AIMD-94-136 (September 1994).

161. GAO, *Improving Government Performance*, pp. 26–27.

162. See Kettl, *Sharing Power*, chap. 6, for an analysis.

163. Vice President Gore did, however, emphasize the importance of learning in a speech, "Overcoming Cynicism about Change in the Federal Government," remarks prepared for the Seventh Annual National Conference on Federal Quality, Washington, July 13, 1994.

164. Paul Holley, "Pilot Program At Local VA Is 'Reinventing' Government," *Milwaukee Business Journal*, April 23, 1994, p. 2.

165. Interview with the author.

166. Interview with the author.

167. On "low" versus "high" politics, see Charles T. Goodsell, "Did NPR Reinvent Government Reform?" *Public Manager*, vol. 22 (Fall 1993), pp. 7–10.

168. Garry Wills, "Can Clinton Close the Vision Gap?" *New York Times*, November 8, 1992, sec. 4, p. 17.

169. Gore's speech, "Overcoming Cynicism about Change in the Federal Government," identified cynicism as a major challenge to government reform.

170. Quoted by Frederick Rose, "Job-Cutting Medicine Fails to Remedy Productivity Ills at Many Companies," *Wall Street Journal*, June 7, 1994, p. A2.

171. Peter Scott-Morgan, *The Unwritten Rules of the Game* (McGraw Hill, 1994).

172. Rose, "Job-cutting Medicine Fails to Remedy Productivity Ills," pp. A2, A16.

173. *Best Practices in Corporate Restructuring: Wyatt's 1993 Survey of Corporate Restructuring* (Washington: The Wyatt Company, 1993), pp. 9, 11, 43.

174. See Shoop, "From Citizens to Customers."

175. Interview with the author.

176. Light, *Thickening Government*.

177. Interview with the author.

178. Interview with the author.

179. NPR, *From Red Tape to Results*, p. ii (emphasis in original).

180. A very useful comparison of how ideas and practice collide is James Q. Wilson, "Mr. Clinton, Meet Mr. Gore," *Wall Street Journal*, October 28, 1993, p. A22. See also James Q. Wilson, "Reinventing Public Administration," *PS: Political Science and Politics*, vol. 27 (December 1994), pp. 667–73.

Chapter Three

1. See, for example, Theda Skocpol and Kenneth Finegold, "State Capacity and Economic Intervention in the Early New Deal," *Political Science Quarterly*, vol. 97 (Summer 1982), pp. 255–78.

2. Message of December 8, 1829, quoted in J. M. Shafritz and others, *Personnel Management in Government* (New York: Marcel Dekker, 1992), p. 8.

3. Herbert Kaufman, "Emerging Conflicts in the Doctrines of Public Administration," *American Political Science Review*, vol. 50 (December 1956), p. 1057.

4. In a curious way, however, this Jacksonian theory of "control through representation" did anticipate the later belief—identified especially with Woodrow Wilson, so unlike the Jacksonians in most other respects—that a cadre of civil servants representative of "public opinion" could be trusted never to become a distanced, autocratic officialdom. See Woodrow Wilson, "The Study of Administration," in Arthur S. Link, ed., *The Papers of Woodrow Wilson*, vol. 5 (Princeton University Press, 1968), pp. 359–80.

5. For a description of Weberian theory, see Max Weber, "Technical Advantages of Bureaucratic Organization," in H. H. Gerth and C. Wright Mills, eds., *From Max Weber* (New York: Oxford University Press, 1946), pp. 215–16.

6. See Samuel Haber, *Efficiency and Uplift* (University of Chicago Press, 1964), chap. 3.

7. An incidental point may be worth considering. In the thought of Frederick Winslow Taylor there converged two themes in American administrative theory— what might be called the "good man" approach (anticipatory of the human relations and organizational culture theorists) and the approach that emphasizes the way the human materials of an institution are structured. The former approach resonates with the thinking of modern human relations management scholars; the latter became a major theme in classical public administration theory.

Taylor recognized that significant physical efficiencies could be achieved if workers could be taught to maximize the amounts of physical mass that they moved in their jobs. Good workers in Taylor's sense, however, would always be sortable into grades, varying from the excellent to the exceedingly dull and plodding. Workers had to be graduated in organizations according to these grades, and their labors coordinated with one another. The emphasis that Taylor laid on the organizational approach as the essential complement of the development of "good men" was well expressed in his canny use of the baseball analogy. Every member of a baseball team, Taylor argued, must use the best technique for his position; yet proper individual behavior accomplishes nothing on a baseball team unless the organization as a whole is a sound one. From positions—abstractly, impersonally defined, in the manner of Weber's ideal bureaucratic type–one can build structures. And, as Dennis Dresang has emphasized, the focus of the scientific managers on classification specifications and position descriptions remains with us to this day: "Positions, not people, continue to be the fundamental building blocks of personnel management in the public sector." See Dresang, "Whither Civil Service? Wither Civil Service?" paper prepared for the La Follette Institute Program on Public Management, September 30–October 1, 1993, Madison, Wisconsin, p. 5.

8. R. H. Coase, "The Nature of the Firm," *Economica*, n.s., vol. 4 (1937), pp. 386–405.

9. Some would contend that legalism as a technique of administrative control traces back to the selection of Thomas Cooley as the first chairman of this country's first great federal regulatory agency, the Interstate Commerce Commission. Cooley fleshed out the ICC's statutory mandate, setting procedural precedents that inclined the American administrative process toward its reliance on the judicial model (adversarial proceedings, rules of evidence). Arguably judges have, in the years since Cooley set the basic pattern, reduced bureaucratic discretion, often by prescribing and confining the procedures that federal bureaucrats must use in their everyday decisionmaking. But a further effect has been to encrust administration in judge-made rules that control agency agendas and tell bureaucrats how to apply the statutory rules that their chartering legislation requires them to implement.

10. National Performance Review, *From Red Tape to Results: Creating a Government that Works Better and Costs Less: A Report of the National Performance Review* (Government Printing Office, 1993), p. iv.

11. Erwin C. Hargrove and Michael Nelson, *Presidents, Politics, and Policy* (Johns Hopkins University Press, 1984), p. 264.

12. Ira C. Magaziner and Robert B. Reich, *Minding America's Business* (Harcourt Brace Jovanovich, 1982).

13. See Ronald C. Moe, "Traditional Organizational Principles and the Managerial Presidency: From Phoenix to Ashes," *Public Administration Review*, vol. 50 (March–April 1990), pp. 129–40.

14. Ronald C. Moe, *Reorganizing the Executive Branch in the Twentieth Century: Landmark Commissions*, CRS Report 92-293 GOV (Congressional Research Service, March 19, 1992).

15. The dates refer to the completions of each commission's work. Obviously,

the activities of each of these commissions lasted longer than a single year. On the Keep commission, see Oscar Kraines, "The President versus Congress: The Keep Commission, 1905-1909, First Comprehensive Presidential Inquiry into Administration," *Western Political Quarterly*, vol. 23 (March 1970), pp. 5–54. Ronald Moe has identified the Commission on Department Methods, nicknamed for its chairman, Charles H. Keep, as the "first overall effort to review the workings of the executive agencies *from a presidential perspective*" (emphasis added). The preoccupying concerns of the Keep commission members were those of proponents of efficient administration as a field of activity distinct from the framing of policy. It is curious that this feature came to characterize almost all of the subsequent reorganizational study groups of the twentieth century, notwithstanding that a general debunking of the Progressive belief in separating policy and administration gradually emerged as a major theme in administrative thought. According to Moe, "The findings of the Commission stimulated management improvements in many bureaus and in such fields as accounting and costing, archives and records management, simplification of paperwork, and improvements in personnel, administration, procurement, supply, and contracting procedures." Ronald C. Moe, *The Hoover Commissions Revisited* (Boulder, Colo.: Westview Press, 1982), p. 9.

16. *Message of the President of the United States on Economy and Efficiency in the Government Service*, Doc. 458, U. S. House of Representatives, 62 Cong. 2 sess. (GPO, 1912). Out of this important study group, headed by Frederick A. Cleveland, director of the prestigious Bureau of Municipal Research in New York, came two important themes: "explicit attention to the management function within the federal government" (the words are Beryl Radin's) and the call for adoption of an executive budget (though *national budget* is the term actually used in the committee report). However, much of the original theory of executive budgeting was subordinate to an intended emphasis on management. That was true among members of the Taft commission, was manifestly and explicitly true among President Roosevelt's Brownlow committee, and underlay the later Ash council's recommendation that the management function of the Bureau of the Budget not only be upgraded but underscored by renaming the president's budget agency the Office of Management and Budget. See Beryl A. Radin, "The Search for the M: Federal Management and Personnel Policy," in Patricia W. Ingraham and David H. Rosenbloom, eds., *The Promise and Paradox of Civil Service Reform* (University of Pittsburgh Press, 1992), pp. 42–43.

17. President's Committee on Administrative Management, *Report* (GPO, 1937).

18. Commission on Organization of the Executive Branch of the Government, *General Management of the Executive Branch* (GPO, 1949).

19. Luther Gulick and Lyndahl Urwick, eds., *Papers on the Science of Administration* (New York: Institute of Public Administration, 1937), pp. 129–31.

20. *Message of the President of the United States on Economy and Efficiency in Government Service*, p. 16. Aaron Wildavsky has underscored the scorn that the original Progressives and their intellectual heirs shared for line-item budgeting. Yet because line-item budgeting is arguably the technique best calculated to achieve legislative control and facilitate the reviewability of administrative actions by the courts, it is also consistent with the rule of law tradition and an emphasis on public law. In other words, the emphasis on performance and program budgeting may have displayed a theme that was difficult to reconcile with other aspects of the classical tradition. See Aaron Wildavsky, *The New Politics of the Budgetary Process* (Harper-Collins, 1992), pp. 56–67.

21. Wallace S. Sayre, "Premises of Public Administration: Past and Emerging," *Public Administration Review*, vol. 18 (Spring 1958), p. 103.

22. This larger body includes the volume by Gulick (a member of Brownlow's three-man study group) and Urwick, with contributions from such other notables of the profession as Henri Fayol, Mary Parker Follett, and James Mooney.

23. President's Committee on Administrative Management, *Report*, p. 5.

24. Lyndahl Urwick, "Organization as a Technical Problem," in Gulick and Urwick, eds., *Papers on the Science of Administration*, p. 49.

25. See Peri Arnold, "Reform's Changing Role: The National Performance Review in Historical Context," paper prepared for the Woodrow Wilson International Center for Scholars, April 12, 1994.

26. Donald F. Kettl, "The Perils—and Prospects—of Public Administration," *Public Administration Review*, vol. 50 (July–August 1990), p. 411.

27. Curtis Ventriss, "Contemporary Issues in American Public Administration Education: The Search for an Educational Focus," *Public Administration Review*, vol. 51 (January–February 1991), pp. 4–14.

28. Arthur M. Schlesinger, Jr., *A Thousand Days* (Houghton-Mifflin, 1965), pp. 679–80.

29. In several federal executive departments, the cabinet-level secretary is commonly thought of as a presidential adviser and framer of policy, while the deputy secretary "runs the department." This pattern has, for example, been the familiar one in State, Defense, and to some extent, Treasury. Although this statement of the pattern is only impressionistic and supportable at best with anecdotal evidence, it is consistent with the theme identified with Stephen Hess's work on executive organization.

30. Stephen Hess, *Organizing the Presidency* (Brookings, 1976).

31. Peri E. Arnold, *Making the Managerial Presidency* (Princeton University

Press, 1986), especially pp. 359–64; and David Broder, "Reinvention Dissenters," *Washington Post*, March 16, 1994, p. A19.

32. See Richard E. Neustadt, *Presidential Power* (Wiley, 1980), chap. 3; and Richard E. Neustadt and Ernest R. May, *Thinking in Time* (Free Press, 1986), chap. 3 and p. 219.

33. U.S. Commission on Organization of the Executive Branch of the Government, *Final Report to the Congress* (GPO, June 1955).

34. James Fesler, "Administrative Literature and the Second Hoover Commission Reports," *American Political Science Review*, vol. 51 (March 1957), p. 150. Herbert Emmerich suggested that the lack of a definitive administrative model may have resulted, in part at least, from the relative absence of academic experts on the second Hoover commission task force staffs. The "intellectual deracination" of public administration had begun. See Herbert Emmerich, *Federal Organization and Administrative Management* (University of Alabama Press, 1971), p. 109.

35. See Moe, *Hoover Commissions Revisited*, p. 126.

36. The story has been told with incomparable lucidity and insight by Walter Millis, Harvey C. Mansfield, and Harold Stein in *Arms and the State* (New York: Twentieth Century Fund, 1958).

37. See Arnold, "Reform's Changing Role," pp. 14–17.

38. Office of Management and Budget, *Papers Relating to the President's Departmental Reorganization Program* (GPO, 1971).

39. See Richard P. Nathan, *The Plot That Failed: Nixon and the Administrative Presidency* (Wiley, 1975), especially pp. 59, 62, 85.

40. The term was coined by Charles E. Lindblom and David Braybrooke in *A Strategy of Decision* (Free Press, 1963), p. 51.

41. For a highly critical reading of the significance of Carter's reviews of federal organization and procedures, see Moe, "Traditional Organizational Principles," pp. 132–33.

42. President's Private-Sector Survey on Cost Control, *A Report to the President* (GPO, 1984).

43. See Moe, *Hoover Commissions Revisited*, p. 96.

44. See Graham T. Allison, Jr., "Public and Private Management: Are They Fundamentally Alike in All Unimportant Respects?" in Richard J. Stillman II, ed., *Public Administration* (Houghton Mifflin, 1992), p. 282.

45. NPR, *From Red Tape to Results*, pp. 2, 3, 93–94.

46. Laurence E. Lynn, Jr., "Government Lite," *American Prospect*, no. 16 (Winter 1994), p. 140.

47. No précis of modern administrative thought is complete if it excludes attention to certain seminal works that did not originate in publicly commis-

sioned studies of the governmental bureaucracy but that nevertheless decisively influenced the intellectual climate of public administration and contemporary organizational theory. Most important among these complementary works were those belonging to the so-called human relations approach. See F. J. Roethlisberger and W. J. Dickson, *Management and the Worker* (Harvard University Press, 1939); Abraham H. Maslow, *Toward a Psychology of Being* (Princeton, N.J.: Van Nostrand, 1962); and Douglas McGregor, "The Human Side of Enterprise," in Warren G. Bennis and Edgar H. Schein, eds., *Leadership and Motivation: Essays of Douglas McGregor* (MIT Press, 1966). A further important offshoot was the organizational culture approach, which in turn led directly by way of Peters and Waterman's *In Search of Excellence* and Osborne and Gaebler's *Reinventing Government* to the NPR. See Thomas J. Peters and Robert H. Waterman, Jr., *In Search of Excellence: Lessons from America's Best-Run Companies* (Harper and Row, 1982); and David Osborne and Ted Gaebler, *Reinventing Government: How the Entrepreneurial Spirit Is Transforming the Public Sector* (Addison-Wesley, 1992).

48. First published as chapter 1 in James Willard Hurst, *Law and the Conditions of Freedom in the Nineteenth Century United States* (University of Wisconsin Press, 1956). The Gore report's emphasis on cutting red tape, empowering administrators (for example, by providing improved technology), and subjecting them to both the opportunities and disciplines of marketlike mechanisms is the bureaucratic equivalent of the basic "release of energy" schema that Hurst set forth as the early American vision for society as a whole.

49. Charles H. Levine and Rosslyn S. Kleeman, "The Quiet Crisis of the Civil Service: The Federal Personnel System at the Crossroads," in Patricia W. Ingraham and Donald F. Kettl, eds., *Agenda for Excellence: Public Service in America* (Chatham, N.J.: Chatham House, 1992), p. 224.

50. John Meacham, "What Al Gore Might Learn the Hard Way," *Washington Monthly* (September 1993), pp. 16–20; and David Segal, "What's Wrong with the Gore Report," *Washington Monthly* (November 1993), pp. 18–23.

51. In Mike Causey, "A Stake in the Buyouts," *Washington Post*, May 9, 1994, p. B2.

52. Stephen Barr, "Bureaucracy Review Opens with a Rally," *Washington Post*, April 16, 1993, p. A23.

53. The imagery is that of Frederick Winslow Taylor's version of the "good man" theory all over again, but with the innovativeness of the individual workers substituted for their programmed efficiency.

54. H. George Frederickson, "Painting Bull's Eyes around Bullet Holes," *Governing*, vol. 6 (October 1992), p. 13.

55. See John J. DiIulio, Jr., Gerald Garvey, and Donald F. Kettl, *Improving Government Performance: An Owner's Manual* (Brookings, 1993), pp. 39–40.

56. Moe, *Reorganizing the Executive Branch in the Twentieth Century*, p. 54.

57. Hargrove and Nelson, *Presidents, Politics, and Policy*, pp. 197–98.

58. See John J. DiIulio, Jr., and Richard P. Nathan, eds., *Making Health Reform Work: A View from the States* (Brookings, 1994).

59. See, for example, Jeffrey L. Pressman and Aaron Wildavsky, *Implementation: How Great Expectations in Washington Are Dashed in Oakland*, 2d ed. (University of California Press, 1979).

60. The need for which is the real point, for example, of Steven Kelman— significant if only because Kelman has joined the Clinton administration and signed on as one of the many born-again reinventers in that group. See Steven Kelman, *Procurement and Public Management* (Washington: American Enterprise Institute, 1990).

61. Which is the real point of John J. DiIulio, Jr., ed., *Deregulating the Public Service* (Brookings, 1994).

Chapter Four

1. National Performance Review, *From Red Tape to Results: Creating a Government that Works Better and Costs Less: A Report of the National Performance Review* (Government Printing Office, 1993), p. i.

2. National Performance Review, *Department of Agriculture: Accompanying Report of the National Performance Review* (GPO, 1993), pp. 1, 11; Kevin Merida, "House Passes Agriculture Reform Bill," *Washington Post*, September 29, 1994, p. A21; and Stephen Barr, "Inside Agriculture—Closing of Field Offices Opens Lawmakers' Eyes," *Washington Post*, September 30, 1994, p. A21.

3. Espy succeeded in getting the USDA reorganization plan passed, but was forced to resign his position as secretary soon thereafter because of allegations that he had improperly accepted gifts from companies that had dealings with the department. See Kevin Merida, "House Passes Agriculture Reform Bill: Restructuring to Give Espy Broad Authority," *Washington Post*, September 29, 1994, p. A21; Ann Devroy, "Agriculture Secretary Espy Resigns: Amid Ethics Probes, Ex-Congressman Will Leave to Fight for 'My Good Name,'" *Washington Post*, October 4, 1994, p. A1; and Bob Benenson, "Long-Delayed Reorganization, Crop Insurance Bill Cleared," *Congressional Quarterly Weekly Report*, October 8, 1994, pp. 2871–72.

4. Much of the information in this chapter about the departmental NPR activities was obtained in interviews with staff members involved in each department's efforts. The interviews were held between January and May 1994.

5. U.S. Department of Agriculture, "Team USDA Summary," internal memo, September 7, 1993, pp. 1–2.

6. NPR, *From Red Tape to Results*, pp. 134–35.

7. General Accounting Office, *Management Reform: GAO's Comments on the National Performance Review's Recommendations*, OCG-94-1 (December 1993), p. 14.

8. National Performance Review, *Department of the Interior: Accompanying Report of the National Performance Review* (GPO, 1993), p. 1.

9. Ibid., p. 64.

10. U.S. Department of the Interior, "Quick Fixes, Moving Forward," *Solutions: Special Update on Interior's National Performance Review*, December 1993, p. 2.

11. NPR, *From Red Tape to Results*, pp. 143–44.

12. Department of Interior, *Solutions*, December 1993, p. 4.

13. The White House, "Performance Agreement between The President of the United States William Jefferson Clinton and The Secretary of The Interior Bruce Babbitt," March 18, 1994.

14. National Performance Review, *Agency for International Development: Accompanying Report of the National Performance Review* (GPO, 1993), p. 1, and data from AID personnel office. The numbers given here are for direct-hire staff only and do not include contract employees.

15. NPR, *From Red Tape to Results*, p. 134.

16. Michael Hammer and James Champy, *Reengineering the Corporation: A Manifesto for Business Revolution* (Harper Business, 1993).

17. Agency for International Development, internal memo, December 21, 1993.

18. See Guy Gugliotta, "Moral of the Story at AID: Stress is Good," *Washington Post*, May 24, 1994, p. A19.

19. National Performance Review, *Department of Health and Human Services: Accompanying Report of the National Performance Review* (GPO, 1993), p. 1.

20. NPR, *From Red Tape to Results*, pp. 141–42.

21. Ibid.

22. U.S. Department of Health and Human Services, "Update on the HHS Continuous Improvement Program," internal memo, undated, unpaged.

23. This is not surprising since the SSA accounts for about half the department's budget and staff. Department of Health and Human Services, *Continuous Improvement Program News Bulletin*, vol. 1 (January 1994), p. 2.

24. Ibid., p. 1.

25. National Performance Review, *Department of Labor: Accompanying Report of the National Performance Review* (GPO, 1993), p. 1.

26. Ibid., pp. 91–92.

27. U.S. Department of Labor, "Reinventing Government, Reinventing DOL," internal memo, undated, p. 3.

28. NPR, *From Red Tape to Results*, pp. 145–47.

29. GAO, *Management Reform*, p. 112.

30. "Performance Agreement Between President of the United States William Jefferson Clinton and Department of Labor Secretary Robert Reich," reported in Frank Swoboda, "A Working Agreement: Reich Sets Some Goals for His Employees," *Washington Post*, March 24, 1994, p. A27.

31. National Performance Review, *Department of Housing and Urban Development: Accompanying Report of the National Performance Review* (GPO, 1993), p. 1.

32. U.S. Department of Housing and Urban Development, *Status Report on the Reinventing HUD Initiative and Reinventing HUD Task Force, March 1993–November 1993*, December 1993, pp. 4–5. See also NPR, *Department of Housing and Urban Development*, p. 42.

33. NPR, *From Red Tape to Results*, p. 142.

34. The White House, "Performance Agreement between The President of the United States William Jefferson Clinton and The Secretary of the Department of Housing and Urban Development Henry Cisneros," March 18, 1994.

Chapter Five

1. Executive Order 10988 (1962). Executive Order 11491, issued by President Nixon in 1969, provided the framework for federal labor relations until 1979. For a good discussion of the history of federal unions, see Richard C. Kearney, *Labor Relations in the Public Sector*, 2d ed. (New York: Marcel Dekker, 1992).

2. 5 U.S.C. 7106(a)(1) and (a)(2).

3. 5 U.S.C. 7106(b)(3).

4. 5 U.S.C 7106(b)(1).

5. See Carolyn Ban, Toni Marzotto, and Charles W. Gossett, "The Dynamics of Civil Service Reform: The Case of Labor Management Relations," paper prepared for the 1981 annual meeting of the Association for Public Policy Analysis and Management.

6. General Accounting Office, *Federal Labor Relations: A Program in Need of Reform*, GGD-91-101 (July 1991), p. 43.

7. For an analysis of the air traffic controllers' strike, see Kearney, *Labor Relations in the Public Sector*, pp. 306–09.

8. Ken Hughes, "Running on Empty: Funds, Membership Dip to Critical Low," *Federal Times*, January 22, 1990, p. 1.

9. Kearney, *Labor Relations in the Public Sector*, p. 23.

10. Hughes, "Running on Empty," pp. 1, 12.

11. GAO, *Federal Labor Relations*, pp. 2-3.

12. Ibid., p. 5.

13. Tom Shoop, "Swing Your Partner," *Government Executive*, vol. 26 (March 1994), pp. 31-34.

14. Executive Order 12871 (October 1, 1993).

15. National Partnership Council, *A Report to the President on Implementing Recommendations of the National Performance Review* (January 1994). Appendix D lists the NPC members, Appendixes E and F the membership of the planning group and working groups.

16. Shoop, "Swing Your Partner," p. 31.

17. National Partnership Council, *Report*, p. 20.

18. Ibid., pp. 20-21.

19. Stephen Barr, "Hill Looms as New Source of Anxiety for Work Force," *Washington Post*, November 14, 1994, p. A19.

20. Ibid., p. 11.

21. See also the comments on the National Partnership Council report by the Coalition for Effective Change, letter to Bob Stone of the National Performance Review, March 1, 1994, pp. 11-14. The coalition report raises the concern that the "good government" standard will lead to protracted litigation.

22. National Partnership Council, *Report*, pp. 15-16.

23. 49 FLRA 21 (February 25, 1994).

24. Jim Armshaw, David Carnevale, and Bruce Waltuck, "Union-Management Partnership in the U.S. Department of Labor," *Review of Public Personnel Administration*, vol. 13 (Summer 1993); Stephen L. Atlas, "Team Builders," *Government Executive*, vol. 26 (March 1994), pp. 36-40; and Christy Harris, "Union Counts on Promises in New Labor Partnership," *Federal Times*, February 28, 1994, p. 13.

25. Cited in Christy Harris, "Effort to Rebuild AFGE Off to an Early Start," *Federal Times*, January 24, 1994, p. 8.

26. Toni Marzotto, "Employee Empowerment and Union-Management Partnership: A Dilemma for Reinventing Government?" paper prepared for the 1994 Annual Meeting of the American Society for Public Administration, pp. 6-7.

27. Stephen Barr, "Gore Gets a Warm Reception From Government Union Chiefs," *Washington Post*, February 10, 1994, p. A25.

28. National Performance Review, *From Red Tape to Results: Creating a Government That Works Better and Costs Less: A Report of the National Performance Review* (Government Printing Office, 1993), pp. 67, 68.

29. The General Accounting Office makes this point in a recent analysis of the impact of the budget on federal employees, which is critical of "equal, across-the-board reductions for all agencies and functions . . . [which do] not distinguish

between efficient and wasteful activities and can seriously diminish agencies' capabilities to manage their resources and deliver services to the public." General Accounting Office, *Federal Employment: Impact of the President's Budget on Federal Employees*, T-GGD-94-108 (March 1994), p. 2.

30. Stephen Barr, "Unions, Clinton at Odds on Civil Service Reform," *Washington Post*, December 15, 1994, p. A25.

31. In contrast, the Winter commission recommends that "states and localities should aim for a stable learning budget set at at least *three percent of total personnel costs.*" National Commission on the State and Local Public Service, *Hard Truths, Tough Choices: An Agenda for State and Local Reform: The First Report of the National Commission on the State and Local Public Service* (Albany, 1993), p. 42.

32. According to a recent survey of SES members by the Federal Executive Institute Alumni Association, "when asked about specific National Performance Review recommendations, the most frequent answers were 'do not know' or no response." Leign Rivenbark, "Executives Say Morale Is Sinking," *Federal Times*, June 23, 1994, p. 4.

Chapter Six

1. National Performance Review, *From Red Tape to Results: Creating a Government That Works Better and Costs Less: A Report of the National Performance Review* (Government Printing Office, 1993), p. iii.

2. New Zealand during 1984-90 provides an example of massive governmental restructuring facilitated by the superior cohesiveness of the governing (Labour) party in a two-party parliamentary system. This restructuring occurred without the rhetoric of "entrepreneurship" and "customer service" that enveloped the NPR. See Jonathan Boston and other, eds., *Reshaping the State: New Zealand's Bureaucratic Revolution* (Auckland: Oxford University Press, 1991).

3. The decentralization of Congress today is easily overstated in certain respects. The Democratic majority leadership of the House of Representatives has created (and been allowed to create) formidable powers for structuring the legislative process. See Barbara Sinclair, "House Majority Party Leadership in an Era of Legislative Constraint," in Roger H. Davidson, ed., *The Postreform Congress* (Saint Martin's Press, 1992), pp. 91–126.

4. R. Douglas Arnold, *The Logic of Congressional Action* (Yale University Press, 1990).

5. On policy-related motivations for committee membership, see Richard F. Fenno, Jr., *Congressmen in Committees* (Little, Brown, 1973), chap. 1.

6. Martha Derthick, *Agency under Stress: The Social Security Administration in American Government* (Brookings, 1990).

7. Matthew D. McCubbins and Thomas Schwartz, "Congressional Oversight Overlooked: Police Patrols versus Fire Alarms," *American Journal of Political Science*, vol. 28 (February 1984), pp. 165–79. However, some conditions do favor a more systematic "police patrol" approach. See Joel D. Aberbach, *Keeping a Watchful Eye: The Politics of Congressional Oversight* (Brookings, 1990), chap. 4. See also Christopher H. Foreman, Jr., *Signals from the Hill: Congressional Oversight and the Challenge of Social Regulation* (Yale University Press, 1988).

8. Stephen Barr, "Hill Leaders Reprove GSA Chief on Yielding Authority," *Washington Post*, March 25, 1994, p. A21.

9. Robert Marshall Wells, "More Funds to Poorer Schools Likely to Be Rejected," *Congressional Quarterly Weekly Report*, March 5, 1994, p. 552.

10. NPR, *From Red Tape to Results*, apps. A, C.

11. For the examples given, see ibid., pp. 17, 97.

12. Ibid., pp. 95–99.

13. Richard Polenberg, *Reorganizing Roosevelt's Government: The Controversy over Executive Reorganization, 1936–1939* (Harvard University Press, 1966), chaps. 4, 5.

14. On the Nixon administration's efforts in this regard, see Richard P. Nathan, *The Plot That Failed: Nixon and the Administrative Presidency* (Wiley, 1975).

15. Peri E. Arnold, "The First Hoover Commission and the Managerial Presidency," *Journal of Politics*, vol. 38 (February 1976), pp. 46–70. As Arnold explains, Hoover may have opposed the New Deal but believed deeply in the institutional presidency that facilitated it.

16. Political scientist Peri E. Arnold has written that "after the middle 1970s, executive reorganization was posed by presidents as a weapon *against* government. Presidents Carter, Reagan, and now Clinton, initiated executive reorganization in the spirit of scourging government. Now executive reorganization was driven by a view of government as a failed enterprise." See Arnold, "Reform's Changing Role: The National Performance Review in Historical Context," paper prepared for the Woodrow Wilson International Center for Scholars, April 12, 1994.

17. Michael Isikoff, "Reno Appoints Freeh Peacemaker at Justice," *Washington Post*, October 22, 1993, p. A21; and Pierre Thomas, "Proposal to Merge Firearms Bureau into FBI Is Scrapped," *Washington Post*, November 25, 1993, p. A20.

18. Kenneth J. Cooper, "Hill Turf Fights May 'Reinvent' Gore Proposals; Long Loyalties, Parochial Politics Appear Likely to Reshape the Recommended Changes," *Washington Post*, September 13, 1993, p. A19.

19. Michael Isikoff, "Reno, in Speech, Says She Opposes DEA-FBI Merger," *Washington Post*, October 20, 1993, p. A27. Espy aggressively promoted major reinvention but concluded, in the words of a Senate report on a departmental reorganization bill, that "there is a comprehensive farm to table approach to food

safety that only the USDA can undertake." See *Department of Agriculture Reorganization Act of 1994*, S. Rept. 103-241, 103 Cong. 2 sess. (GPO, 1994), p. 6.

20. Chris Harvey, "Officials Rise in Defense of Military Med School," *Washington Post*, June 2, 1994, p. Md 1.

21. Martin Tolchin, "Clinton Air Traffic Control Plan Suffers Setback," *New York Times*, May 4, 1994, p. A21.

22. See Polenberg, *Reorganizing Roosevelt's Government*.

23. Mike Mills, "Clinton and Gore Hit the Road to Build a Better Bureaucracy," *Congressional Quarterly Weekly Report*, September 11, 1993, pp. 2381, 2384. See also William V. Roth, Jr., "Maintaining the Momentum," *Public Manager*, vol. 22 (Winter 1993–94), pp. 15–18.

24. Richard L. Berke, "The Good Son," *New York Times Magazine*, February 20, 1994, pp. 33–34; and Stephen Barr, "Managers Urged to Abandon Cynicism of Workplace 'Culture,'" *Washington Post*, March 30, 1994, p. A17.

25. On the appeal of government reform among Perot voters, see Fred Barnes, "Gored," *New Republic*, September 20, 1993, p. 12.

26. David Wessel and Timothy Noah, "Gore vs. Grace: Dueling Reinventions Show How Clinton, Reagan Views of Government Differ," *Wall Street Journal*, September 8, 1993, p. A14.

27. General Accounting Office, *Management Reform: GAO's Comments on the National Performance Review's Recommendations*, OCG-94-1 (December 1993).

28. Office of the Press Secretary, The White House, "Remarks Announcing Federal Procurement Reforms and Spending Cut Proposals," *Weekly Compilation of Presidential Documents*, vol. 29 (November 1, 1993), p. 2174.

29. Letter (and enclosures) to House Majority leader Richard A. Gephardt from Robert D. Reischauer, director, Congressional Budget Office, dated November 15, 1993. See also Steven Greenhouse, "Savings Vastly Overestimated in Streamlining Plan, Agency Reports," *New York Times*, November 17, 1993, p. A22.

30. P.L. 103-62. See *Congressional Record*, June 23, 1993, pp. S7739–40; and Stephen Barr, "Legislation Would Judge Agencies by How Their Own Goals Are Met," *Washington Post*, May 5, 1993, p. A19.

31. Jonathan Walters, "The Benchmarking Craze," *Governing*, vol. 7 (April 1994), pp. 33–37.

32. Laurence E. Lynn, Jr., *Managing the Public's Business: The Job of the Government Executive* (Basic Books, 1981), chap. 4.

33. Donald F. Kettl, "Measuring Performance When There Is No Bottom Line: A Discussion Paper on Performance Measurement and Budgeting," paper prepared for a conference of the Brookings Institution's Center for Public Management, April 19, 1994, p. 3.

34. *Government Performance and Results Act of 1993*, H. Rept. 103-106, pt. 1, 103 Cong. 1 sess. (GPO, 1993), p. 13; and *Government Performance and Results Act of 1993*, S. Rept. 103-58, 103 Cong. 1 sess. (GPO, 1993), pp. 7–8.

35. Foreman, *Signals from the Hill*, chap. 5.

36. Stephen Barr, ". . . as 252,000 Becomes the Magic Number in Job-Reduction Plan," *Washington Post*, November 11, 1993, p. A21.

37. Stephen Barr, "U.S. Budget May Force Layoffs," *Washington Post*, January 30, 1994, p. A1.

38. Stephen Barr, "Under Pressure to Cut, Agencies Look to Buyouts," *Washington Post*, January 31, 1994, p. A4; and Barr, "'Buyouts' Pitch Comes In High," *Washington Post*, February 2, 1994, p. A17.

39. Stephen Barr, "Last-Ditch Effort Set on Buyout Impasse," *Washington Post*, February 28, 1994, p. A15.

40. Stephen Barr, "Personnel Office Launches First Non-Defense RIFs over Budget," *Washington Post*, February 18, 1994, p. A23.

41. Mike Causey, "The Outs Are In," *Washington Post*, March 16, 1994, p. D2; Stephen Barr, "Conferees Approve 'Buyout' Measure For U.S. Workers," *Washington Post*, March 16, 1994, p. A17; and Stephen Barr and Helen Dewar, "Senate Passes Buyout Plan," *Washington Post*, March 25, 1994, p. A1. The legislation is P.L. 103-226, the Federal Workforce Restructuring Act of 1994.

42. Like buyouts, deficit politics complicated the bill's floor consideration as H.R. 3400 became a vehicle for high-profile proposals to cut federal spending. See generally *Congressional Record*, November 23, 1993, pp. H10721-893. A well-publicized but defeated alternative enjoyed the bipartisan sponsorship of Timothy Penny, Democrat of Minnesota, and John Kasich, Republican of Ohio. The Penny-Kasich amendment promised some $90 billion in cuts. On the helium program proposal, see *Government Reform and Savings Act of 1993*, H. Rept. 103-366, pt. 5, 103 Cong. 1 sess. (GPO, 1993), p. 10. On the Merchant Marine Academy proposal, see ibid., pt. 7, p. 4.

43. "Senate Passes Diminished Bill on 'Reinventing Government,'" *Congressional Quarterly Weekly Report*, October 1, 1994, p. 2794.

44. *Congressional Record*, September 28, 1994, pp. S13623–26.

45. *Congressional Record*, October 3, 1994, pp. H10496–99. See also "Statement on Signing the Government Management Reform Act of 1994," *Weekly Compilation of Presidential Documents*, vol. 30 (October 17, 1994), pp. 2006–07. The act is P.L. 103-356.

46. "Remarks on Signing the Federal Acquisition Streamlining Act of 1994," *Weekly Compilation of Presidential Documents*, vol. 30 (October 17, 1994), pp. 2000–03. The act is P.L. 103-355.

47. Pat Towell, "Political Knots Complicate Plan to Simplify Purchasing," *Congressional Quarterly Weekly Report*, February 26, 1994, p. 487.

48. An example of analysis originating outside the government is Steven Kelman, *Procurement and Public Management* (Washington: AEI Press, 1990). Kelman became head of the Office of Federal Procurement Policy in the Clinton administration.

49. P.L. 101-510, the National Defense Authorization Act for fiscal year 1991.

50. *Congressional Record*, October 26, 1993, p. S14384.

51. See statements of Steven Kelman, administrator, Office of Federal Procurement Policy, and John M. Deutch, undersecretary of defense for acquisitions and technology, before a joint hearing of the Senate Committees on Governmental Affairs and Armed Services, February 24, 1994, pp. 8, 12.

52. William H. Gregory, "Buyers Beware," *Government Executive*, vol. 26 (April 1994), p. 34.

53. Stephen Barr, "Government Streamliners Target Wage-Control Law," *Washington Post*, April 22, 1994, p. A23.

54. See, for example, comments of Senator David Pryor, Democrat of Arkansas, in Towell, "Political Knots Complicate Plan to Simplify Purchasing."

55. *Reinventing the U.S. Department of Agriculture*, Hearing before the Information, Justice, Transportation, and Agriculture Subcommittee of the House Committee on Government Operations, 103 Cong. 1 sess. (GPO, 1993), pp. 6, 36.

56. Kevin Merida, "Agriculture, Reclamation Embrace Major Reorganization: Senate Supports Department Change," *Washington Post*, April 14, 1994, p. A29; and *Department of Agriculture Reorganization Act of 1994*, S. Rept. 103-241.

57. "Statement on Signing the Federal Crop Insurance Reform and Department of Agriculture Reorganization Act of 1994," *Weekly Compilation of Presidential Documents*, vol. 30 (October 17, 1994), pp. 2005-06. The law is P.L. 103-354.

58. See National Performance Review, *Creating a Government That Works Better and Costs Less—A Status Report* (September 1994), pp. 125-26, for a listing of twenty-one such laws as of September 1, 1994.

59. "Analysis of H.R. 3400–Comparison of Bill Introduced and as Passed by the House," NPR internal draft, December 21, 1993.

60. Stephen Barr, "House Votes to Protect Veterans Affairs From Cuts," *Washington Post*, April 29, 1994, p. A38, and Barr, "Downsizing Reinvention," *Washington Post*, May 2, 1994, p. A17.

61. *Congressional Record*, September 22, 1994, p. H9555.

62. NPR, *From Red Tape to Results*, p. 17.

63. Testimony of Thomas E. Mann in *The Vice President's National Performance*

Review–Recommending a Biennial Budget Process, Hearing before the Subcommittee on Legislation and National Security of the House Committee on Government Operations, 103 Cong. 1 sess. (GPO, 1993), pp. 72–81; and Louis Fisher and Albert J. Kliman, "The Gore Report on Budgeting," *Public Manager*, vol. 22 (Winter 1993–94), p. 19.

64. Paul Glastris, "Whose Government is Gored?" *New Republic*, October 11, 1993, p. 33; and Jon Meacham, "What Al Gore Might Learn the Hard Way," *Washington Monthly* (September 1993), p. 19.

65. Louis Fisher, "Micromanagement by Congress: Reality and Mythology," in L. Gordon Crovitz and Jeremy A. Rabkin, eds., *The Fettered Presidency: Legal Constraints on the Executive Branch* (Washington: American Enterprise Institute for Public Policy Research, 1989), pp. 139–57; and Christopher H. Foreman, Jr., "Legislators, Regulators, and the OMB: The Congressional Challenge to Presidential Regulatory Relief," in James A. Thurber, ed., *Divided Democracy: Cooperation and Conflict between the President and Congress* (Washington: Congressional Quarterly Press, 1991), pp. 123–43.

66. Among Gore's first legislative triumphs was his successful sponsorship of the scandal-generated Infant Formula Act of 1980, despite the Carter administration's assertion that new statutory protections were unnecessary. During the Reagan years, Gore proved himself an adept and tenacious critic of administration regulatory initiatives. See Foreman, *Signals from the Hill*, chap. 2.

67. Fisher, "Micromanagement by Congress," p. 147; and *INS* v. *Chadha*, 462 U.S. 919, 952 (1983).

Index